Nick Vandome

Apple Computing for Seniors

Covers OS X El Capitan (10.11)
and iOS 9

In easy steps is an imprint of In Easy Steps Limited
16 Hamilton Terrace · Holly Walk · Leamington Spa
Warwickshire · United Kingdom · CV32 4LY
www.ineasysteps.com

Second Edition

Printed and bound in the United Kingdom

ISBN 978-1-84078-723-8

Contents

1 Apple Macs and More

Apple Mac computers are renowned for their ease-of-use, stability and security, with good reason. This chapter looks at the types of Macs and their general functions. It also shows how you can expand your Apple computing through the use of the online iCloud service.

The World of Apple

Apple, the makers of Mac computers and mobile devices such as the iPhone and the iPad, was founded in California in 1976 by Steve Jobs, Steve Wozniak and Ronald Wayne. Originally called Apple Computer, the initial emphasis of the company was very much on personal computers. After some innovative early machines, Steve Jobs decided that the next Apple computer had to have a Graphical User Interface (GUI). This is a computer that can be controlled by the user with a device such as a mouse or a joystick. In many ways, this was the breakthrough that has shaped the modern face of personal computing.

Mac users are usually very devoted to the Apple brand and support it with very enthusiastic fervor.

The first Macintosh computer using a GUI was released in 1984. The sales of the first Mac were good, particularly because of its strength using graphics and for desktop publishing. However, shortly afterwards, Steve Jobs left Apple which was the beginning of a downturn for the company. The increasing development of Microsoft Windows and IBM-compatible PCs became a real threat to the existence of Apple.

The rise of the iMac

During the 1990s, Apple experienced several commercial setbacks, and the company was in trouble. However, shortly afterwards Steve Jobs returned and, in 1998, the iMac was launched. With its ground-breaking, all-in-one design, and bright, translucent colors, it transformed people's attitudes towards personal computers.

The New icon pictured above indicates a new or enhanced feature introduced with the latest version of OS X El Capitan.

Apple goes mobile

The iMac was followed in 2001 by the iPod, a portable digital music player. Like the iMac, this caught the public's imagination, and Apple has exploited this with dramatic effect with the addition of products such as iTunes, iPhone, iPad and its OS X operating system. Much of this has been aimed at capturing market share in the lucrative mobile computing sector, which has expanded rapidly during the 21st century and is now a key area for digital hardware and software manufacturers.

The death of Steve Jobs in October 2011 created a potential challenge for Apple, but the company has built on his legacy with several updates to its flagship products such as the iPhone and the iPad and also regular updates to its operating systems, which are currently iOS 9 for mobile devices and OS X El Capitan for desktops and laptops.

In 2015, Apple released its latest digital device, the Apple Watch. This is designed to work in conjunction with the iPhone, and has sensors that can monitor functions such as heart rate and number of steps taken.

Up in the iCloud

Apple's products are not created in isolation, though: the aim is to create a seamless experience whether using a Mac computer, an iPhone or an iPad, and ensure that content from one device can easily be accessed and opened on another device. This is done largely through the online iCloud service, which can be used to store and backup content from Apple devices and then make this content available to other compatible Apple devices. This is done with a unique Apple ID and can be used to view items such as photos, documents, calendars, address books and notes on Mac computers, iPhones, iPads and iPod Touches.

See Chapter Nine for details about using devices with iOS 9 and also linking devices together with iCloud.

Although this book focuses on the use of Mac computers, it also covers using mobile Apple devices with iOS 9 and also the iCloud service.

Computing is no longer a standalone activity on a single device, and Apple has created a range of products to help with all of your computing needs, whether you are using a Mac computer, an iPhone, an iPad or an iPod Touch, or a combination of all three.

About Mac Computers

As with most things in the world of technology, there is a wide range of choice when it comes to buying a Mac computer. This includes the top-of-the-range Mac Pro, which is a very powerful desktop computer, to the MacBook Air, which is a laptop that is thin enough to fit into an envelope – if required! In between these two extremes is a variety of desktops and laptops that can match most people's computing needs. For the senior user, some of the best options are:

All new Macs come with the latest Mac operating system pre-installed. At the time of printing this is OS X (pronounced "ten"), or 10.11 to be precise, known as El Capitan.

Desktop

As a good, all-purpose desktop computer, the iMac is hard to beat. This is the machine that helped to turn around Apple's fortunes in the 1990s and it remains one of its most popular computers.

The iMac is a self-contained computer which means the hard drive and the monitor are housed together as a single unit. There are two models that offer different levels of computing power and different monitor sizes: a 21.5-inch model and a 27-inch model. Both models come with wireless connectivity for Wi-Fi connection to the internet. There is also a 27-inch Retina 5K Display model which boasts a higher quality screen.

There are two versions of the latest 21.5-inch iMac: one with an LED-backlit screen; and one with a Retina 4K Display for even greater clarity.

Another desktop option is the Mac Mini, which is a smaller, cheaper computer that consists of just the hard drive. This means that you have to buy the mouse, keyboard and monitor separately.

This is a reasonable option if your computing needs are mainly email, the internet and word processing. For anything more, the iMac is a better option.

The latest versions of the Mac Mini (2015) come with either a 1.4GHz, 2.6GHz or 2.8GHz processor, 500GB or 1TB of storage and 4GB or 8GB of memory (both configurable up to 16GB).

Laptop

More and more people are using laptops these days, as mobile computing takes over from static desktops. In the Mac range, the MacBook is probably the best all-round option. Although not as powerful as the iMac, it has enough computing power for most people's needs. The MacBook Pro comes in 13- and 15- inch models, both with Retina Display high resolution screens. The MacBook Air is ultra-thin and a great option for when traveling: it is available in 11- and 13-inch models.

If you plan on traveling a lot with a laptop, the MacBook Air may feel a bit flimsy due to its very thin design. However, it is surprisingly robust.

About Apple iCloud

Cloud computing is an attractive proposition and one that has gained greatly in popularity in recent years. As a concept, it consists of storing your content on an external computer server. This not only gives you added security in terms of backing up your information, it also means that, with your unique login ID, the content can then be shared over a variety of devices.

The standard iCloud service is free and this includes an iCloud email address and 5GB of online storage. Extra storage can be purchased, up to 1TB (terabyte). (*Correct at the time of printing.*)

iCloud is Apple's consumer cloud computing product that consists of online services such as email, a calendar, notes, contacts and saving documents. iCloud provides users with a way to save and backup their files and content to the online service and then use them across their Apple devices such as other Mac computers, iPhones, iPads and iPod Touches.

For details about using System Preferences on your Mac, see page 17.

About iCloud

iCloud can be set up from this icon within System Preferences:

You can use iCloud to save and share the following between your different devices, with an Apple ID:

- Music
- Photos
- Documents
- Apps
- Books
- Calendars
- Notes
- Reminders
- Backups

There is also a version of iCloud for Windows, which can be accessed for download from the Apple website at **www.apple.com/icloud/setup/pc.html**

When you save an item to the iCloud it automatically sends it to all of your other compatible devices; you do not have to do anything, iCloud does it all for you.

Setting up iCloud

To use iCloud with OS X El Capitan on your Mac you first need to have an Apple ID. This is a service you can register for to be able to access a range of Apple facilities, including iCloud. You can register with an email address and a password. When you first start using iCloud you will be prompted for your Apple ID details. If you do not have an Apple ID you can apply for one at this point:

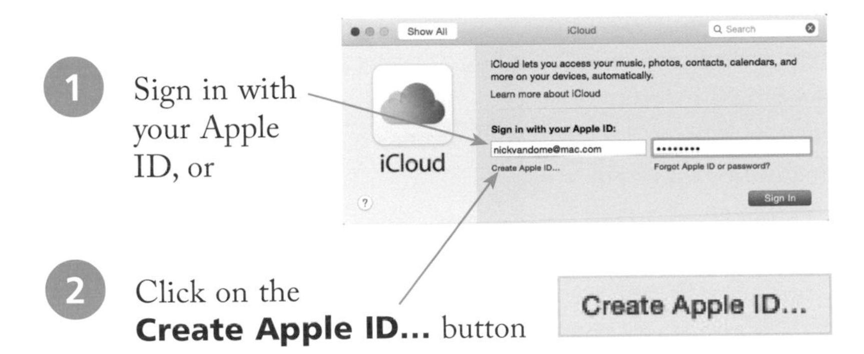

1. Sign in with your Apple ID, or
2. Click on the **Create Apple ID...** button

For more information about using iCloud and linking a Mac to mobile devices such as an iPhone and an iPad, see Chapter Nine.

Setting up iCloud

To use iCloud:

1. Open System Preferences and click on the **iCloud** button

2. Check on the items you want included within iCloud. All of these items will be backed up and shared across all of your Apple devices

When you have an Apple ID and an iCloud account, you can also use the iCloud website to access your content. Access the website at **www.icloud.com** and log in with your Apple ID details.

Inside a Mac

Operating system

The Mac operating system (the software that is the foundation of how the computer works) is known as OS X (pronounced "ten"). This is now on version 10.11, which is more commonly known as El Capitan. This is based on UNIX, a system that is both secure and robust.

Hot tip

To find out more about your current operating system, click on the Apple symbol at the top left of the screen and click on **About This Mac**.

OS X is not only easy to use, it also has a very attractive graphical interface. This is created by a technology known as Quartz and the interface itself is known as Aqua, which is a set of graphics based on the theme of water. The OS X El Capitan interface is immediately eye-catching as soon as any Mac is turned on.

Storage

The iMac, Mac Mini and MacBook ranges have innovative storage solutions to ensure that you can save your documents, photos, music, videos, and more, as quickly and as efficiently as possible. This is done through either a traditional hard drive, or flash storage, or a combination of the two using the Fusion Drive storage option. Flash storage has no moving parts and is up to five times faster than a traditional hard drive. This means that your Mac will start up more quickly, apps will open more quickly, and viewing and saving multimedia items such as photos and videos will also be quicker. iMacs and Mac Minis have a combination of hard drive and flash storage, while MacBooks rely solely on flash storage.

Don't forget

The range of Mac computers have a minimum of 4GB of onboard memory for dealing with the operations of the computer. This is in the form of memory chips and more memory can be added to iMacs, Mac Minis and MacBooks.

Processors

The range of Mac computers use either dual-core or quad-core Intel processors for optimum speed of operation. Quad-core processors are available in iMacs.

Ports and Slots Explained

Every Mac computer has a number of ports and slots for different functions to be performed or additional devices to be attached. Some of these are the same for iMacs, Mac Minis and MacBooks, while others are specific to particular models, depending on their functionality.

USB ports

These are the ports that are used to connect a variety of external devices such as digital cameras, memory card readers, pen drives or external hard drives. On most Macs there are a minimum of two USB ports.

Thunderbolt ports

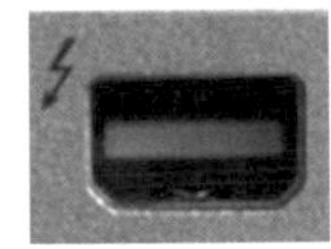

These are ports for transferring data at high speeds, up to 12 times faster than FireWire. FireWire was used on some previous models of Macs and, at the time of printing, is still available on the Mac Mini. Thunderbolt ports can be used to attach external devices and also be used to connect a Thunderbolt screen to a MacBook.

SD card

This is a slot that can be used to download content from an SD card. This is usually for photos or videos.

HDMI ports

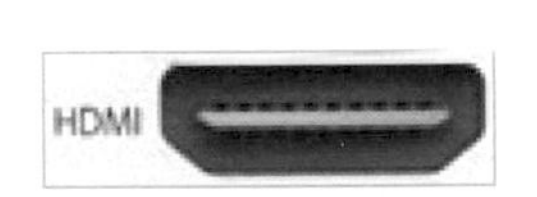

These are ports for connecting your Mac to another screen, such as a High Definition (HD) TV.

Ethernet port

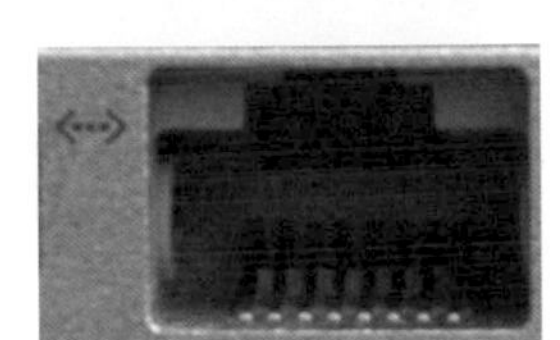

This is for the connection of an Ethernet cable, for a cable or broadband internet connection. This is now only available on the iMac and Mac Mini as the MacBook range relies on Wi-Fi for internet connections.

iMacs, Mac Minis and the MacBook range no longer have an internal CD/DVD drive. However, an external one can be attached via a USB cable.

USB stands for Universal Serial Bus and, at the time of printing, the latest version is USB 3.

The latest models of iMacs and MacBooks do not have a FireWire port. However, a FireWire-to-Thunderbolt adapter can be used if you have FireWire devices.

The Mac Desktop

The first thing to do with your new Mac is to turn it on. This is done by pressing this button once (on the MacBook this is on the body next to the keyboard; on the iMac it is at the back of the screen).

If the Finder is not showing, click on this icon on the Dock. The Dock is the collection of icons at the bottom of the screen.

The first thing you will see is the Mac Desktop. This is the default layout and, as we will see in the next few pages, this can be customized to your own preferences.

Some of the specific elements of the Desktop are:

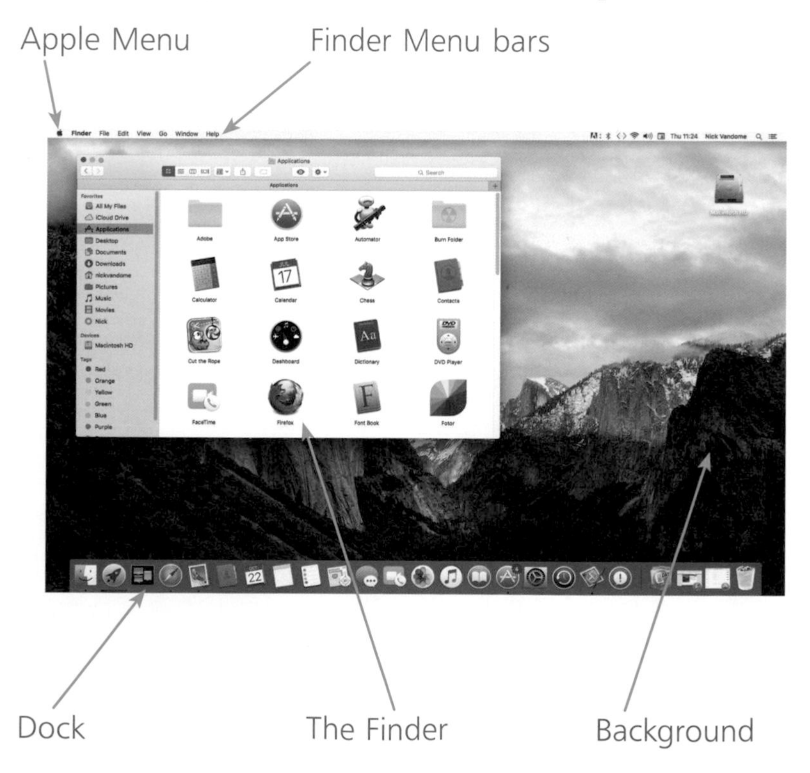

The Finder Sidebar (the panel at the left-hand side of the Finder) is semi-transparent and shows some of the background behind it.

Customizing Your Mac

All of us have different ideas about the way we want our computers set up, in terms of layout, colors, size and graphics. Macs allow a great deal of customization so that you can personalize yours to genuinely make it feel like your own computer.

The customization features are contained within the System Preferences. To access these:

1. Click here on the Dock (for more details about working with the Dock see pages 30-33)

2. The **System Preferences** folder contains a variety of functions that can be used to customize your Mac

Click on the **Show All** button at the top of the **System Preferences** folder to show all of the items in the folder, regardless of which element you are currently using.

Use the **General** option to customize items such as the color of buttons and menus.

Changing the Background

Background imagery is an important way to add your own personal touch to your Mac. (This is the graphical element upon which all other items on your computer sit.) There are a range of background options that can be used. To select your own background:

You can select your own photographs as your Desktop background, once you have loaded them onto your Mac. To do this, select the **Pictures** folder in Step 3 (underneath the **Apple** section) and browse to the photograph you want.

Click on the **Screen Saver** tab to select options for what is displayed on the screen when your Mac is not in use.

Screen Saver

1. Click on this icon in the **System Preferences** folder

2. Click on the **Desktop** tab

Desktop

3. Select a location from where you want to select a background

▼Apple
Desktop Pictures
Nature
Plants
Art
Black & White
Abstract
Patterns
Solid Colors

4. Click on one of the available backgrounds

5. The background is applied as the Desktop background imagery

Changing the Screen Size

For most computer users, the size at which items are displayed on the screen is a crucial issue: if items are too small this can make them hard to read and lead to eye strain; too large and you have to spend a lot of time scrolling around to see everything.

The size of items on the screen is controlled by the screen's resolution, i.e. the number of colored dots displayed in an area of the screen. The higher the resolution, the smaller the items on the screen; the lower the resolution, the larger the items. To change the screen resolution:

1. Click on this button in the **System Preferences** folder

2. Click on the **Display** tab

3. Click on the **Default for display** button to let your Mac select the most appropriate resolution

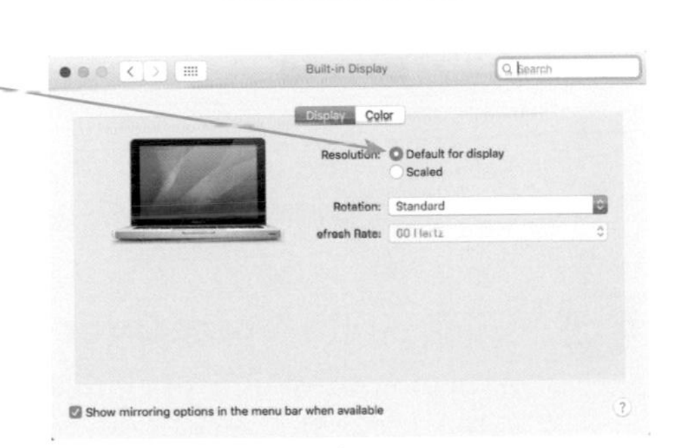

4. Click on the **Scaled** button and select a resolution setting to change the overall screen resolution

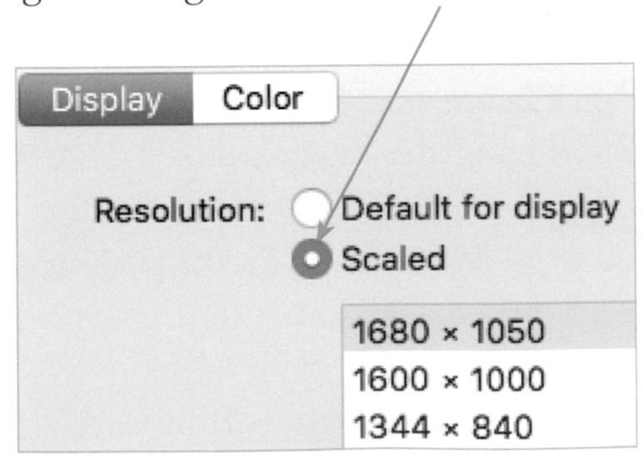

A higher resolution makes items appear sharper on the screen, even though they appear physically smaller.

Making Things Accessible

In all areas of computing it is important to give as many people access to the system as possible. This includes users with visual impairments and also people who have problems using the mouse and keyboard. In OS X, this is achieved through the Accessibility System Preferences. To use these:

Experiment with the VoiceOver function, if only to see how it operates. This will give you a better idea of how visually-impaired users access information on a computer.

1. Click on this button in the **System Preferences** folder

2. Click on the **Display** button for options for changing the display colors, contrast, and increasing the cursor size

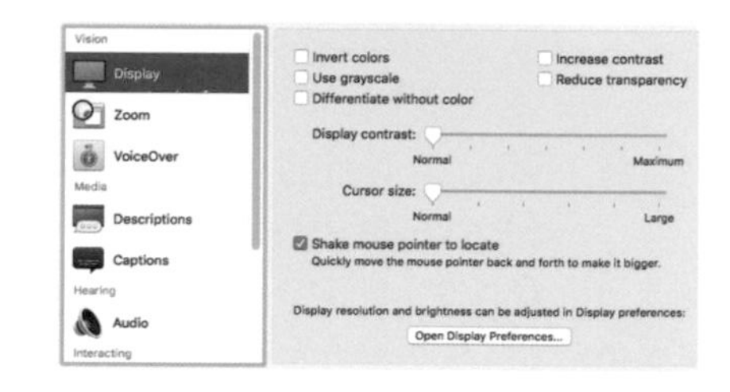

The Audio, Keyboard, and Mouse & Trackpad accessibility options have links to additional options within their own System Preferences.

3. Click on the **Zoom** button for options to zoom in on the screen
4. Click on the **VoiceOver** button to enable VoiceOver, which provides a spoken description of what is on the screen
5. Click on the **Audio** button to select an on-screen flash for alerts and how sound is played
6. Click on the **Keyboard** button to access options for customizing the keyboard
7. Click on the **Mouse & Trackpad** button to access options for customizing these devices
8. Click on the **Dictation** button to select options for using spoken commands

Another option in the Accessibility window is for **Switch Control**, which enables a Mac to be controlled by a variety of devices, including the mouse, keypad and gamepad devices.

The Spoken Word

El Capitan not only has numerous options for adding text to documents, emails and messages; it also has a dictation function so that you can speak what you want to appear on screen. To set up and use the dictation feature:

1. Click on this button in the **System Preferences** folder

2. By default, Dictation is Off

3. Click on the **On** button to enable dictation

4. Click on the **Enable Dictation** button

5. Once Dictation has been turned On, it can be accessed in relevant apps by selecting **Edit > Start Dictation** from the menu bar

6. Start talking when the microphone icon appears. Click **Done** when you have finished recording your text

7. Click on the **Text to Speech** tab to make selections for dictation

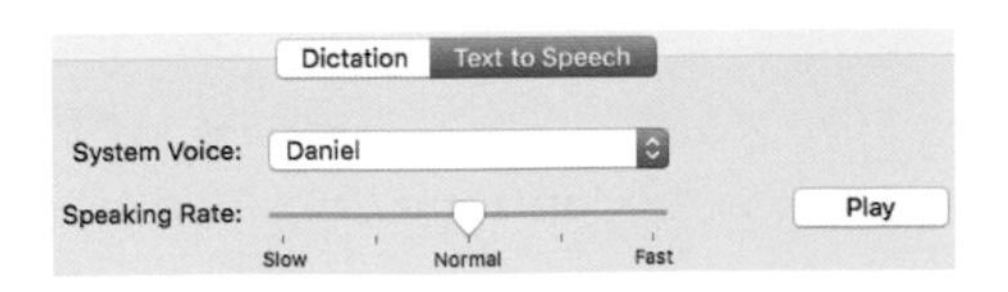

Punctuation can be added with the dictation function, by speaking commands such as 'comma' or 'question mark'. These will then be converted into the appropriate symbols.

Shutting Down and Sleeping

When you are not using your Mac you will want to either shut it down or put it to sleep. If you shut it down this may close all of your applications and open files. This is the best option if you are not going to be returning to your Mac for a reasonable length of time (say, more than one day).

If you put the Mac to sleep, it will retain your current work session so that you can continue when you wake up the Mac. This option is useful if you know you will be returning to your Mac within a few hours.

The process for shutting down or putting a Mac to sleep is very similar in both cases:

1. Click on this icon on the main Menu bar 

2. Click on either **Sleep**, **Restart...** or **Shut Down...**

3. If you are shutting down, a window appears asking you to confirm your request

Are you sure you want to shut down your computer now?
If you do nothing, the computer will shut down automatically in 50 seconds.
Reopen windows when logging back in
Cancel
Shut Down

4. Click on the **Shut Down** button

Hot tip

To wake up a Mac from sleep, simply move the mouse, or tap on a key on the keyboard (the Ctrl key is a good one to use as this will not affect any open files).

Hot tip

Check on the **Reopen windows when logging back in** box when you shut down. This ensures that the next time you turn on your Mac, it will resume at the place where you closed it, i.e. all open apps and files will appear in their previous state.

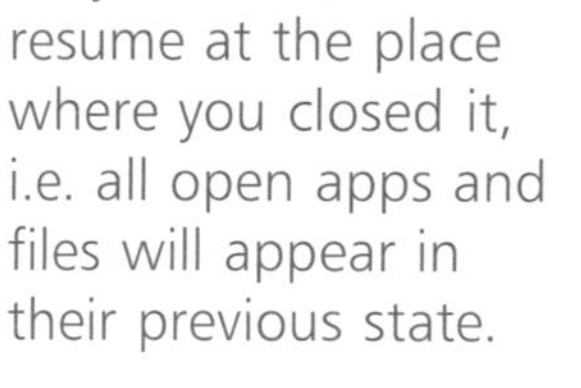

2 Finding Your Way Around

This chapter looks at two of the most important functions on the Mac: the Finder and the Dock. It shows how to use these to access and view items. It also shows how to work with apps and obtain new ones from the online Mac App Store. Ways of navigating around are covered, including Split View.

Finder: the Core of Your Mac

One of the most basic requirements of any computer is that you can easily and quickly find the applications and documents that you want to use. On Macs, a lot of this work is done through the aptly-named Finder, with the transparent sidebar. This is the area on your Mac which you can use to store, organize and display files, folders and applications. It is an area that you will return to frequently whenever you are using your Mac. To access the Finder:

By default, a home folder is created in the Finder when you first set up your Mac. This will contain all of your own folders and files. Some of these folders will also be in the Finder Sidebar. These are just shortcuts to these items.

1. Click on this icon on the Dock (this is one element of the Dock that cannot be removed)

2. The Finder window has a Sidebar and a main window area

3. The Sidebar can be used to create folders and categories for a variety of items

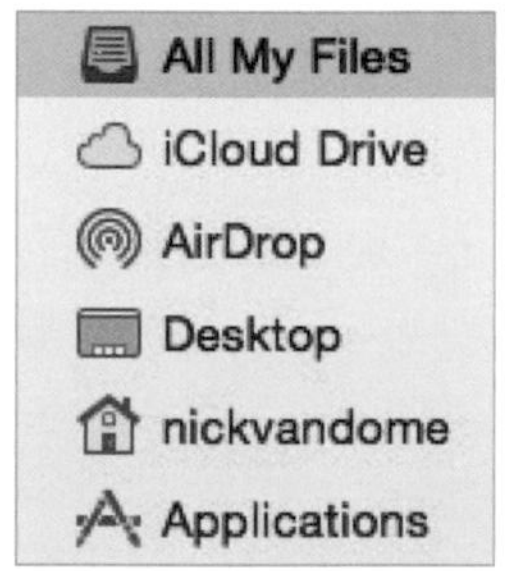

4. The main window displays items within the selected location

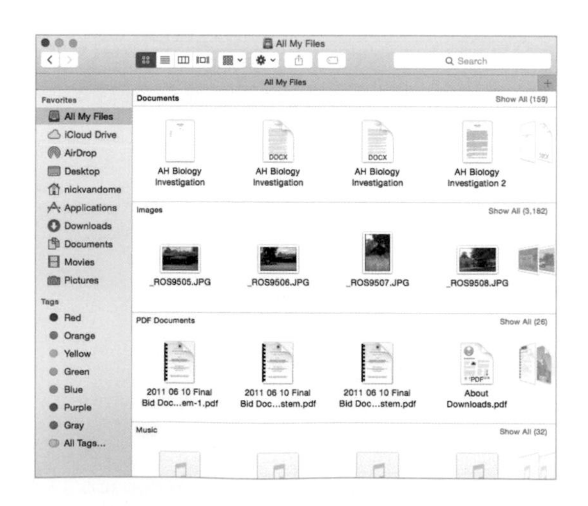

The first link on the Finder Sidebar is **All My Files**. This lists all of the latest files that have been created or saved to your Mac. This is an excellent way to view your most recent files.

Using the Sidebar

The Sidebar is the left-hand panel of the Finder, which can be used to access items on your Mac:

1. Click on a button on the Sidebar

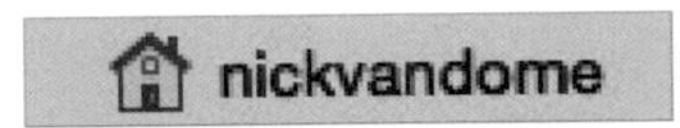

2. Its contents are displayed in the main Finder window

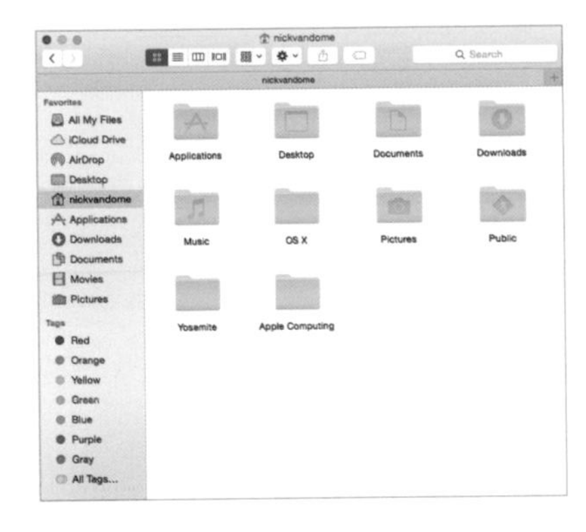

When you click on an item in the Sidebar, its contents are shown in the main Finder window to the right.

Adding to the Sidebar

Items that you access most frequently can be added to the Sidebar. To do this:

1. Drag an item from the main Finder window onto the Sidebar

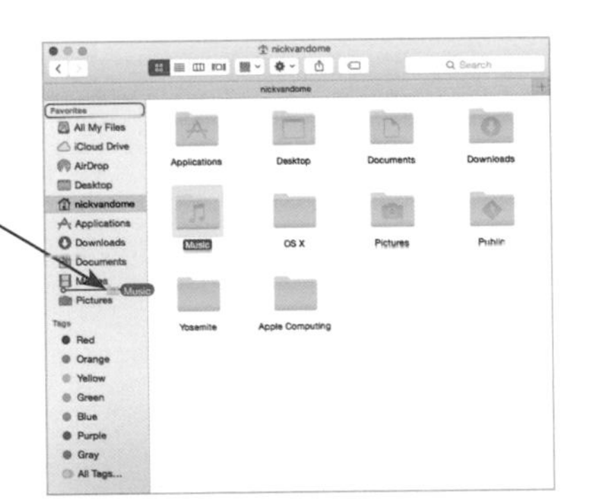

2. The item is added to the Sidebar. You can do this with apps, folders and files

Items can be removed from the Sidebar by dragging them away from it. They then disappear in a satisfying puff of smoke. This does not remove the item from your Mac, just the Finder Sidebar.

...cont'd

Viewing items in the Finder

Items within the Finder can be viewed in a number of different ways:

In Icons view it is possible to view the icons at different sizes. To do this, click on the cog icon next to the view icon and select **Show View Options**. Then drag the Icon size slider for the appropriate size.

1. Click on this button to view items as icons 

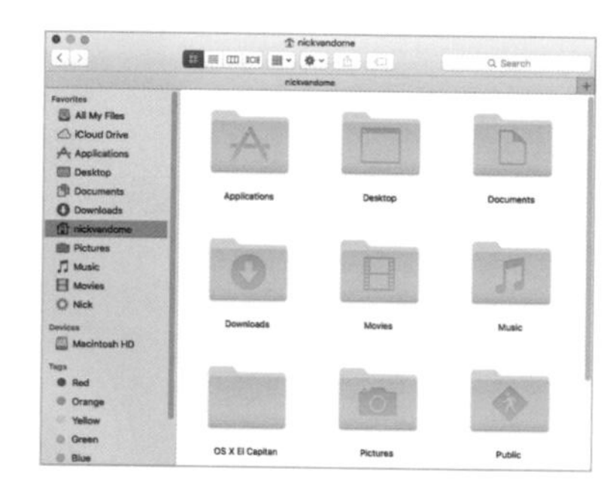

2. Click on this button to view items as a list 

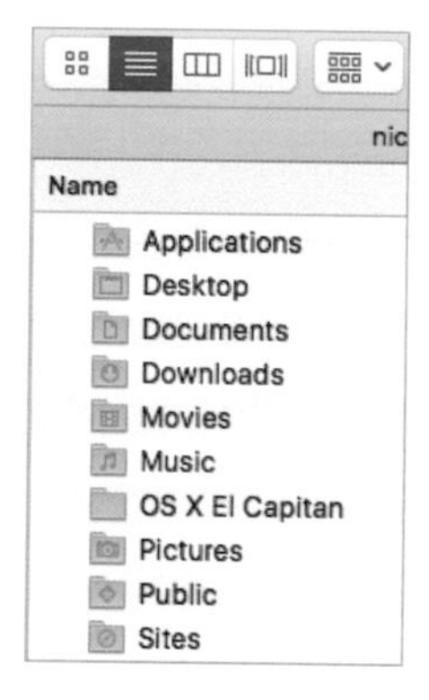

Click on this button to access Cover view, which displays a large graphic in the main Finder window, of the selected item.

3. Click on this button to view items in columns 

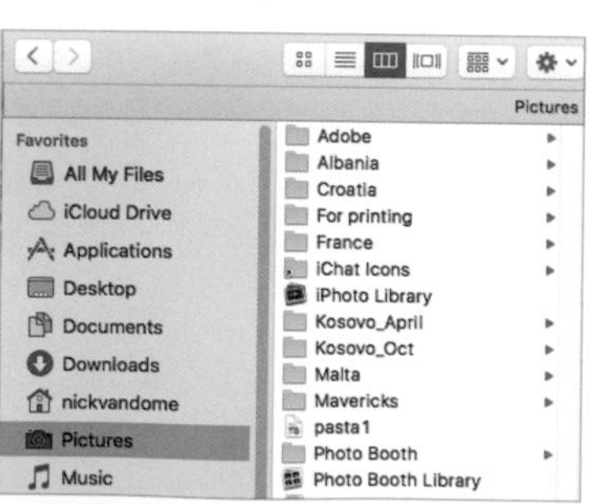

Quick Look

Through a Finder option called Quick Look, it is possible to view the content of a file without having to first open it. To do this:

1. Select a file within the Finder

2. Press the space bar
3. The contents of the file are displayed without it opening in its default app

4. Click on the cross to close Quick Look 

In Quick Look it is even possible to preview videos or presentations without having to open them in their default app.

Finder Tabs

Tabs in web browsers are now well established, where you can have several pages open within the same browser window. This technology is incorporated in the Finder in OS X El Capitan with the use of Finder Tabs. This enables different folders to be open in different tabs within the Finder so that you can organize your content exactly how you want. To do this:

1. Select **View > Show Tab Bar** from the Finder menu bar

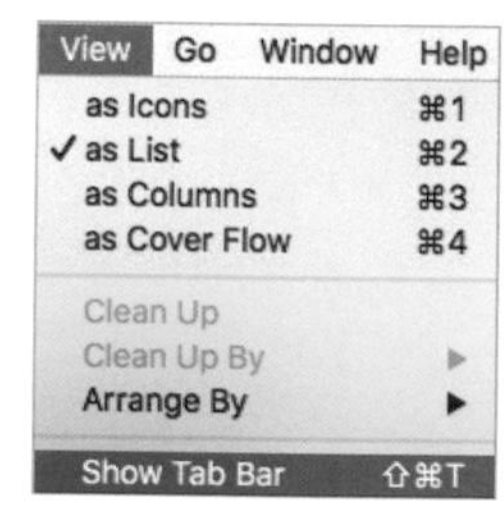

Each time a new tab is opened, it displays the contents of the **All My Files** window, regardless of what is displayed in the previous tab window.

2. A new tab is added here to the Finder

3. Click on this button to view the new tab

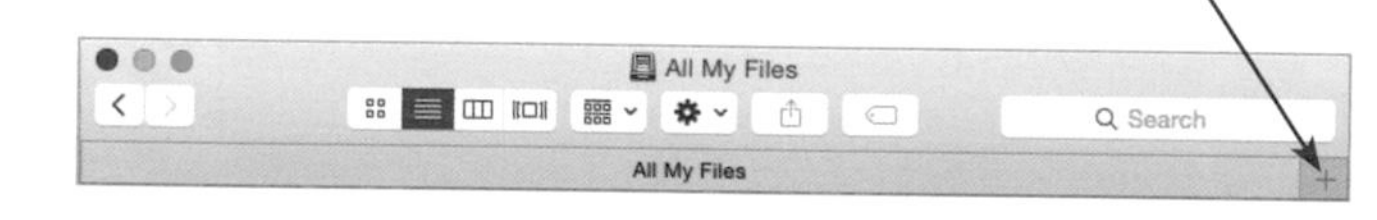

4. At this point, the content in the new tab is displayed for the **All My Files** window. Select another folder to display its content in the new tab

The view for each tab can be customized, without affecting the content in other tabs.

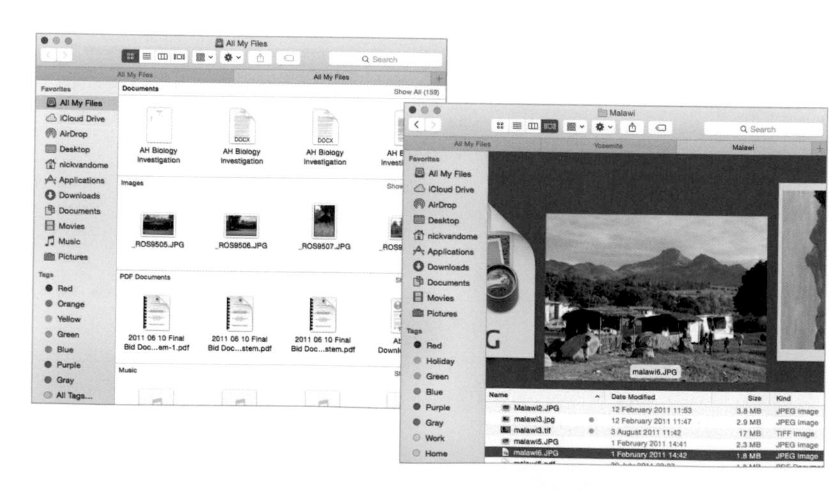

Finder Tags

When creating content in OS X El Capitan you may find that you have documents of different types that cover the same topic. With the Finder Tags function it is possible to link related content items through the use of colored tags.

1. The tags are listed in the Finder Sidebar

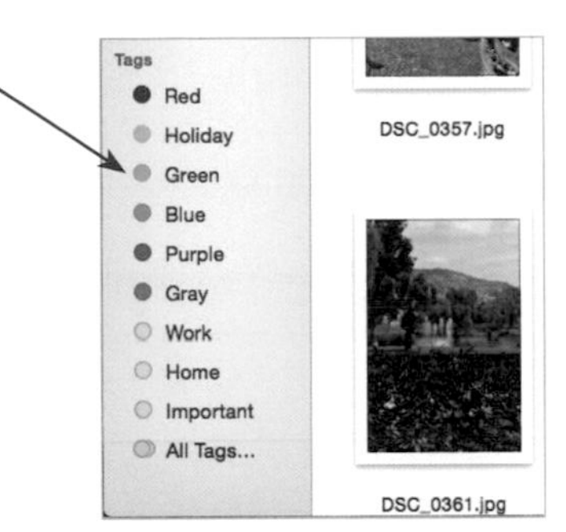

2. To give tags specific names, Ctrl + click on one and click on the **Rename** link

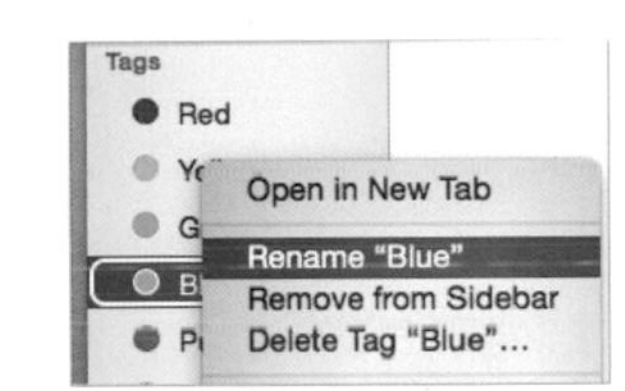

3. To add tags, select the required items in the Finder window

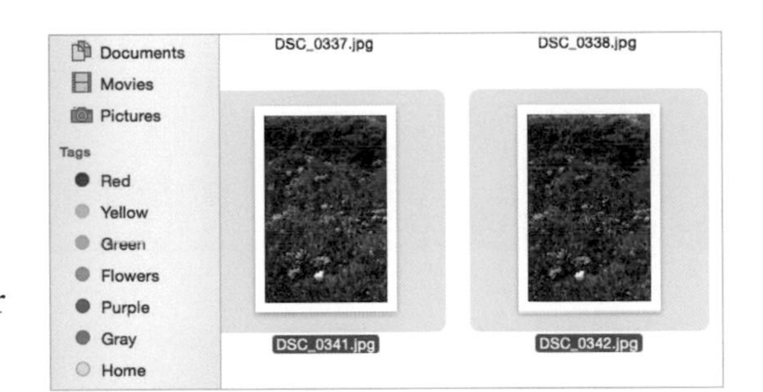

4. Drag the selected items over the appropriate tag

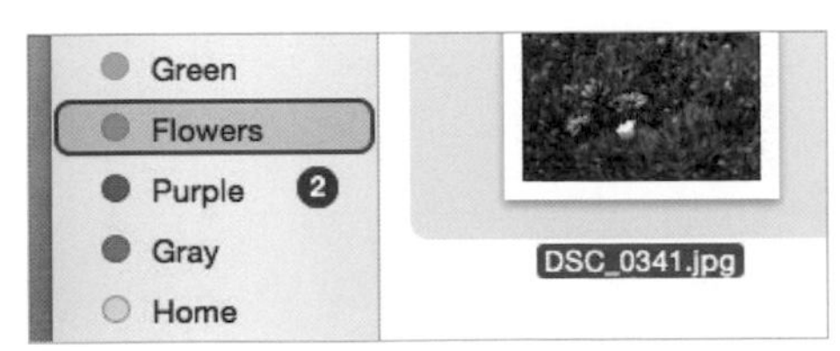

5. The tags are added to the selected items. Click on a tag to view all of the linked files

Tags can be added to documents using some apps including Pages, Numbers and Keynote.

Tags can also be added to items by Ctrl + clicking on them and selecting the required tag from the menu that appears. Also, they can be added from this button on the main Finder toolbar.

Using the Dock

The Dock is the collection of icons that, by default, appears along the bottom of the Desktop. If you choose, this can stay visible permanently. The Dock is a way to quickly access the apps and folders that you use most frequently. The two main things to remember about the Dock are:

- It is divided into two: apps go on the left of the dividing line; all other items go on the right
- It can be edited in a number of ways

Items on the Dock can be activated by clicking on them once, rather than double-clicking.

The more icons that are added to the Dock, the smaller they will all become.

By default, the Dock appears at the bottom of the screen, but it can also be positioned at the left- or right-hand side of the screen.

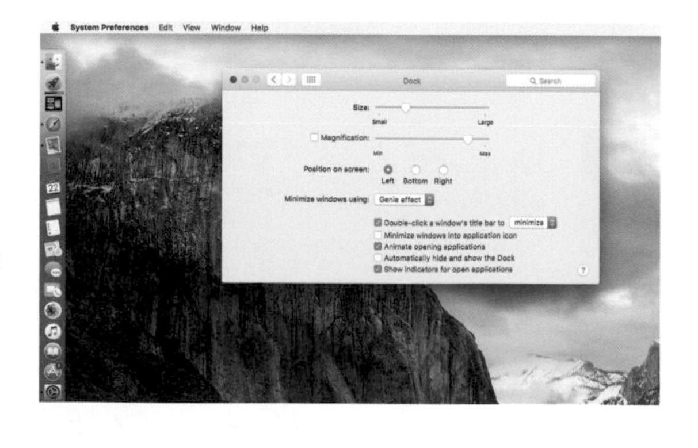

Customizing the Dock

The Dock can be modified in numerous ways. This can affect both the appearance of the Dock and the way it operates. To set Dock preferences:

1. Select **Apple Menu > System Preferences** from the Menu bar

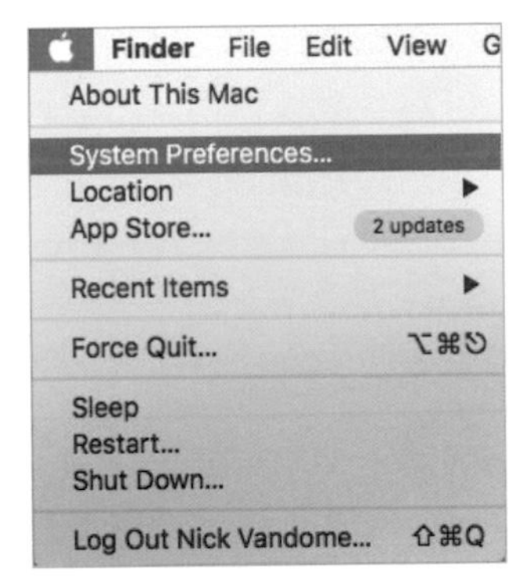

2. Click on the **Dock** button

3. The options for customizing the Dock are displayed. Drag this slider to change the size of the icons on the Dock

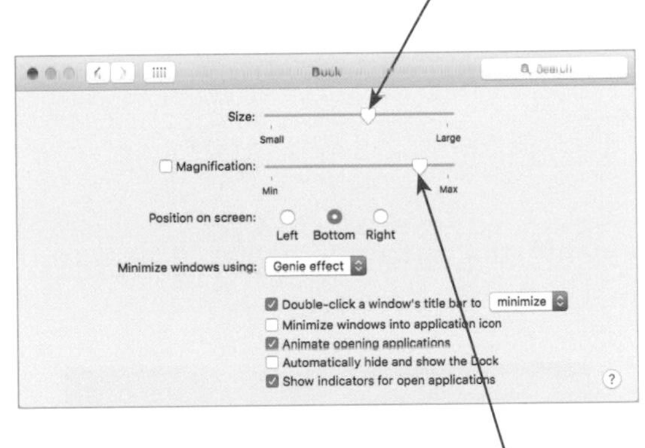

4. Check on the **Magnification** box and drag this slider to specify how much larger an icon becomes when the cursor is passed over it

The **Apple Menu** is accessed from the Apple icon that is always visible at the top left of the screen.

Select **Left**, **Bottom** or **Right** under **Position on screen** to position the Dock.

If you select the **Automatically hide and show the Dock** option for the Dock then it is hidden unless you pass the cursor over the bottom of the screen (or wherever it is hidden). However, this can become annoying as the Dock then appears and disappears at times you do not want it to.

...cont'd

Adding and removing items

To add items to the Dock:

Removing items from the Dock does not remove them from your Mac. The items on the Dock are only a reference to the actual locations of the items.

1. For apps, drag their icons onto the Dock, to the left of the dividing line

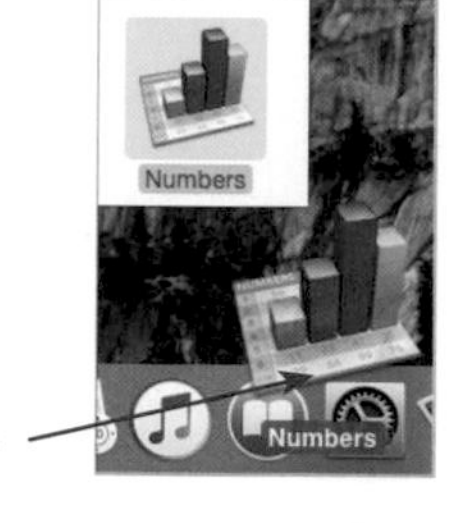

2. For folders or files, drag their icons onto the Dock, to the right of the dividing line

3. To remove items from the Dock, drag them off the Dock and release over the Desktop: they will disappear in a satisfying puff of smoke

Dock menus

Each Dock item has its own contextual menu that has commands relevant to that item. To access these:

If an app window is closed, the app remains open and the window is placed within the app icon on the Dock. If an item is minimized it goes on the right of the Dock dividing line.

1. Click and hold beneath a Dock item
2. The contextual menu is displayed next to the Dock item. Click on a command as required

Stacking items

To save space on the Dock it is possible to add folders to it, from where the folders' contents can be accessed. This is known as Stacks. By default, Stacks for documents and downloaded files are created on the Dock. To use Stacks:

1. Stacked items are placed at the right-hand side of the Dock

2. Click on a Stack to view its contents

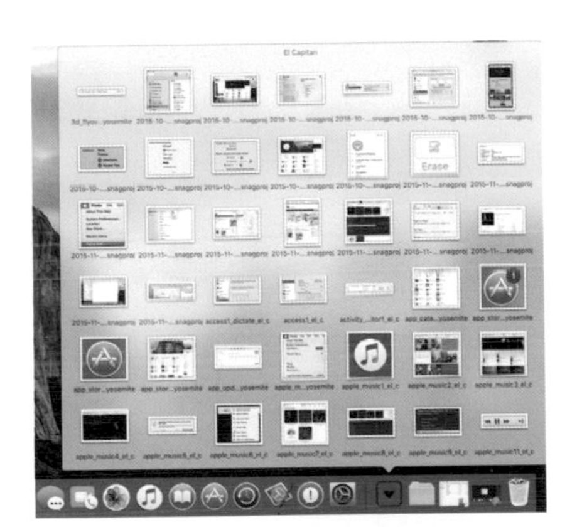

3. Stacks can be viewed as a grid, or

4. As a fan, depending on the number of items it contains, or

5. As a list. Click on a folder to view its contents within a Stack. Click on files to open them in their relevant app

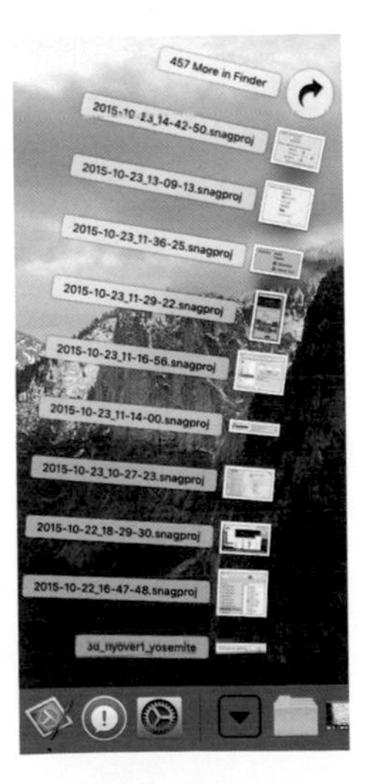

To create a new Stack, drag a folder to the right-hand side of the Dock, i.e. to the right of the dividing line.

Move the cursor over a Stack and press Ctrl + click to access options for how that Stack is displayed.

Mission Control

Mission Control is a function in OS X El Capitan that helps you organize all of your open apps, full screen apps and documents. It also enables you to quickly view the Desktop. Within Mission Control there are also Spaces, where you can group together similar types of documents. To use Mission Control:

Click on a window in Mission Control to access it and exit the Mission Control window.

1. Click on this button on the Dock, or from the Launcher

2. All open files and apps are visible via Mission Control

The top row of Mission Control contains the Dashboard, the Desktop and any full-screen apps.

All windows are now shown individually.

3. If there is more than one window open for an app they will each be shown separately

Any apps or files that have been minimized or closed do not appear within the main Mission Control window. Instead, they are located to the right of the dividing line on the Dock.

4. Move the cursor over the top of the Mission Control window to view the different Spaces and any apps in full-screen mode

Launchpad

Even though the Dock can be used to store shortcuts to your applications, it is limited in terms of space. The full set of applications on your Mac can be found in the Finder, but OS X El Capitan has a feature that allows you to quickly access and manage all of your applications. These include the ones that are pre-installed on your Mac, and also any that you install yourself or download from the Apple App Store. This feature is called Launchpad. To use it:

Apps can be opened from within the Launchpad by clicking or tapping on them once. If they are opened from the **Applications** folder in the Finder, this has to be done by double-clicking or tapping.

1. Click once on this button on the Dock

2. All of the apps are displayed

Drag one app over another in the Launchpad to create a new folder. This can be done with similar types of apps to group them together. A default name is given to the folder, but this can be changed by clicking on it (at the top of the folder when it is created) and typing a new name.

3. Similar types of apps can be grouped together in individual folders. By default, the Utilities are grouped in this way

Mac Apps

In addition to the Launchpad, Mac programs (apps) are located in the Applications folder. This is located within the Finder. To view and access the available apps:

1. Click on the **Applications** button in the Finder

2. The currently-installed apps are displayed

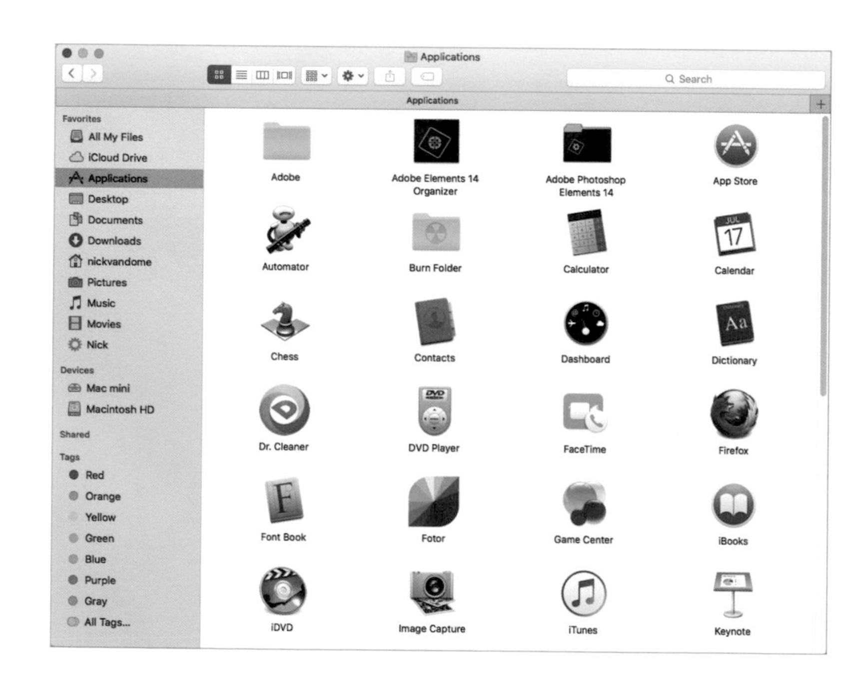

3. To open an app, double-click on its icon

Items other than apps can be added to the Applications folder, but it is better to keep it for this specific use.

Apps can be added to the Dock by dragging their icons there from the Applications folder.

The App Store

The App Store is another OS X app. This is an online facility where you can download and buy new apps. These cover a range of categories such as productivity, business and entertainment. When you select or buy an app from the App Store, it is downloaded automatically by Launchpad and appears here next to the rest of the apps.

To buy apps from the App Store you need to have an Apple ID and account. If you have not already set this up, it can be done when you first access the App Store. To use the App Store:

The App Store is an online function so you will need an Internet connection with which to access it.

1. Click on this icon on the Dock or within the Launchpad

2. The Homepage of the **App Store** contains the current top-featured apps

3. Your account information and **Quick Link** categories are listed at the right-hand side of the screen

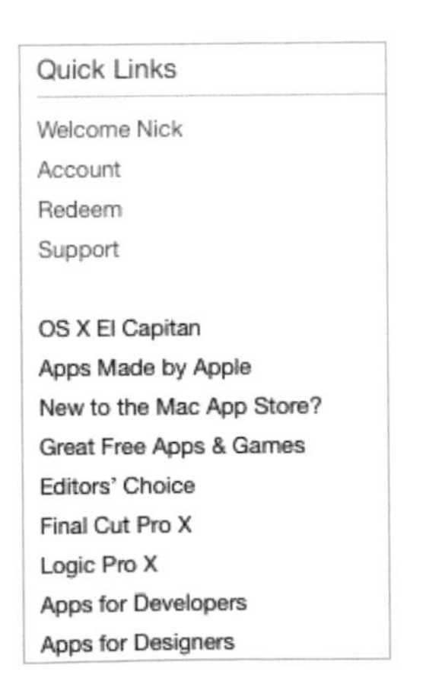

You can set up an Apple ID when you first set up your Mac or you can do it when you register for the App Store or another app that requires an Apple ID, such as buying music from the iTunes Store.

Downloading Apps

The App Store contains a wide range of apps: from small, fun apps, to powerful productivity ones. However, downloading them from the App Store is the same regardless of the type of app. The only differences are whether they require payment or not and the length of time they take to download. To download an app from the App Store:

Apps can be searched for according to specific categories, by clicking on the **Categories** button on the top toolbar of the App Store window.

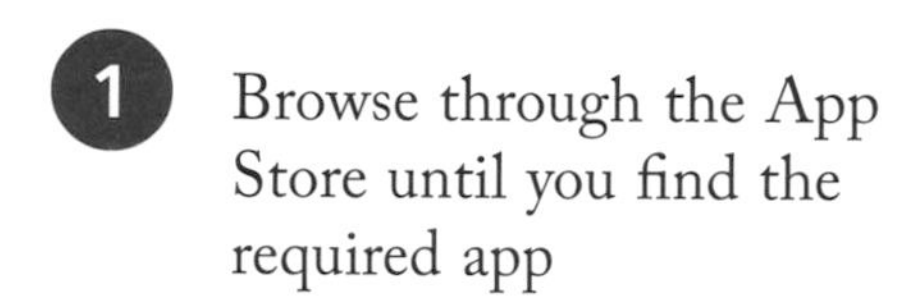

1. Browse through the App Store until you find the required app

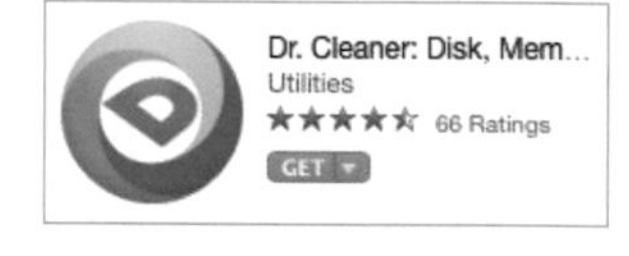

2. Click on the app to view a detailed description about it

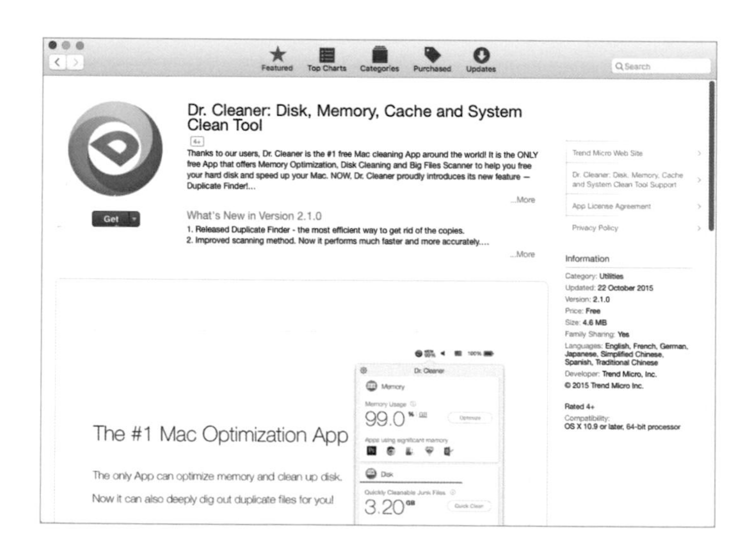

When downloading apps, start with a free one so that you can get used to the process before you buy paid-for apps.

3. Click on the button underneath the app icon to download it. If there is no charge for the app, the button will say "Free"

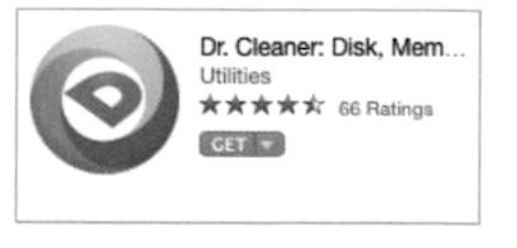

4. If there is a charge for the app, the button will say **Buy App**

5. Click on the **Install App** button

6. Enter your **Apple ID** account details to continue downloading the app

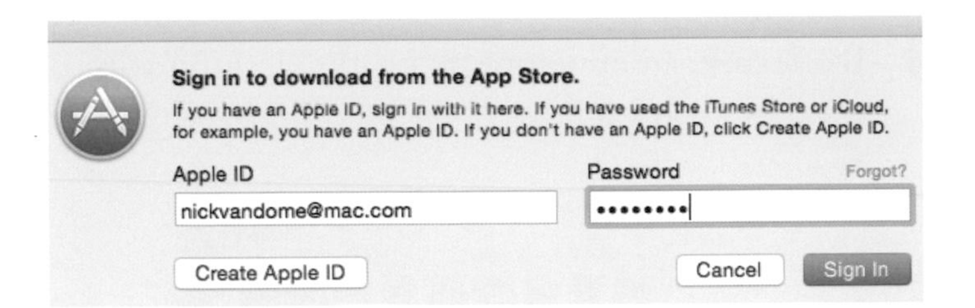

Sign in to download from the App Store.
If you have an Apple ID, sign in with it here. If you have used the iTunes Store or iCloud, for example, you have an Apple ID. If you don't have an Apple ID, click Create Apple ID.
Apple ID
Password
Forgot?
nickvandome@mac.com
Create Apple ID
Cancel
Sign In

7. The progress of the download is displayed in a progress bar underneath the Launchpad icon on the Dock

8. Once it has been downloaded, the app is available within Launchpad

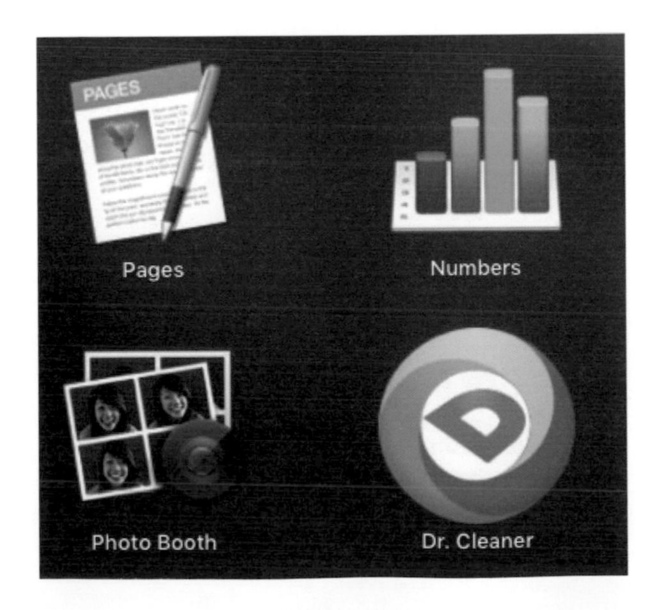

Depending on their size, different apps take differing amounts of time to be downloaded.

As you download more apps, additional screens will be created within the Launchpad to accommodate them.

Full-Screen Apps

When working with apps we all like to be able to see as much of a window as possible. With OS X El Capitan, this is possible with the full-screen app. This allows you to expand an app with this functionality so that it takes up the whole of your monitor or screen with a minimum of toolbars visible. Some apps have this functionality but some do not. To use full-screen apps:

In OS X El Capitan, the Mail app is the latest one to have full-screen functionality added.

1. By default, an app appears on the desktop with other windows behind it

If the button in Step 2 is not visible then the app does not have the full-screen functionality.

2. Click on this button at the top left-hand corner of the app's window

3. The app is expanded to take up the whole window. The main Apple Menu bar and the Dock are hidden

4. To view the main Menu bar, move the cursor over the top of the screen

5. You can move between all full-screen apps by swiping with three fingers left or right on a trackpad or Magic Mouse

For more information about navigating with a trackpad or a Magic Mouse, see pages 44-47.

6. Move the cursor over the top left-hand corner of the screen and click on this button to close the full-screen functionality

Click on an app at the top of the Mission Control window to make it the currently active app.

7. In Mission Control, all of the open full-screen apps are shown in the top row

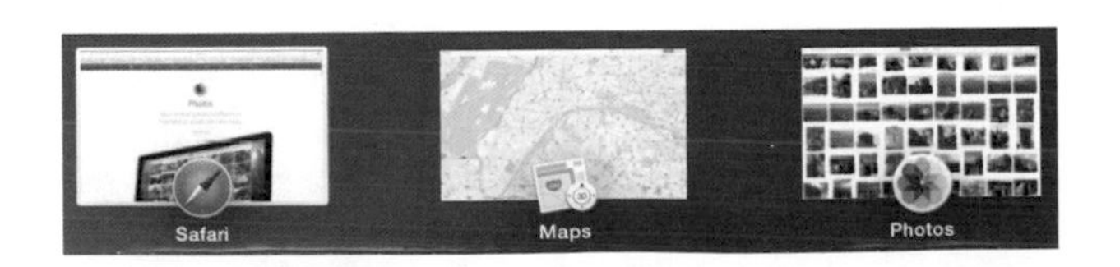

Split View

Split View is a new feature in OS X El Capitan.

When working with computers it can sometimes be beneficial to be able to view two windows next to each other. This can be to compare information in two different windows, or just to be able to use two windows without having to access them from the Desktop each time. In OS X El Capitan, two windows can be displayed next to each other using the Split View feature:

1. By default, all open windows are layered on top of each other, with the active one at the top

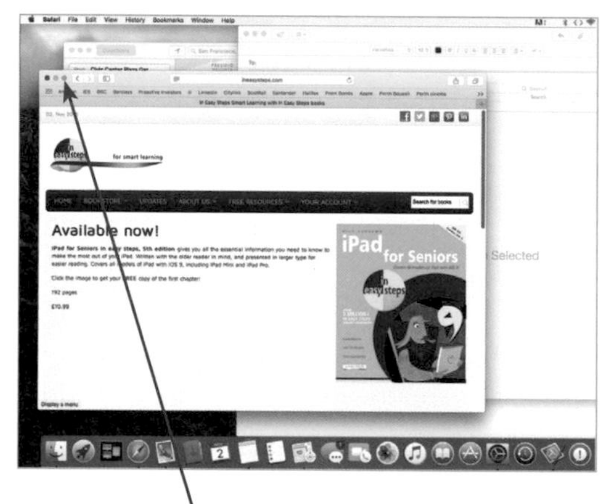

If you click once on the green maximize button this will display the app in full screen mode, rather than holding on it for Split View.

2. Press and hold on the green maximize button to activate Split View. The active window is displayed in the left-hand side of the screen, with thumbnails of the other open apps in the right-hand side

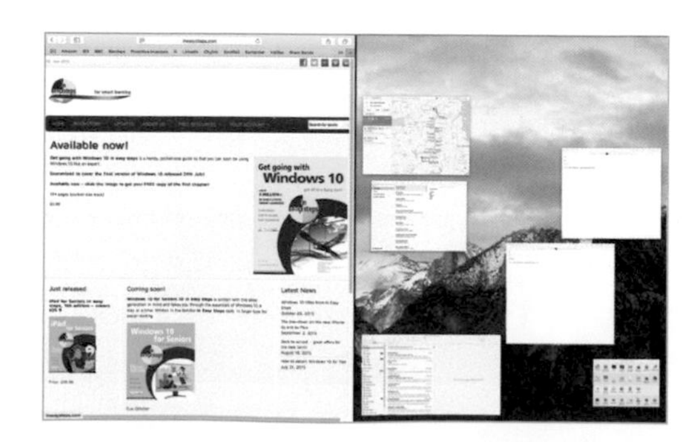

3. Click on one of the apps in the right-hand side in Step 2 to add it as the other Split View panel. Click on each window in Split View to make it active

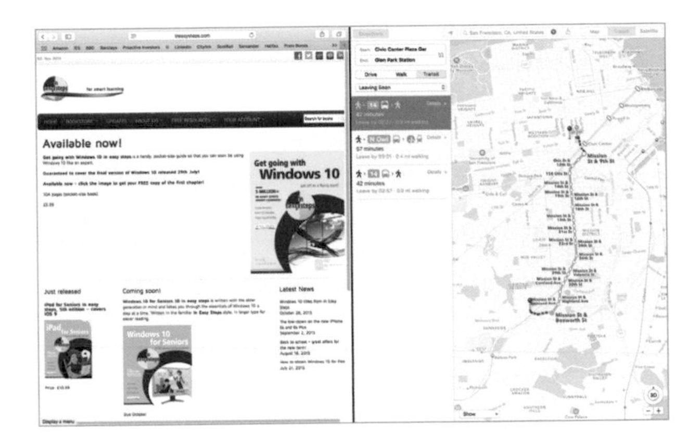

Don't forget

You can work on one panel in Split View, i.e. move through web pages, without affecting the content in the app on the other side.

4. Drag the middle divider bar to resize either of the Split View panels, to change the viewing area

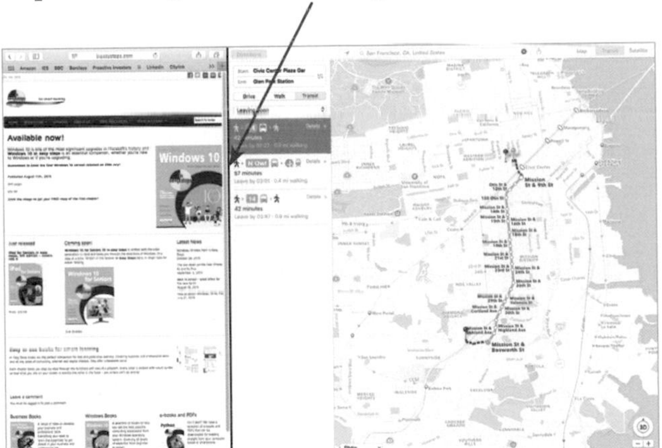

Swap the windows in Split View by dragging the top toolbar of one app into the other window.

5. Move the cursor over the left-hand edge of the window to display the sidebar menu for that app, if it has one

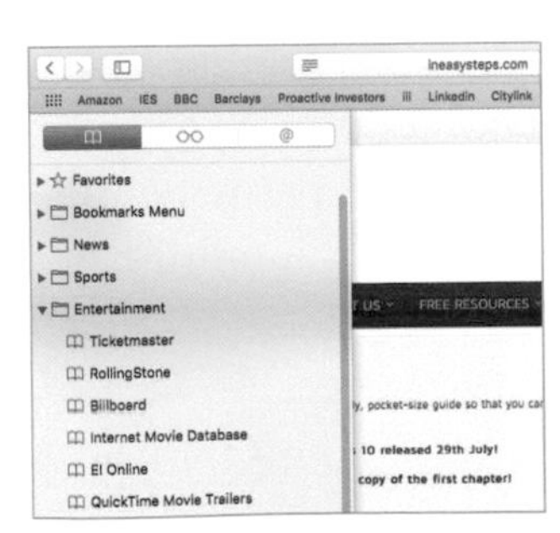

Navigating in OS X

One of the most revolutionary features of OS X is the way in which you can navigate around your applications, web pages and documents. This involves a much greater reliance on swiping on a trackpad or adapted mouse; techniques that have been imported from the iPhone and the iPad. These are known as multi-touch gestures and to take full advantage of these you will need to have one of the following devices:

- **A trackpad**. This will be found on MacBooks.
- **A Magic Trackpad**. This can be used with an iMac, a Mac Mini or a Mac Pro. It works wirelessly via Bluetooth.
- **A Magic Mouse**. This can be used with an iMac, a Mac Mini or a Mac Pro. It can also be used with a MacBook if desired. It works wirelessly via Bluetooth.

Don't forget

If you do not have a trackpad, a Magic Trackpad or a Magic Mouse you can still navigate within OS X El Capitan with a traditional mouse and scroll bars in windows.

All of these devices work using a swiping technique with fingers moving over their surface. This should be done with a light touch; it is a gentle swipe, and no pressure is applied to the device.

The trackpads and Magic Mouse do not have any buttons in the same way as traditional devices. Instead, specific areas are clickable so that you can still perform left- and right-click operations.

Working with scroll bars

In OS X El Capitan, scroll bars in web pages and documents are more reactive to the device being used on the computer.

By default, with a Magic Trackpad, a trackpad or a Magic Mouse, scroll bars are only visible when scrolling is actually taking place. However, if a mouse is being used they will be visible permanently, although this can be changed for all devices. The full list of these multi-touch gestures is shown on page 47.

Multi-Touch Preferences

Some multi-touch gestures only have a single action, which cannot be changed. However, others have options for changing the action for a specific gesture. This is done within the Trackpad preferences, where a full list of multi-touch gestures is shown:

Point & Click Preferences

1. Access the **System Preferences** and click on the **Trackpad** button

2. Click on the **Point & Click** tab

3. The actions are described on the left, with a graphic explanation on the right

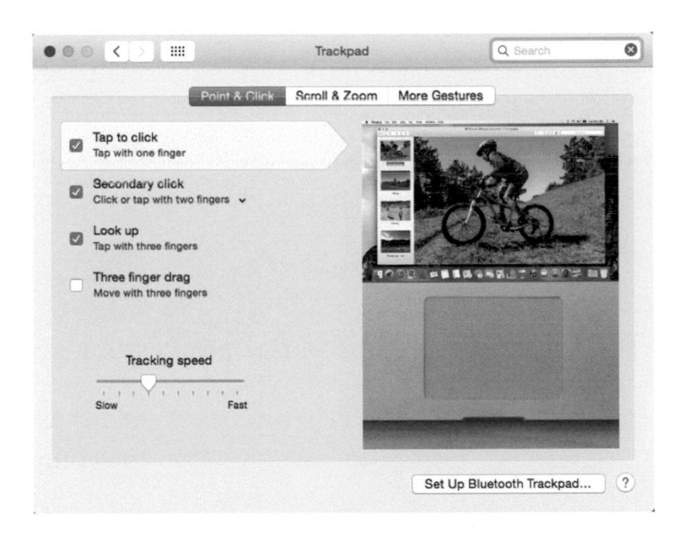

4. If there is a down-arrow next to an option, click on it to change the way an action is activated

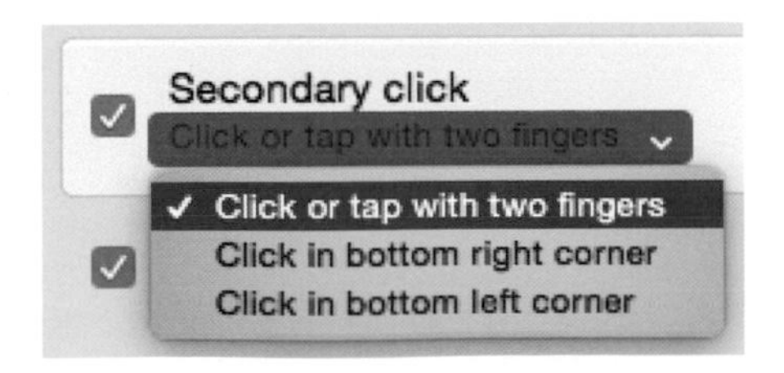

When setting multi-touch preferences try to avoid having too many gestures using the same number of fingers, in case some of them override the others.

...cont'd

Scroll & Zoom Preferences

1. Click on the **Scroll & Zoom** tab

2. The actions are described on the left, with a graphic explanation on the right

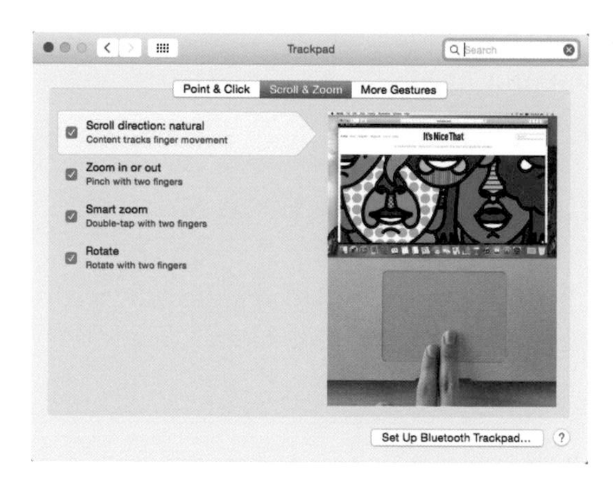

Move the cursor over one of the actions in the left-hand panel to view an animated effect of the action in the right-hand panel.

More Gestures Preferences

1. Click on the **More Gestures** tab More Gestures

2. The actions are described on the left, with a graphic explanation on the right

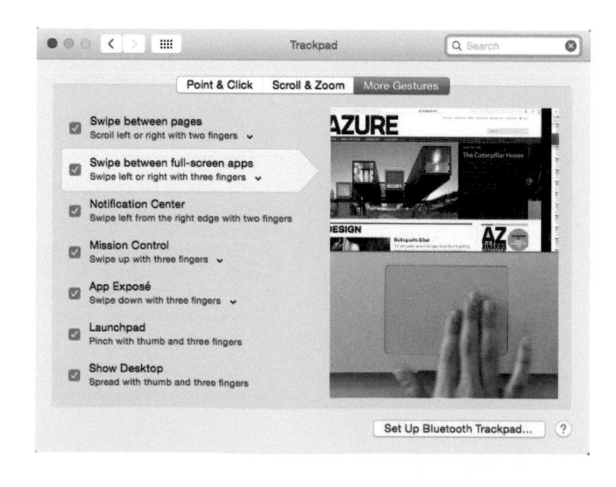

There will be some slightly different gestures for the trackpad, Magic Trackpad and the Magic Mouse.

Multi-Touch Gestures

The list of trackpad multi-touch gestures (relevant ones for a Magic Mouse are in brackets) are:

Point & Click

- Tap to click – tap once with one finger (same for the Magic Mouse)
- Secondary click – click or tap with two fingers (single-click on the right of the Magic Mouse)
- Look up – double-tap with three fingers
- Three finger drag – move with three fingers

Scroll & Zoom

- Scroll direction – content tracks finger movement, with two fingers (one finger with the Magic Mouse)
- Zoom in or out – pinch or spread with two fingers
- Smart zoom – double-tap with two fingers (double-tap with one finger with the Magic Mouse)
- Rotate – rotate with two fingers

More Gestures

- Swipe between pages – scroll left or right with two fingers (scroll left or right with one finger with the Magic Mouse)
- Swipe between full-screen apps – swipe left or right with three fingers (swipe left or right with two fingers with the Magic Mouse)
- Access Mission Control – swipe up with three fingers (double-tap with two fingers with the Magic Mouse)
- Access Launchpad – pinch with thumb and three fingers
- Show Desktop – spread with thumb and three fingers

For the multi-touch gestures there does not have to be a great deal of pressure applied for scrolling, zooming and swiping.

Removing Items

As you work on your Mac you will have some files, folders and apps that you definitely want to keep, and others that you would like to remove. To do this:

Beware

Some apps take up a lot of space on the hard drive. If you do not need an app, it is worth thinking about removing it. But make sure you still have a copy of any non-App Store apps (like Adobe suite, for example) in case you ever need to re-install it at a later date.

1. In the Finder, click on the item you want to remove

2. Drag it onto the **Trash** icon on the Dock

Don't forget

If you have downloaded apps from the App Store you will be able to re-install them from there by downloading them again.

3. To empty all of the items from the Trash, select **Finder > Empty Trash...** from the Menu bar

Finder File Edit View
About Finder
Preferences... ⌘,
Empty Trash... ⇧⌘⌫

Beware

Only empty the trash if you are sure you do not want any of the files or folders which are in there.

3 Organizing Your Mac

Keeping everything organized on a computer can be a bit of a headache. This chapter shows how to work with files and folders on your Mac, and details some useful apps, such as those for an address book, making notes and setting reminders.

Creating Files

There are generally two ways for creating files on a Mac. One is to generate a new file within the app you are using and then save this into a folder. The other is to import files that have already been created, such as digital photographs.

Don't forget

See pages 66-73 for more information on working with digital photographs.

Creating new files

The process for creating new files is essentially the same for all apps:

1. Open the app you want to use
2. Select **File > New** from the app's Menu bar

3. Depending on the app, there may be a properties window that can be used to define various elements of the file being created. Some apps also have templates that can be used as the basis of the document you want to create

4. Add the required content to the file

Always save new files once they have been created, and keep saving them at regular intervals (**File > Save** from the app's Menu bar) so that you do not lose any work.

Sharing Files

It is possible to share a range of files from the Finder, using the Share button. This can be used to share a selected item, or items, in a variety of ways appropriate to the type of file that has been selected. For instance, a photo will have options including the photo-sharing site Flickr, while a text document will have fewer options. To share items directly from the Finder:

The Share button is available from many apps throughout El Capitan. This means that there is increased functionality for sharing items. For instance, you can share web pages from Safari or share photos from the Photos app.

1. Locate and select the item(s) that you want to share

2. Click on the **Share** button on the Finder toolbar and select one of the options

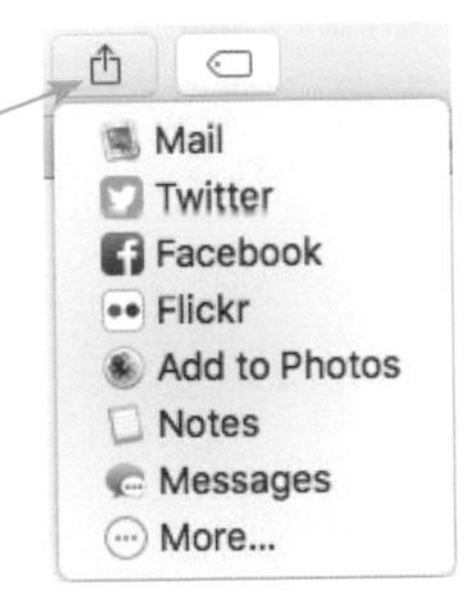

3. For some of the options, such as Twitter, Facebook and Flickr, you will be asked to add an account. If you already have an account you can enter the details or, if not, you can create a new account

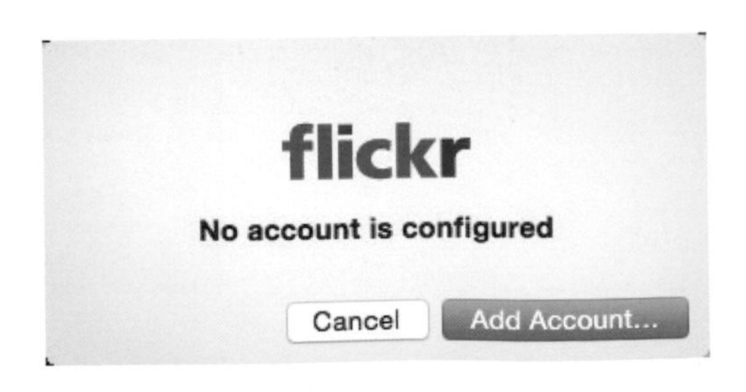

To the left of the Share button on the Finder is a button for changing the arrangement of items within the Finder. Click on this button to access arrangement options such as Name, Kind, Date and Size.

Opening Items

It is possible to open items on your Mac from the Dock, from the Finder or from the Launchpad.

From the Dock

1. Click on an item once to open it (app) or make it active (file)

From the Finder

1. Browse to the item you want to open
2. Double-click on the required item to open it

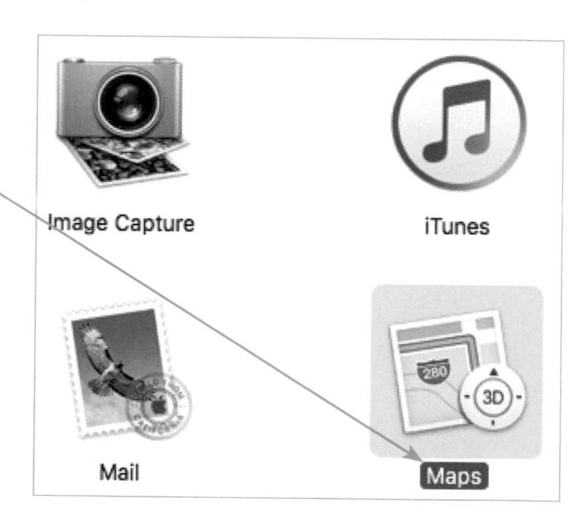

From the Launchpad

1. Click on this button on the Dock

2. Click on the required item to open it

Beware

Files can be saved onto the Desktop and opened from there. However, if there are too many items on the Desktop this can increase the time it takes the Mac to boot up and be ready for use after it has been turned on.

Don't forget

Folders and files can be opened from the Dock (if they have been added there) and the Finder. However, only apps can be opened from the Launchpad.

Creating a Folder Structure

As you create more and more files on your Mac it can become harder to find what you are looking for. To try to simplify this, it is a good idea to have a robust folder structure. This gives you a logical path to follow when you are looking for items. To create a folder structure:

Macs use spring-loaded folders. This means that if you drag a file over a folder and hold it there, the folder will automatically open. As long as you keep the mouse button held down, you can do this through as many layers as there are in a folder structure.

1. In the Finder, click on the **Documents** button

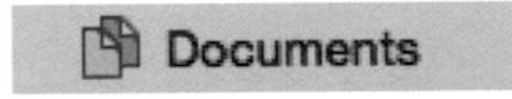

2. In the main Finder window Ctrl + click and select **New Folder**

3. Enter a name for the new folder

4. Double-click on the new folder to open it

5. Initially, the folder is empty. Repeat Steps 2, 3 and 4 to create as much of a folder structure as required

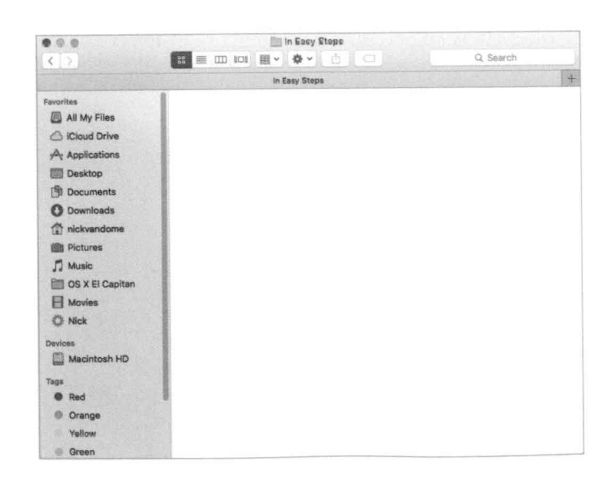

Create folders for different types of content, to keep the Finder as organized as possible.

Compiling an Address Book

Having an address book on your Mac is an excellent way to keep track of your family and friends and it can also be used within other apps, such as the Mail app for email. To create an address book:

1. Click on this icon on the Dock, or in the Launchpad

2. Click on an existing contact here

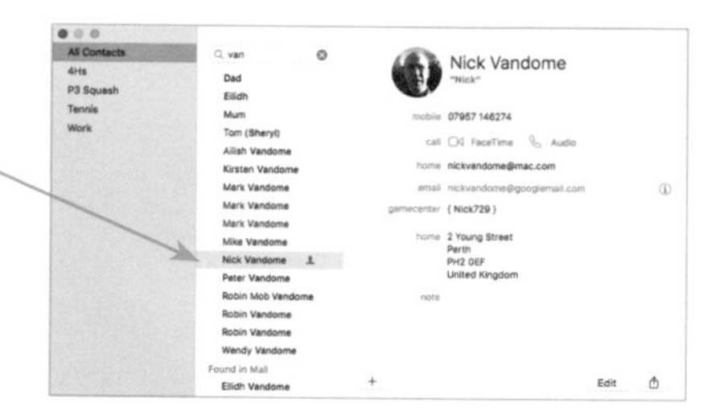

3. Their details are displayed in the right-hand window

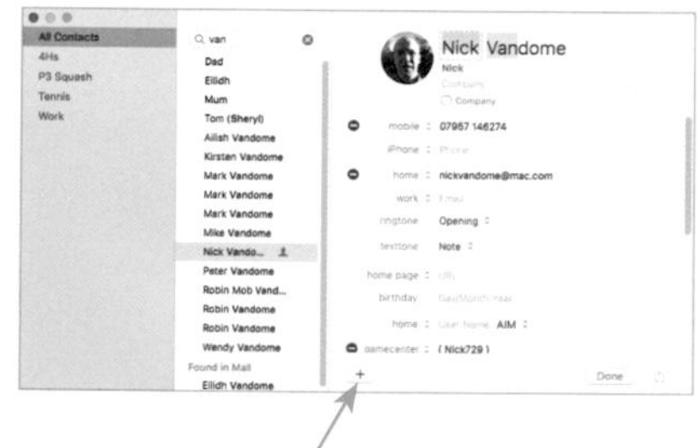

4. Click here under the Name panel to add a new contact

5. Enter the person's details

6. Click on the **Done** button to finish the entry

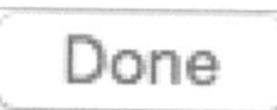

Don't forget

You can edit an individual's entry at any time by clicking on their name and clicking on the **Edit** button. Click on the **Done** button once you have finished updating their details.

Hot tip

If a contact has been added to the Address Book and their details include an email address, then you can enter them as a recipient for an email in the Mail app by typing the first two or three letters of their name: suggestions will appear and you can select their email address from here.

Adding a Calendar

Electronic calendars are now a standard part of modern life, and on the Mac this function is performed by the Calendar app. To create a calendar:

1. Click on this icon on the Dock, or in the Launchpad

2. Select whether to view the calendar by day, week, month or year

3. Click on the **Today** button to view the current day. Click on the forward or back arrows to move to the next day, week, month or year

Calendars and address books can be backed up and shared with the online iCloud service. See Chapter Nine for more details about iCloud.

To add new events:

1. Select a date and double-click on it, or Ctrl + click on the date and select **New Event**

2. Enter the details for the new event

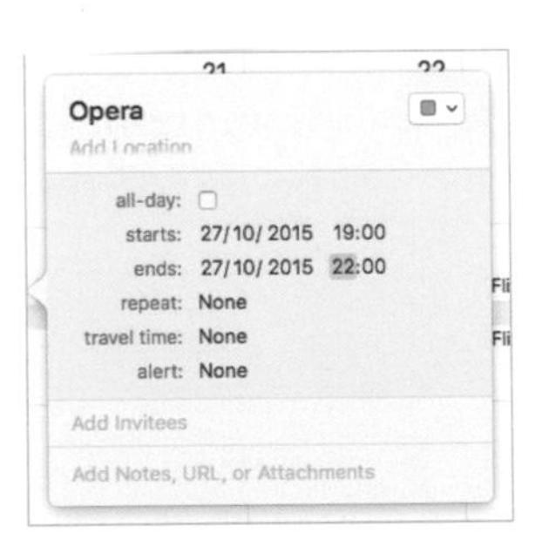

3. Double-click on an item and select options for how it is displayed

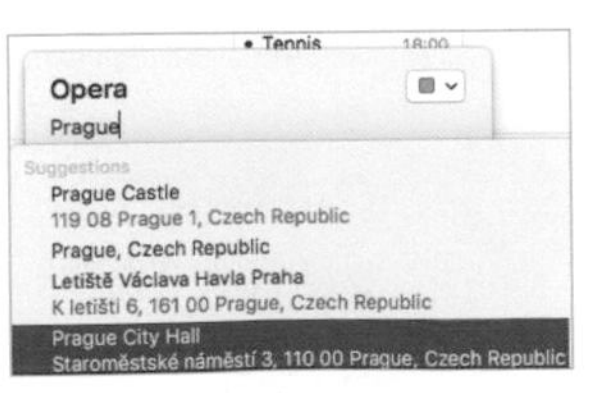

A quick event can be added to a calendar by clicking on this button at the top of the calendar window and entering the details in the **Quick Event** window that appears.

Making Notes

It is always useful to have a quick way of making notes of everyday things, such as shopping lists, recipes or packing lists for traveling. With OS X El Capitan, the Notes app is perfect for this task. To use it:

1. Click on this icon on the Dock, or in the Launchpad

2. The right-hand panel is where the note is created. The middle panel displays a list of all notes

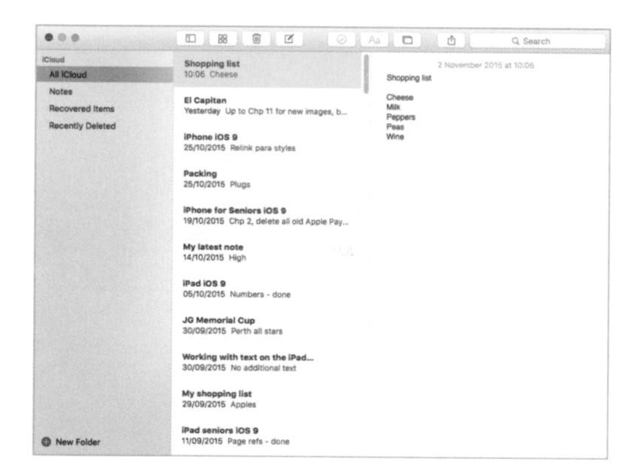

3. Click on this button to add a new note

4. As more notes are added, the most recent appears at the top of the list in the middle panel

5. Click on this button to show or hide the left-hand panel in the Notes app, which displays the notes folders

Enable iCloud for Notes so that all of your notes will be backed up and also available on all of your iCloud-enabled devices. You will also be able to access them by signing in to your account with your Apple ID at www.icloud.com

The first line of a note becomes its heading in the notes panel.

Hot tip

Click on this button to view the Attachments Browser to view all of the items you have added to your notes. You can then select an item for a new note.

Formatting notes

There are a number of formatting options for the Notes app:

There are new formatting options for the Notes app in OS X El Capitan.

1. Enter a line of text and click on this button to add a radio button

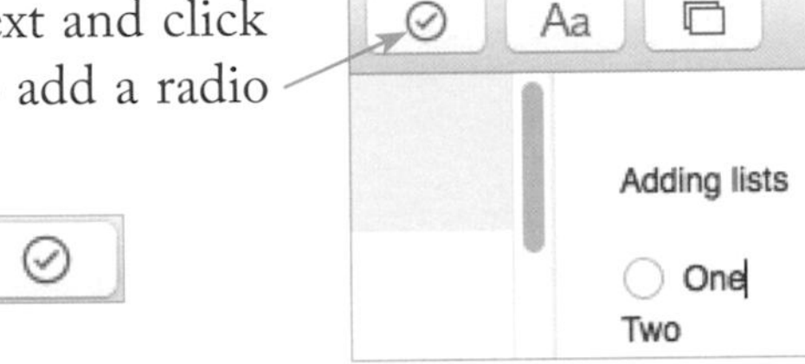

2. Click on the radio button to add a tick, to indicate that an item has been completed

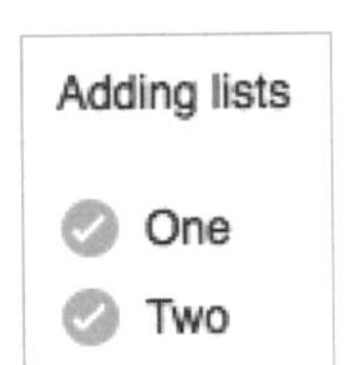

Click on the **Share** button to share a note using a range of other apps.

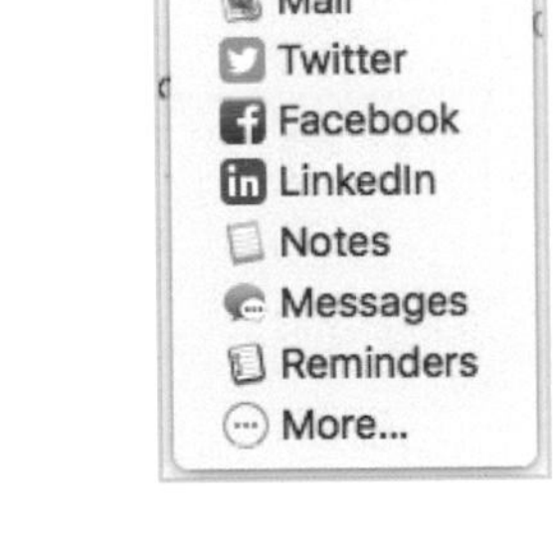

3. Drag over a piece of text and click on this button to access formatting options for it

4. Click on this button to add photos and videos to a note. Navigate to the required item and drag it into the note from the Photo Browser

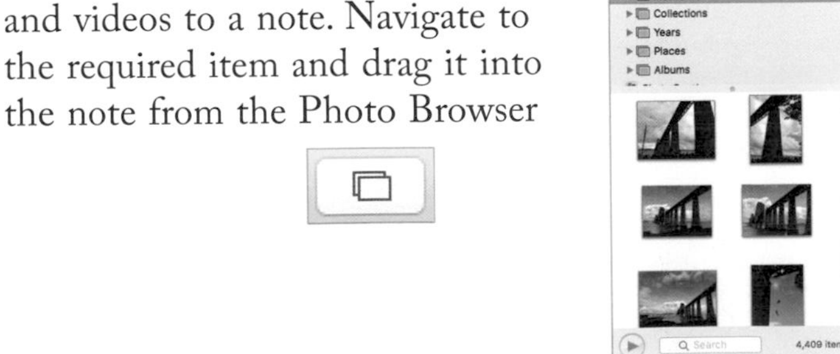

Content can be added to notes from a range of other apps, such as Safari or the Photos app, by clicking on the **Share** button and selecting **Notes** as the option.

Setting Reminders

Another useful app for staying organized is Reminders. This enables you to create lists for different topics and then set reminders for specific items. A date and time can be set for each reminder and, when this is reached, the reminder appears on your Mac screen (and in the Notification Center). To use Reminders:

As with Notes, iCloud makes your reminders available on all of your Apple devices, i.e. your Mac, iPad, iPhone and iPod Touch.

1. Click on this icon on the Dock, or in the Launchpad

2. Lists can be created for different categories of reminders. The Reminder lists are located in the left-hand panel. Click on a list name to add lists here

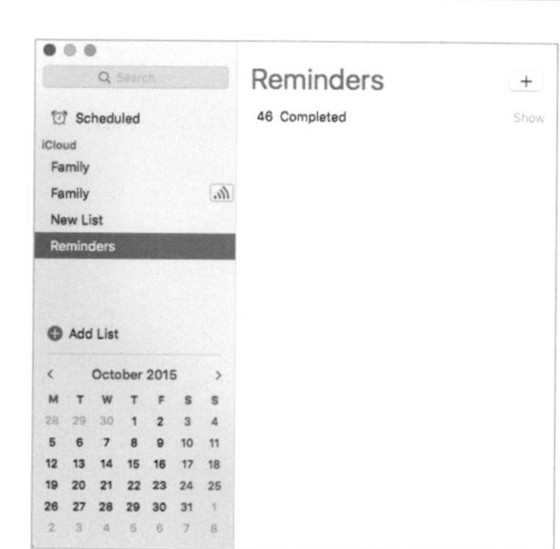

Hot tip

Roll over a reminder name to access the 'i' symbol for adding details to the reminder.

3. Click on this button to add a new reminder, or click on a new line

4. Enter text for the reminder

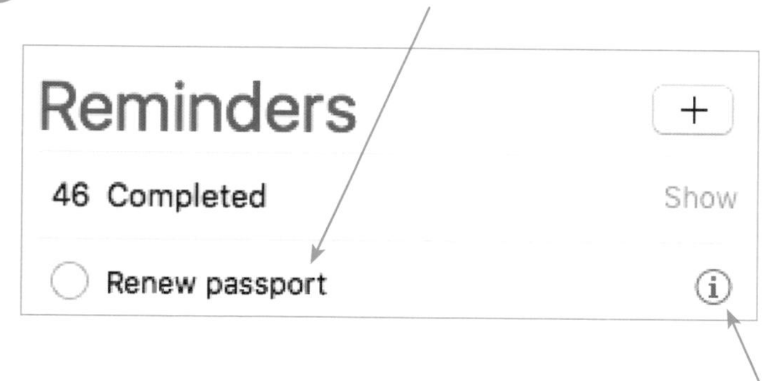

5. Click on this button to add details for the reminder

6. Check on this button to add a time and date for the reminder

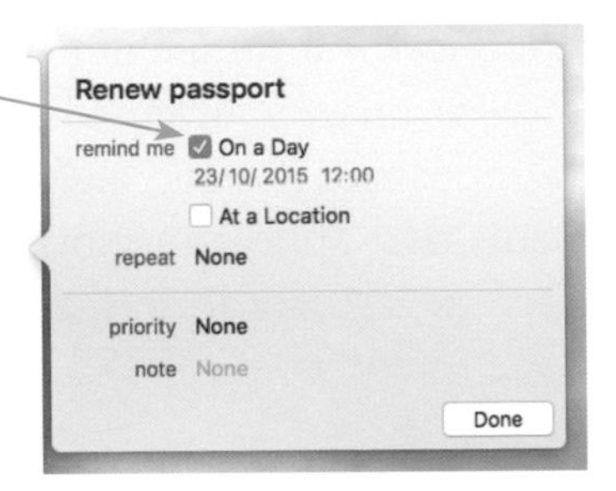

7. Click on the date and select a date for when you want the reminder alert. Do the same for the time, by typing a new time over the existing one

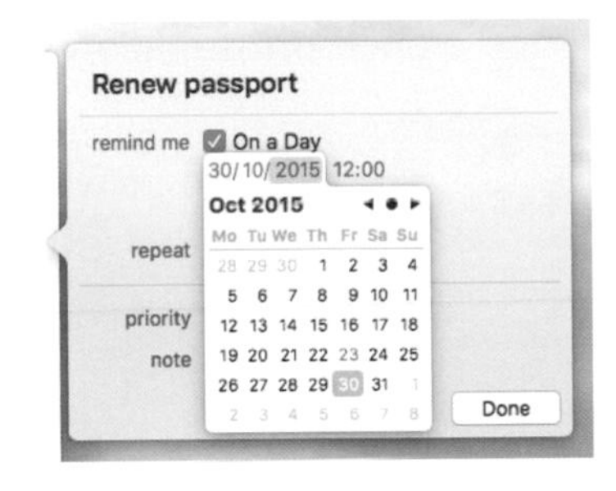

8. If required, add details for a repeat reminder and a priority level

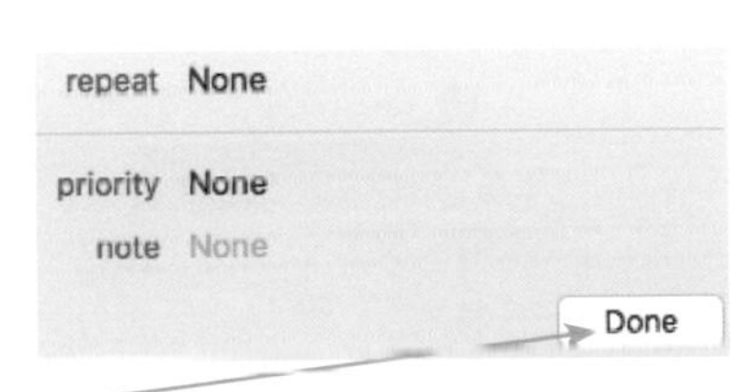

9. Click on the **Done** button

10. The reminder is set for the specified date and time. This will appear on the screen when the time arrives and also in the Notification Center, if it is set up for Reminders (see pages 60-61)

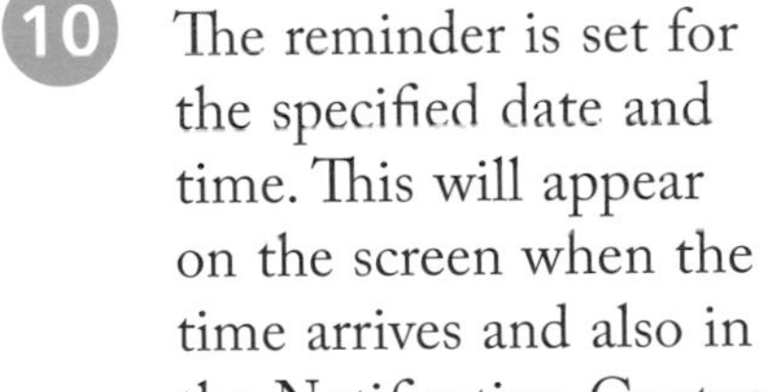

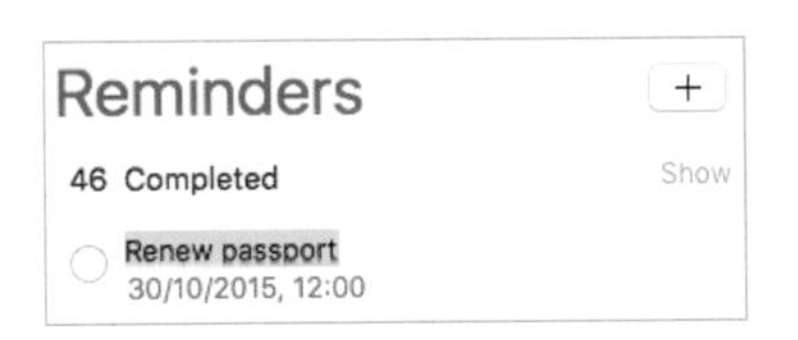

11. Check on this box to move a reminder to the Completed list

For a recurring reminder, click on the **Repeat** link at Step 8 and select a repeat option from None, Every Day, Every Week, Every 2 Weeks, Every Month, Every Year.

Getting Notifications

The Notification Center option provides a single location to view all of your emails, messages, updates and alerts. It appears at the top right-hand corner of the screen. The items that appear in Notifications are set up within System Preferences. To do this:

1. Open **System Preferences** and click on this icon

2. The items that will appear in the Notification Center are listed here. Click on an item to select it and set its notification options

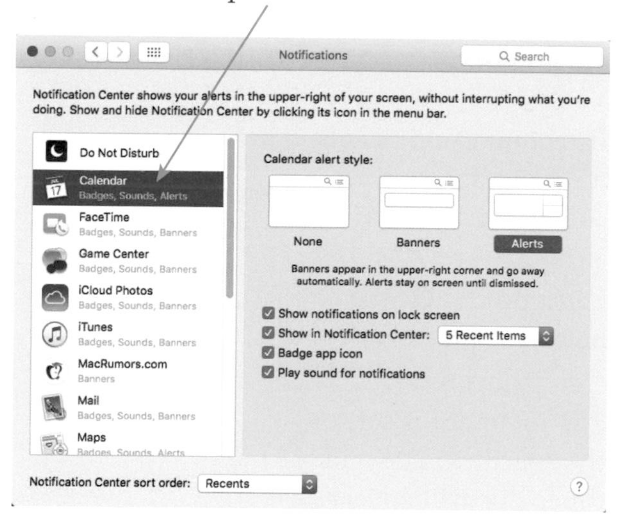

3. To disable an item so that it does not appear in the Notification Center, select it as above and check off the **Show in Notification Center** box

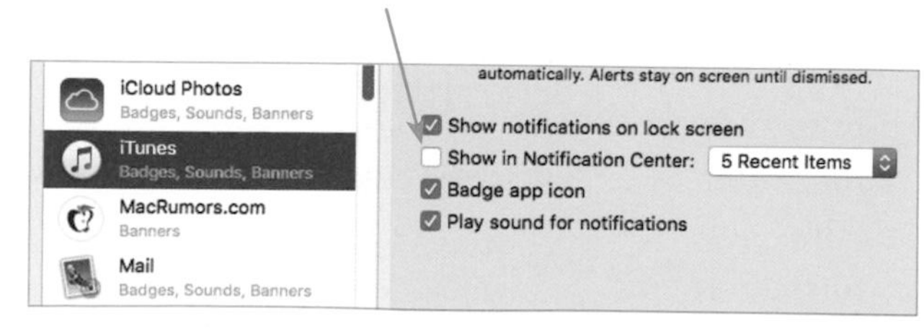

Twitter feeds and Facebook updates can also be set up to appear in the Notification Center.

Do not set up too many notifications, otherwise you may be bombarded with messages.

Viewing Notifications

Notifications appear in the Notification Center. The way they appear can be determined in the System Preferences:

1. Select an alert style. A banner alert comes up on the screen and then disappears after a few seconds

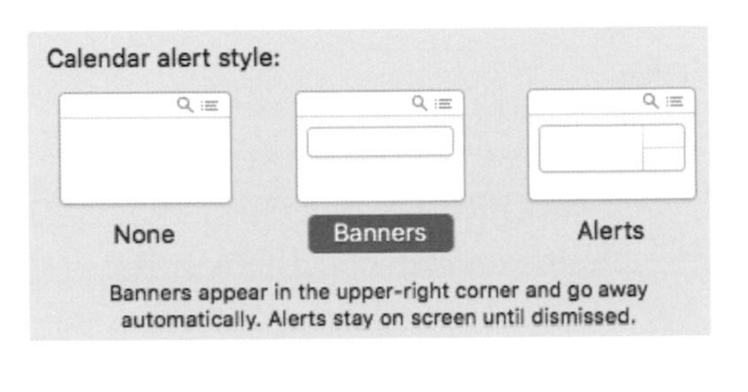

Hot tip

The Notification Center can also be displayed with a trackpad or Magic Trackpad by dragging with two fingers from right to left, starting from the far right edge.

2. The **Alerts** option shows the notification; it stays on screen until dismissed (such as this one for reminders)

3. Click on this button in the top right-hand corner of the screen to view all of the items in the Notification Center. Click on it again to hide the Notification Center

Don't forget

Software updates also appear in the Notification Center, when they are available.

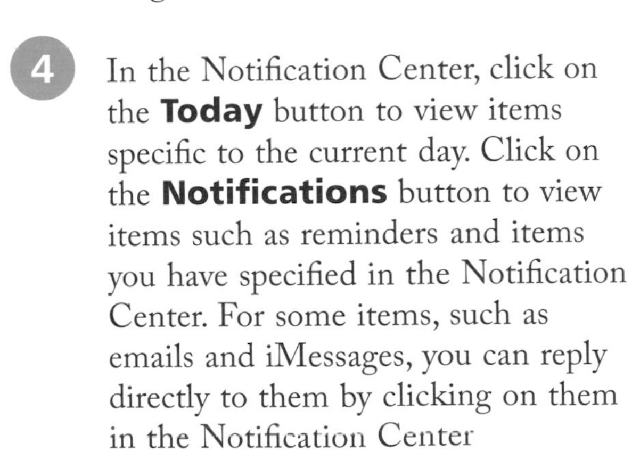

4. In the Notification Center, click on the **Today** button to view items specific to the current day. Click on the **Notifications** button to view items such as reminders and items you have specified in the Notification Center. For some items, such as emails and iMessages, you can reply directly to them by clicking on them in the Notification Center

Finding Things

On Macs it is also possible to search your folders and files, using the built-in search facilities. This can be done either through the Finder or with the Spotlight app.

When entering search keywords try to be as specific as possible. This will cut down on the number of unwanted results.

Using Finder

1. In the Finder window, enter the search keyword(s) in this box and select the search criteria. The results are shown in the Finder

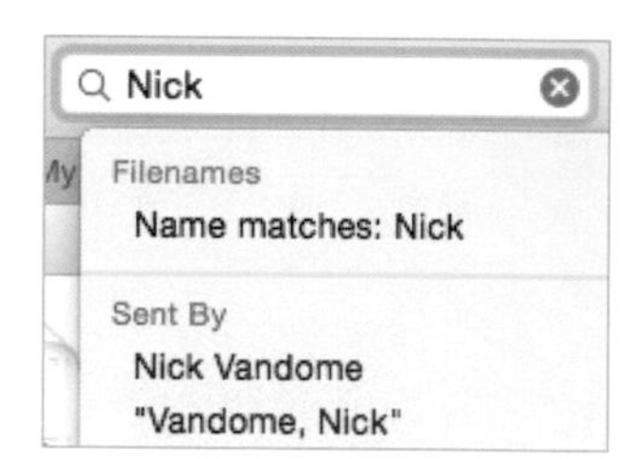

2. Select the areas over which you want the search performed, e.g. Home folder or Documents

Both folders and files will be displayed in the Finder as part of the search results.

3. Double-click on a folder to see its contents or double-click on a file to open it

Using Spotlight

The Spotlight search option can also search over your Mac:

The Spotlight window can be moved and resized, and displays a greater range of information.

1. Click on this button in the right corner of the screen on the top toolbar

2. Enter a search word or phrase. Click on an item to view it, including items from the web and Wikipedia

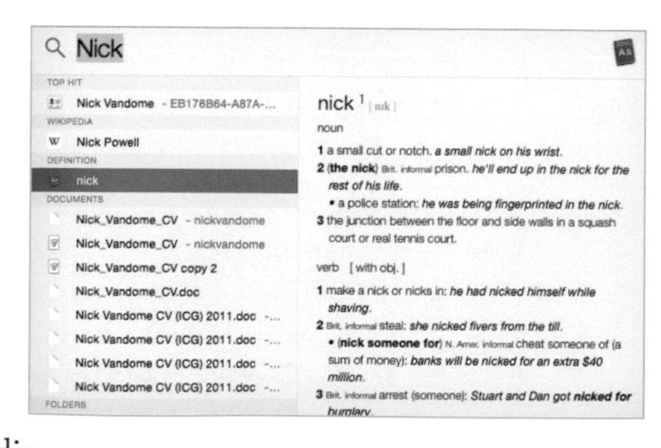

Spotlight search can show results from your Mac, the internet, iTunes, the App Store and also items such as movies nearby and local restaurants.

Adding a Printer

OS X El Capitan makes the printing process as simple as possible, partly by being able to automatically install new printers as soon as they are connected to your Mac. However, it is also possible to install printers manually. To do this:

If you have an old printer your Mac may not identify it and you will have to install the printer driver from the disk that came with the printer, or download it from the website of the printer's manufacturer.

1. Open **System Preferences** and click on the **Printers & Scanners** button

2. Currently installed printers are displayed in the Printers List. Click on this button to add a new printer

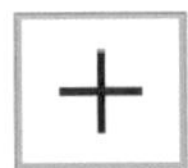

3. Select an available printer

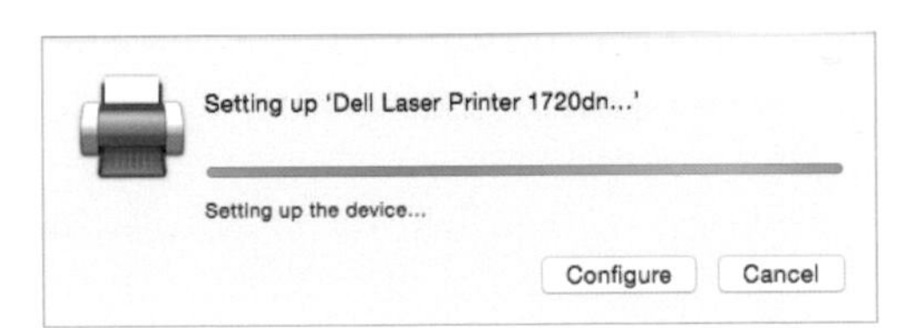

4. Click on the **Add** button to load the printer drivers for the selected printer

5. The printer drivers are added

More than one printer can be added and one will be selected as the default. If you want to use another printer, this will have to be selected manually from the **Print** window when you come to print a document.

6. Once a printer has been installed, documents can be printed by selecting **File > Print** from the Menu bar. Print settings can be set at this point and they can also be set by selecting **File > Page/Print Setup** from the Menu bar in most apps

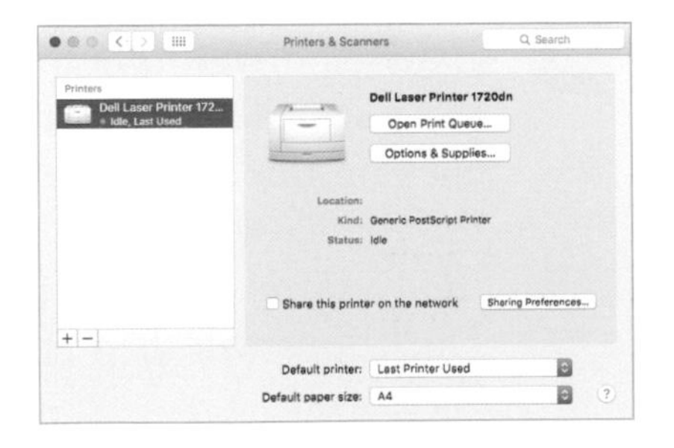

External Drives

Attaching external drives is an essential part of mobile computing: whether it is to back up data as you are traveling or for downloading photos and other items. External drives are displayed on the Desktop once they have been attached and they can then be used for the required task. To do this:

Don't forget

External drives can be items such as flash drives, digital cameras or external hard disks.

1. Attach the external drive. This is usually done with a USB cable. Once it has been attached, it is shown on the Desktop

2. The drive is shown under the **Devices** section of the Finder

3. Perform the required task for the external drive (such as copying files or folders onto it from the hard drive of your Mac computer)

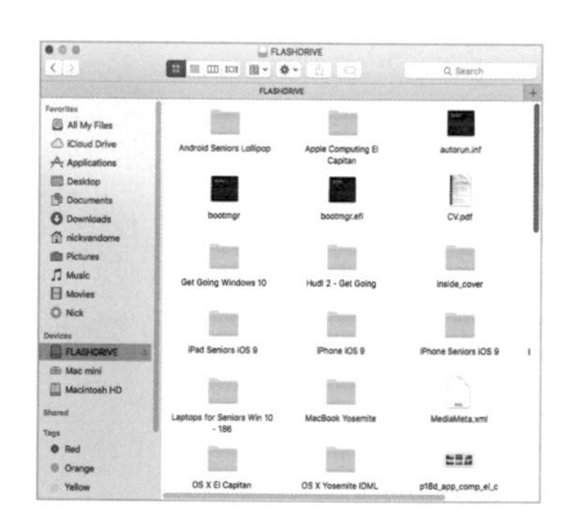

Hot tip

External drives can be renamed by **Ctrl + clicking** on their name in the Finder and overtyping it with a new name.

4. External drives have to be ejected properly, not just pulled out or removed. To do this, click on this button next to the drive in the Finder window, or drag its icon on the Desktop over the Trash icon on the Dock. This will then change into an Eject icon

4 Leisure Time

Leisure time, and how we use it, is a big issue for everyone. For Mac users this is recognized with the iLife suite of apps. This chapter looks at how to use the iLife apps to organize and edit photos, play and download music, create your own music and produce and share home movies. It also covers reading books and listening to the radio.

Using the Photos App

The Photos app is a new feature in OS X.

For a number of years the photo management and editing tool for OS X has been iPhoto. However, in Spring 2015 the Photos app was introduced. iPhoto can still be used, but the Photos app is designed to mirror the one used on iOS 9 devices and integrate more with iCloud, so that you can store all of your photos in the iCloud, and then view and manage them on all of your Apple devices.

If you are using the Photos app, you can specify how it operates with iCloud in the iCloud System Preferences:

1. Click on the **System Preferences** button 

2. Click on the **iCloud** button in the System Preferences window 

3. Check On the **Photos** checkbox

4. Click on the **Options** button for Photos 

5. Select the options for using iCloud with the Photos app. Click on the **Done** button 

The iCloud options for the Photos app are: **iCloud Photo Library**, which uploads your entire photo library to the iCloud; **My Photo Stream**, which uploads photos that are added from the device you are using; and **iCloud Photo Sharing**, which enables you to share photos from the Photos app with family and friends.

Getting started with the Photos app

If you have previously used iPhoto, you can import your photo library into Photos when you start using it:

1. Click on the **Photos** app in the Dock or from the Launchpad

2. Click on the **Get Started** button in the Welcome window

Once the Photos app has been set up and you have imported your photos, you will be able to view your photos immediately, each time you open the Photos app.

3. Select the photo library that you want to import and click on the **Choose Library** button

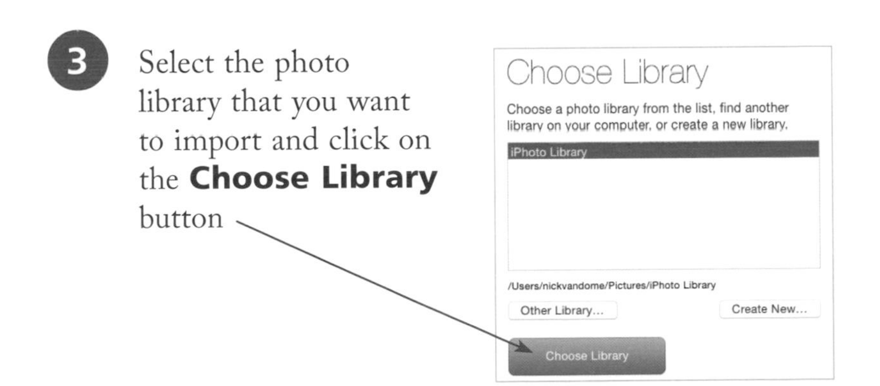

If you have a large number of photos to import, it could take a few minutes to complete the process.

4. The photo library will be prepared so that you can use it with the Photos app

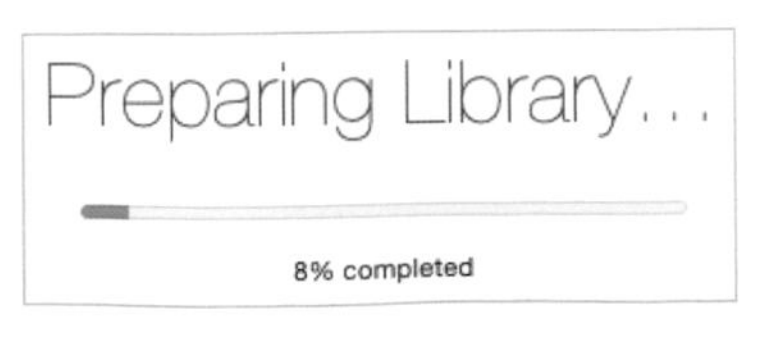

Viewing Photos

The Photos app can be used to view photos according to years, collections, moments or at full size. This enables you to view your photos according to dates and times at which they were taken.

Hot tip

Photos can be imported into the Photos app by selecting **File > Import** from the Menu bar and navigating to the required location within the Finder. This can be used to import photos from your Mac or an external device connected with a USB cable, such as a digital camera, a card reader or a flash drive.

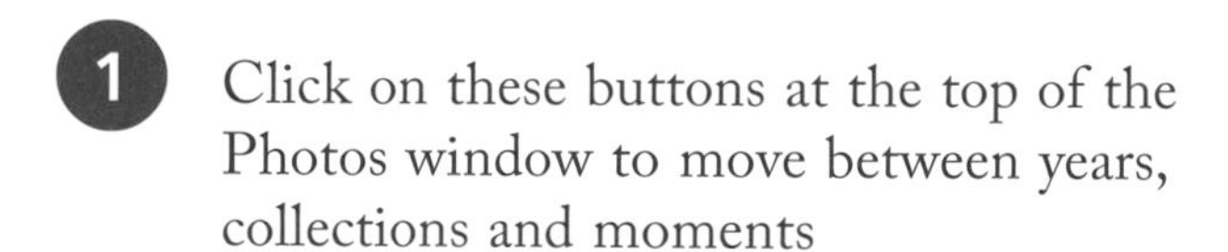

1 Click on these buttons at the top of the Photos window to move between years, collections and moments

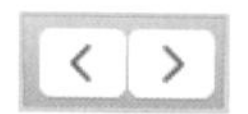

2 Click on the left-hand button in Step 1 to move to **Years** view

3 Click and hold on a thumbnail in Years view to enlarge it

4 Click on a photo within the Years section to view the **Collections**. This displays groups of photos (Moments) taken at the same location

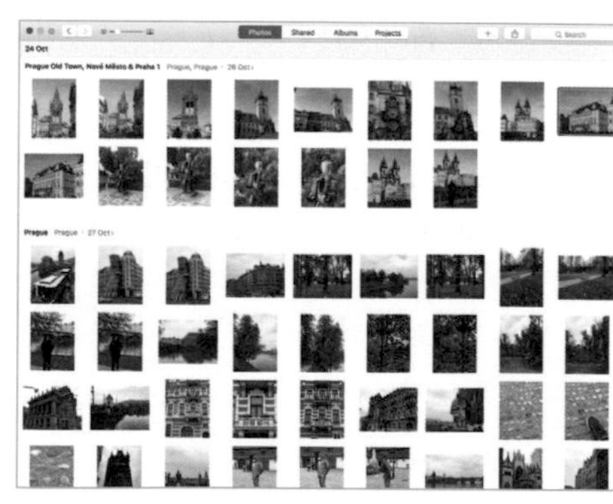

Don't forget

Click on the **Photos** tab at the top of the Photos app window to view your photos in **Years**, **Collections**, **Moments** or full size.

Photos

5. Click on a photo within the Collections section to view specific **Moments**. This displays photos taken at the same time, in the same location

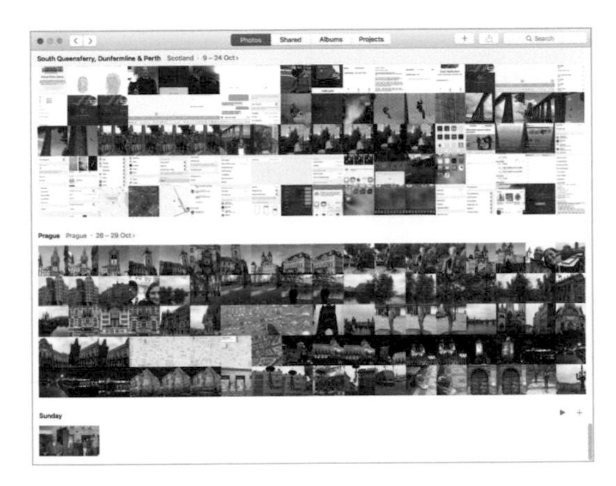

Drag this slider to change the magnification of the photo, or photos, being displayed, in Moments, or at full size view.

6. Double-click on a photo in the Collections or Moments section to view it at full size

Rollover a photo in Collections or Moments view and click on the left-hand icon below to view the relevant photos as a slideshow.

7. For a photo being displayed at full size use these buttons, from left to right, to: add it as a favorite, view information about it, add a new album and create items, share the photo or edit it

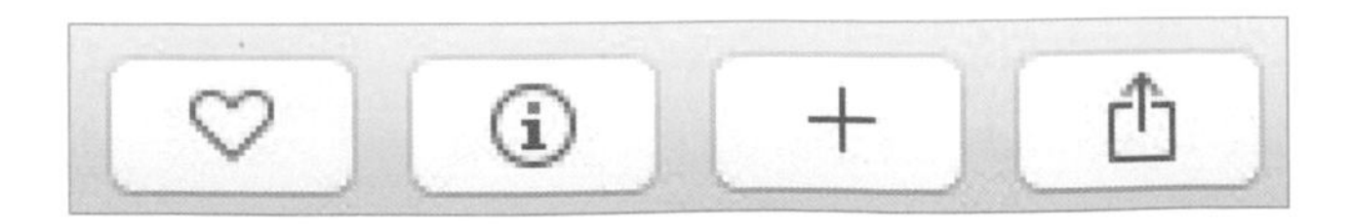

Editing Photos

The Photos app has a range of editing options so that you can fine-tune the appearance of your photos. To do this:

Most photos benefit from some cropping and this is one option that should at least be considered in most cases, to give the main subject more prominence.

Do not overdo color adjustments as this can create an unnatural effect (unless this is what you are aiming for, as it can be effective in its own right).

1. Open a photo at full size and click on the **Edit** button

Edit

2. The editing options include: **Enhance**, for auto color correction; **Rotate** for rotating the image; **Crop** for cropping the image to remove areas you do not want; **Filters**, for adding effects to the whole image (see Step 3); **Adjust**, for manual color editing (see Step 4); and **Retouch**, for removing unwanted items in an image

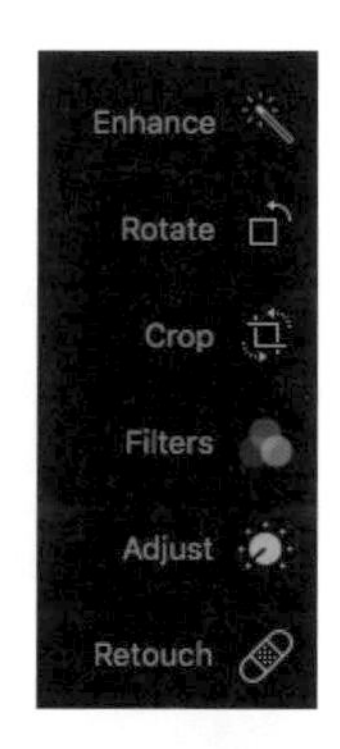

3. Click on the **Filters** button and click on one of the filter effects to apply it to the whole image. Click on the **Done** button to apply the effect

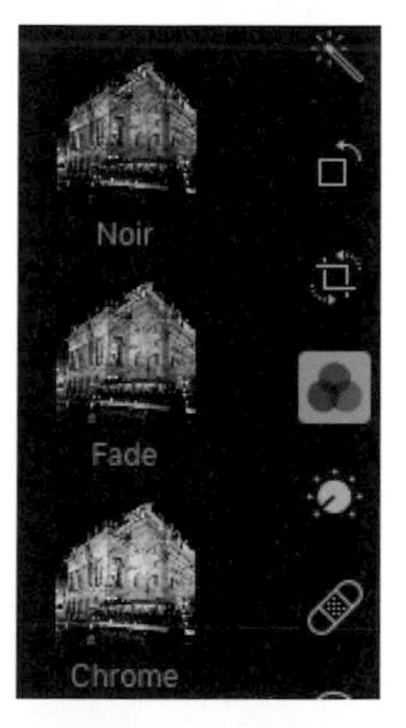

4. Click on the **Adjust** button to apply color editing manually. Drag the white bar to apply the adjustments for the required item. Click on the **Add** button to apply the changes

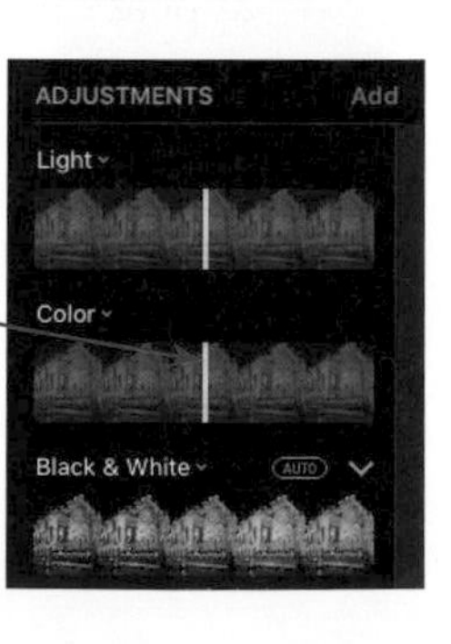

Creating Albums

Albums can be created to organize similar photos within the Photos app, so that you can find and view them in one place. To do this:

1. Click on the **Albums** tab Albums

2. Click on this button and click on the **Album** button

3. Give the album a name and click on the **OK** button

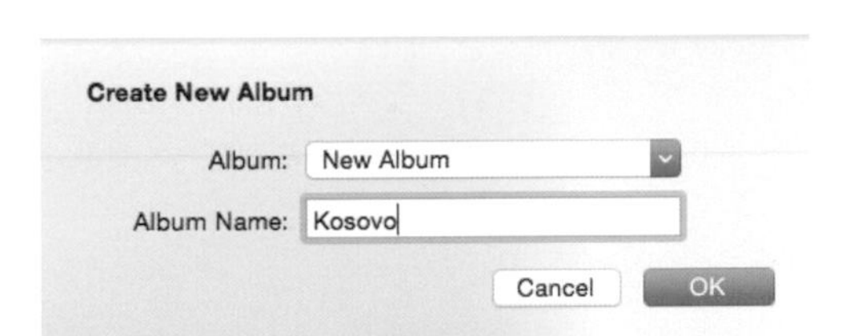

4. Select photos for the album from the main Photos window, and click on the **Add** button

5. The album you have created appears under the **Albums** tab. Also included are albums for **All Photos** (which are all of your photos within iCloud) and **My Photo Stream** (which are the photos that you have added on this device)

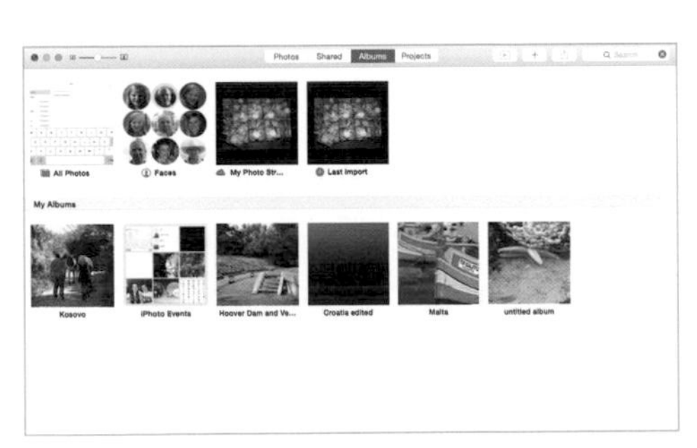

Photo projects can also be created from the Create button in Step 2. Select one of the projects (Book, Calendar or Card) and follow the wizard to create the project.

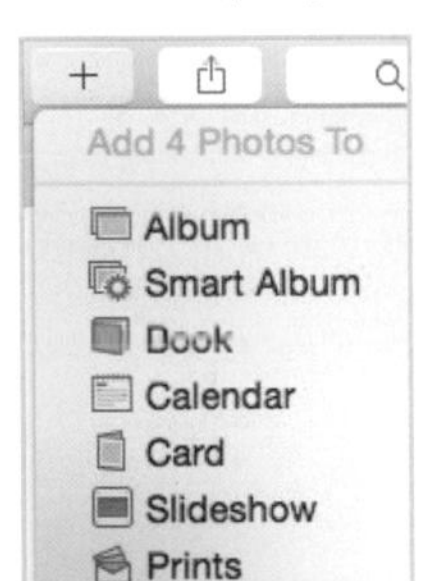

Completed projects can be viewed by clicking on the **Projects** tab at the top of the Photos app window.

Projects

Sharing Photos

Individual photos can be shared with the Photos app. Shared albums can also be created and shared using iCloud.

To share a specific photo:

1. Select it in Moments or open it at full size. Click on this button and select one of the sharing options

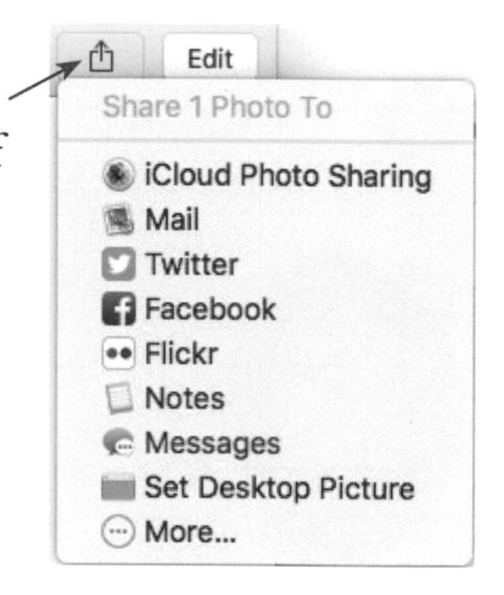

2. To share a photo via iCloud, select the **iCloud Photo Sharing** option in Step 1

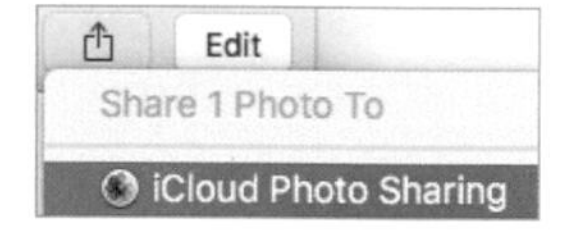

3. Select an existing shared album or click on the **New Shared Album** button to create a new shared album

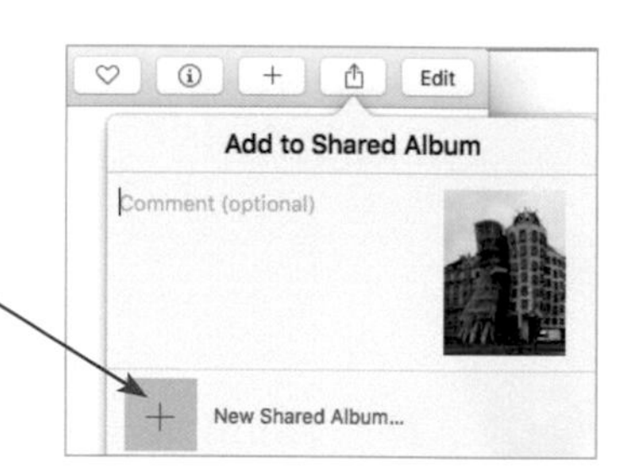

4. Shared albums can also be created in the **Shared** section. Click here, enter the details for the album and the email address of the recipient, and then click on the **Create** button. Photos can then be added in the same way as for a standard album on page 71

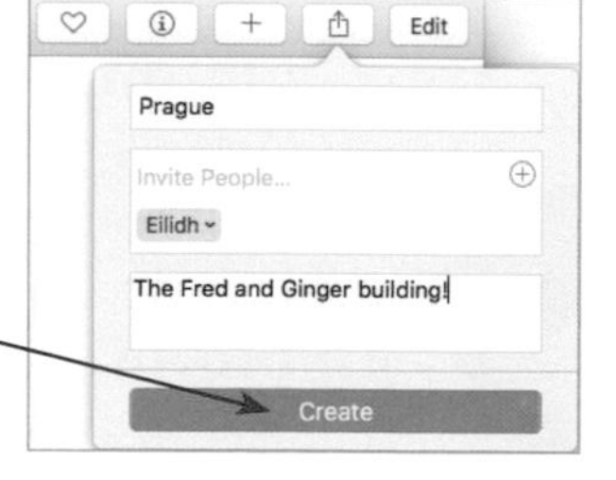

In order to use **iCloud Photo Sharing**, this has to be enabled in the iCloud System Preferences, as shown on page 66.

When you share an album with someone they will be sent an email notification.

Using iPhoto

It is possible to still use the iPhoto app in OS X El Capitan. If you have set up the Photos app you will need to specify that you want to use the photo library that was used by iPhoto. To do this:

1. Click on the **iPhoto** app in the Dock or from the Launchpad

2. Select the **iPhoto Library**

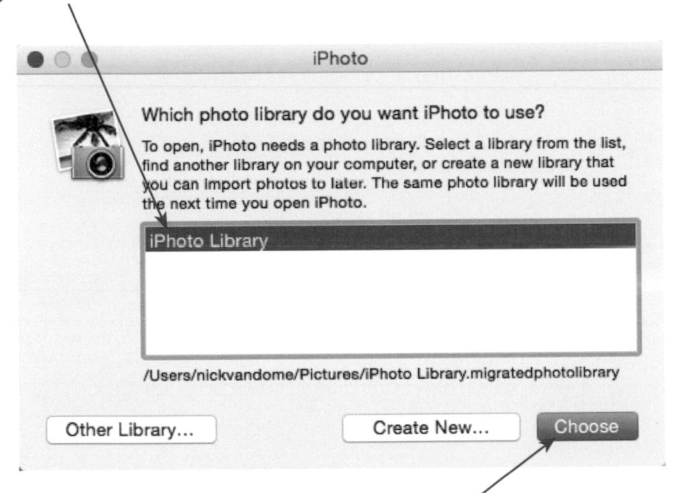

3. Click on the **Choose** button

4. Click on the **Open library in iPhoto** button

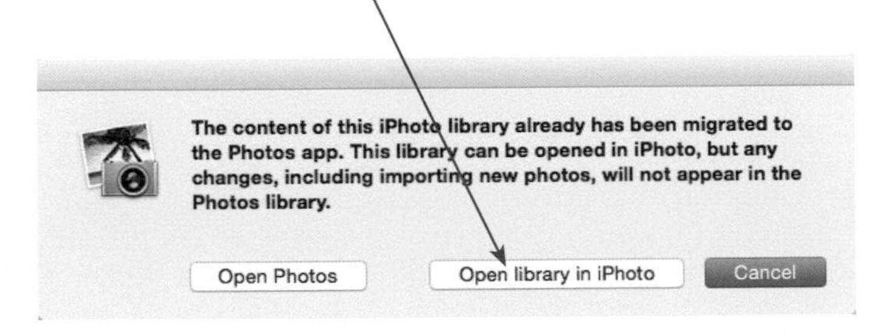

5. Items that are imported into iPhoto, or editing changes, will not appear in the Photos app

The Photos app is intended to supersede iPhoto so it is best to update to it as soon as is practical. While iPhoto can still be used at present, it will probably stop being supported by Apple at some point in the future.

Playing a Music CD

Music is one of the areas that has revived Apple's fortunes in recent years, primarily through the iPod music player and iTunes, and also the iTunes music store, where music can be bought online. iTunes is a versatile app but its basic function is to play digital music and also music CDs. To do this:

iTunes can be accessed by clicking on this icon on the Dock.

1. Insert the CD in an external CD/DVD drive
2. By default, iTunes will open and display this window. Click **No** if you just want to play the CD

3. Click on the CD name

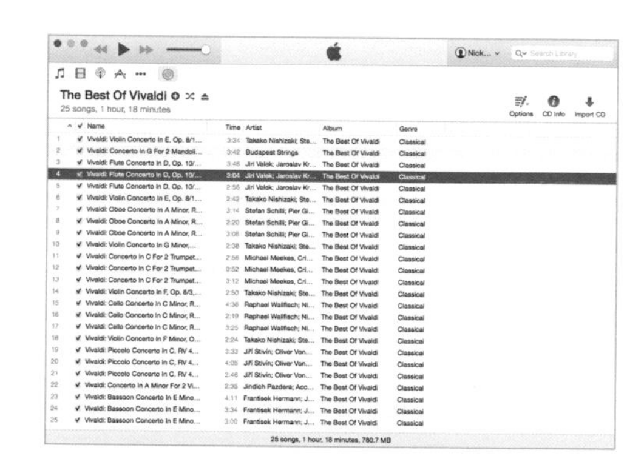

Beware

Never import music and use it for commercial purposes as this would be a breach of copyright.

4. Click on this button to play the whole CD

5. Click on the **Import CD** button if you want to copy the music from the CD onto your hard drive

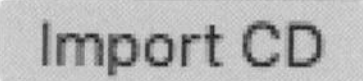

Organizing Your Music

iTunes has a variety of ways to organize your music:

1. Click on the **View > Music** button to see the iTunes categories, within a drop-down menu

View | Controls | Store | Wi
✓ Music ⌘1
Movies ⌘2
TV Shows ⌘3
More ▶

iTunes can also be used to view movies, TV shows, podcasts, and audiobooks that have been bought and downloaded from the **iTunes Store**.

2. Click on this button on the top toolbar and click on the **My Music** heading to see music you have added, either from a CD as shown on the previous page, or bought from the iTunes Store, see pages 76-77

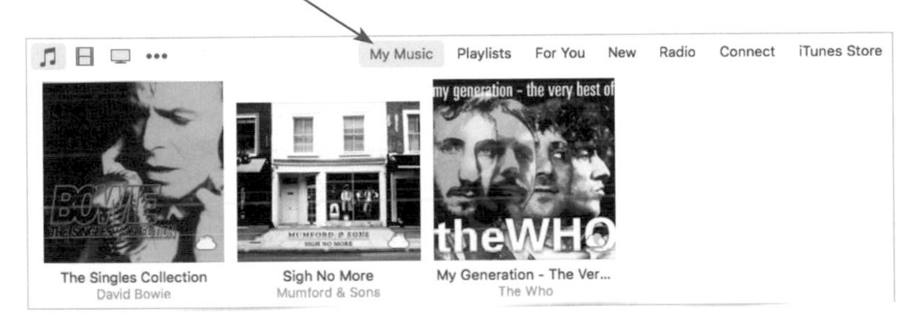

Click on this button on the top toolbar when an album is playing to view all of the tracks that will play.

3. Click on an item to view its details, e.g. the tracks in an album. Double-click on an item to play it

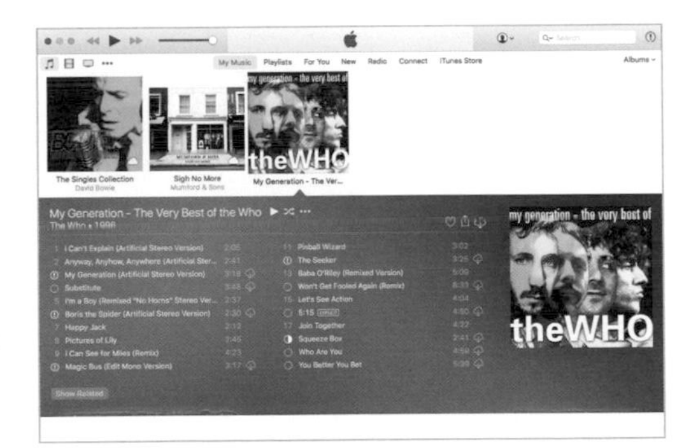

Click on the **Playlists** button on the top toolbar to create your own playlists from your music collection.

Playlists

4. When a song is playing it is displayed at the top of the iTunes window, along with the music controls

Downloading Music

As well as playing music, iTunes can also be used to legally download and buy music, via the iTunes Store. This contains a huge range of music, and you only have to register on the site once. After this, you can download music for use on your Mac and also on mobile Apple devices. To do this:

Never use illegal music download sites. Apart from the legal factor, they are much more likely to contain viruses and spyware.

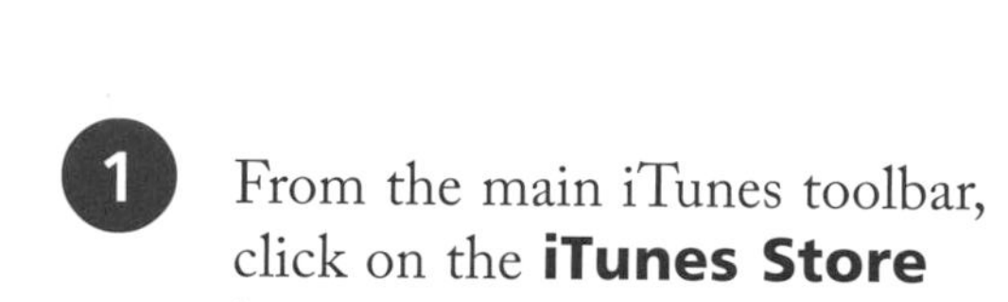

1. From the main iTunes toolbar, click on the **iTunes Store** button

2. The iTunes Store offers music, videos, television apps, audiobooks and podcasts for downloading

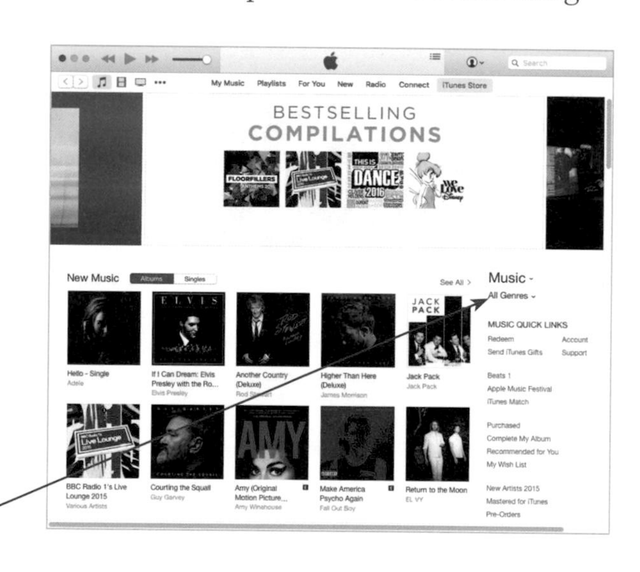

Click on the **Music > All Genres** button in the main iTunes Store window to select specific musical genres to view.

3. Look for items in the iTunes Store either by browsing through the sections of the site, or enter a keyword in the search box at the top of the window

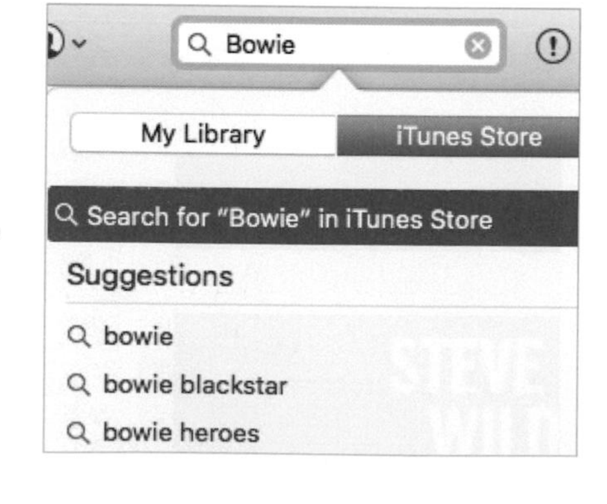

4. Locate an item you want to buy

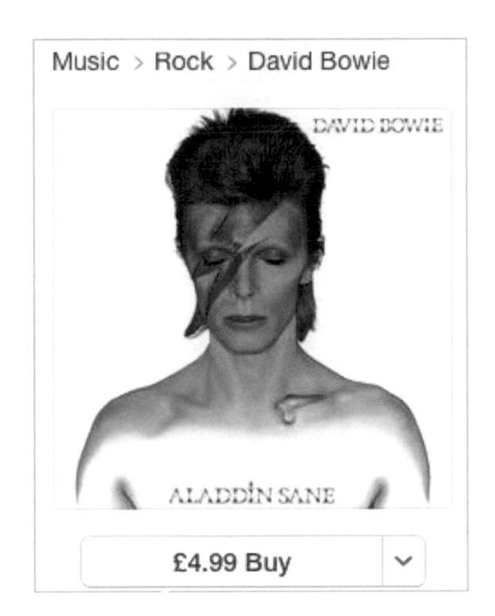

Once you have registered on iTunes, you can then download music from your account to up to five different computers or devices.

5. Click on the **Buy** button (at this point you will have to register with the iTunes Store, if you have not already done so)

6. Once you have registered, you will have to enter a username and password to complete your purchase

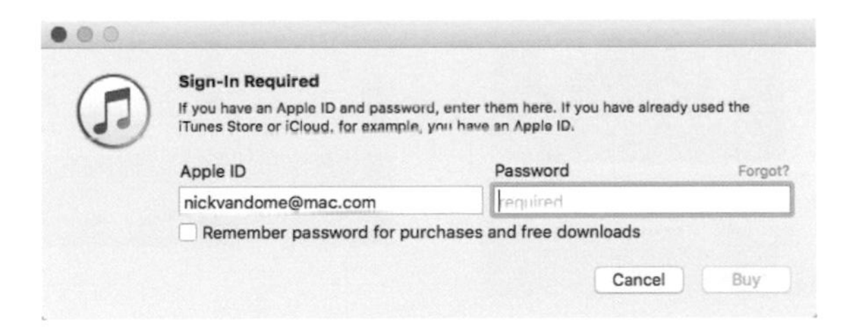

Once items have been bought from the iTunes Store, a record of this is kept there so that they can be downloaded again (free of charge) if you delete them from your Mac computer or digital device.

7. Once the item has been downloaded, it is available through iTunes on your Mac, under the **Playlists > Purchased** button

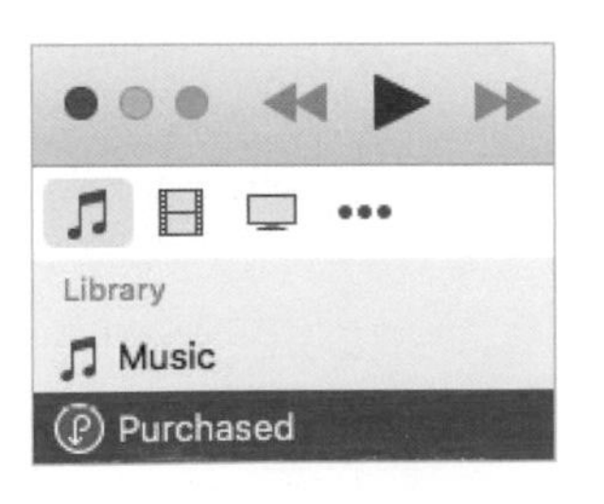

Using Apple Music

Apple Music is a new feature in OS X and iOS.

To end your Apple Music subscription at any point (and to ensure you do not subscribe at the end of the free trial) open **iTunes** and select **Store > View Account** from the menu bar. Log in with your Apple ID and select **Account Info**. Under **Settings** click on the **Subscriptions > Manage** button. Click on the **Edit** button and drag the **Automatic Renewal** button to **Off**. You can then renew your Apple Music membership, if required, by selecting one of the **Renewal Options**.

Apple Music is a new service that makes the entire Apple iTunes library of music available to users. It is a subscription service, but there is a 3-month free trial. Music can be streamed over the internet or downloaded so you can listen to it when you are offline. To start with Apple Music:

1. Click on the **iTunes** icon and click on the **For You** or **New** buttons on the top toolbar. This will start the Apple Music wizard which will start your free 3-month trial, and also ask for some music preferences so that the service can be tailored for you

2. Click on the **For You** or **New** buttons on the top toolbar to view suggested playlists or specific tracks. These can all be played directly using streaming over Wi-Fi

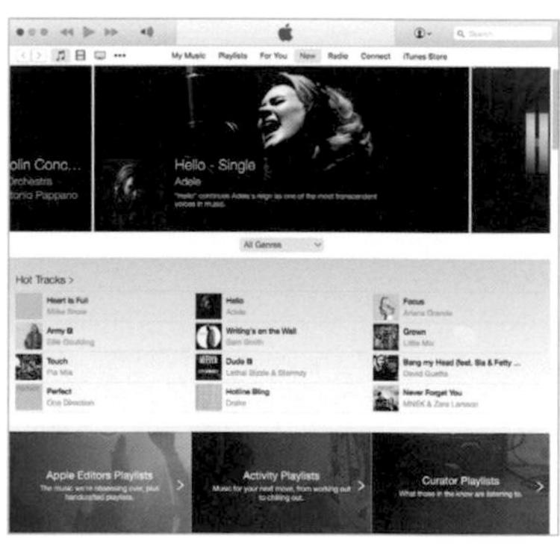

3. Click on individual items to view their details

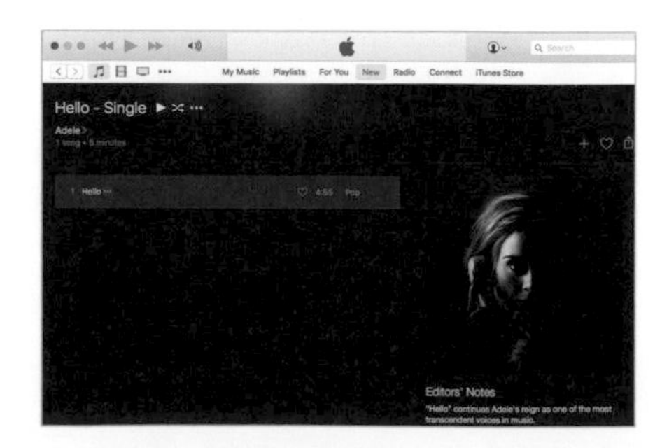

4. Click next to a track or album to access menu options. These include adding it to your own **My Music** section in iTunes, where it can also be played if you are offline, by clicking on the cloud icon next to it

5. Click on the **My Music** button on the top toolbar to view all items here, including those that have been bought from the iTunes Store. The most recent items appear at the top of the window

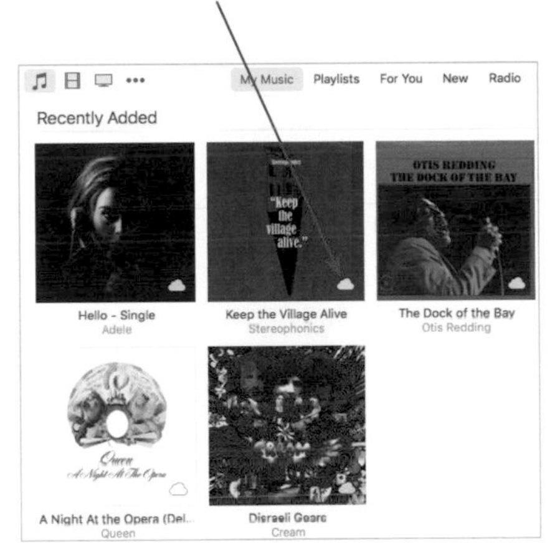

6. Click on items within the **My Music** section to view them. Click on an item to play it

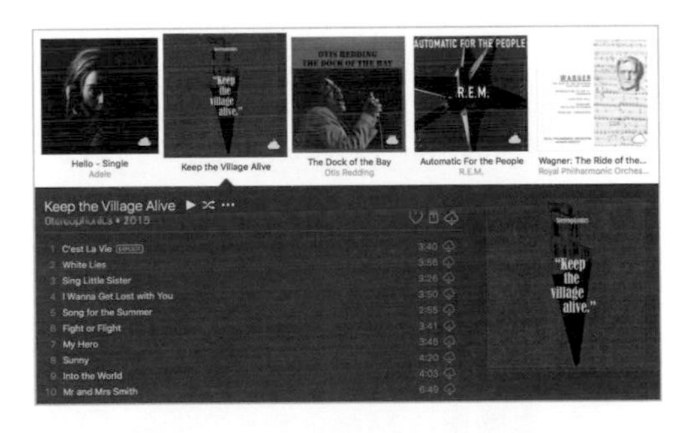

7. The currently playing item is displayed at the top of the iTunes window where it can be managed with the music controls

Numerous radio stations can also be listened to with Apple Music, including Beats 1.

Hot tip

Click on the **Connect** button on the top toolbar to select artists to follow so that you get the latest music information and updates about them.

Earbuds and Headphones

When listening to music there will probably be occasions when you will want to use either earbuds/earpods or headphones to save other people from hearing your music. The choice between the two could have a significant impact on your overall audio experience and comfort.

Earbuds/Earpods

These are essentially small plastic buds that fit inside the ear. The most common example is the earpods supplied with iPods. While these are small and convenient, they do not usually offer the best sound quality and, perhaps more importantly for some people, they can be uncomfortable to use, particularly for prolonged periods.

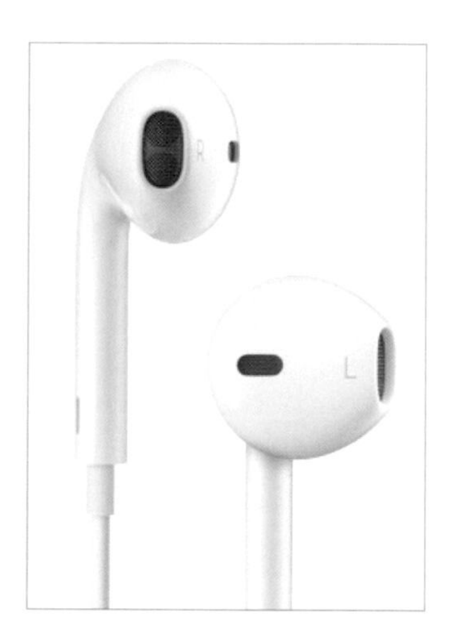

It is worth investing in good quality earbuds/earpods or headphones, otherwise the escape of sound could annoy people around you.

Headphones

These go over the ears, rather than in them, and are generally more comfortable as a result. It is worth investing in a good set of headphones because the sound quality will ensure that it is money well spent. The one downside of headphones is that they can be slightly bulky, but some are designed so that they fold away into a small, compact pouch.

Creating Music

For those who are as interested in creating music as listening to it, GarageBand can be used for this very purpose. It can take a bit of time and practice to become fully proficient with GarageBand, but it is worth persevering with if you are musically inclined and want to compose your own. To use GarageBand:

1. Click on this icon on the Dock or within the Launcher

2. Click on the **New Project** button

3. Select an instrument group and click on the **Choose** button

Choose

4. Select an instrument within the group

5. Select **Window > Show Keyboard** from the menu bar to display the keyboard for inputting music

6. Click on this button to start recording a track, using the keyboard

GarageBand can appear quite complex at first, and it takes a little time to feel comfortable with it.

...cont'd

Click on the arrows at either end of the keyboard to access the other sections of it.

7. Click on the keyboard to record the music

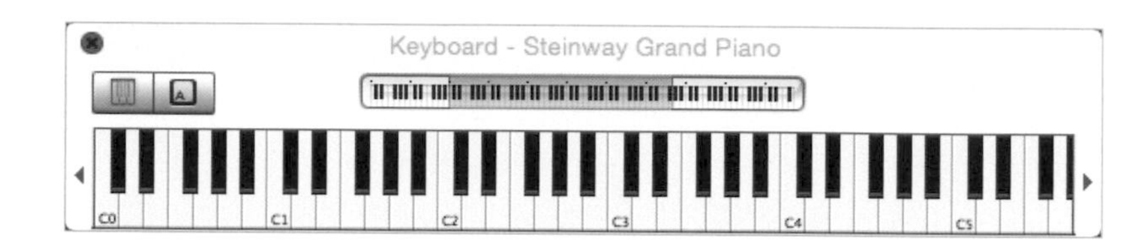

8. The track is placed on the GarageBand timeline

9. Click on this button to view a list of pre-recorded music loops

Click and drag on tracks on the timeline to move their position.

10. A list of loops is displayed. Select a style and an instrument. The available loops are displayed underneath the **Name** tab

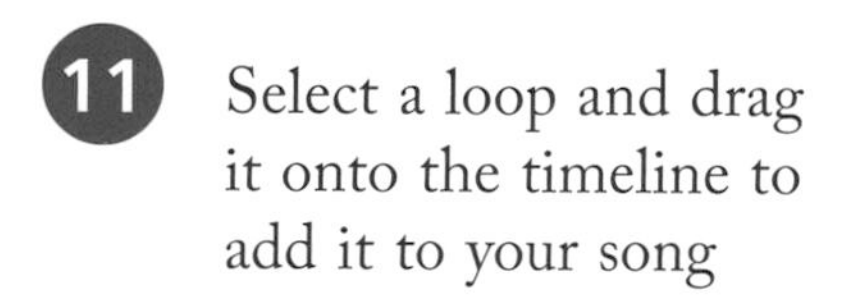

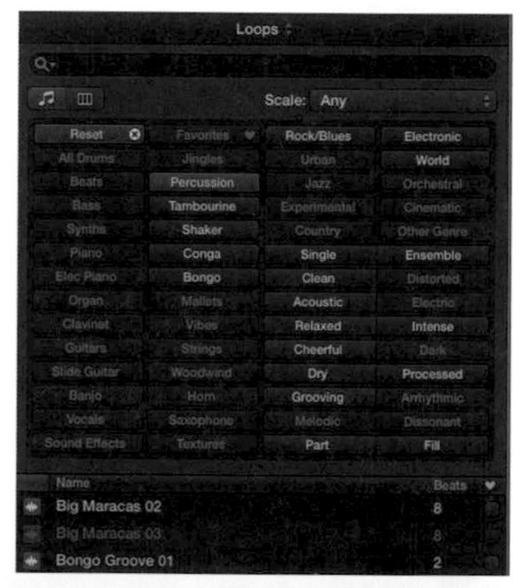

11. Select a loop and drag it onto the timeline to add it to your song

12. The completed song is shown in the timeline. This can consist of several separate tracks

Listening to the Radio

For the radio lover, Internet Radio is available via iTunes. To use this:

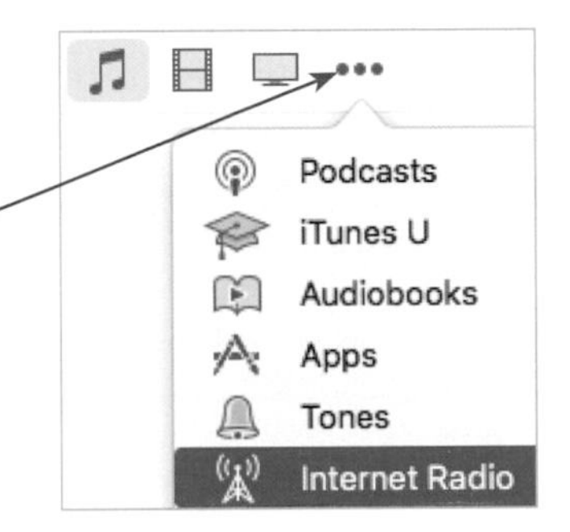

1. Click on this icon on the main iTunes toolbar and click on **Internet Radio**

2. Click on a category of music and click on a radio station to have it streamed over the internet, i.e. the music plays from the station as long as you have an internet connection, it is not downloaded to your Mac

An alternative is to use one of the many radio apps from the App Store.

1. Enter **radio** into the Search box

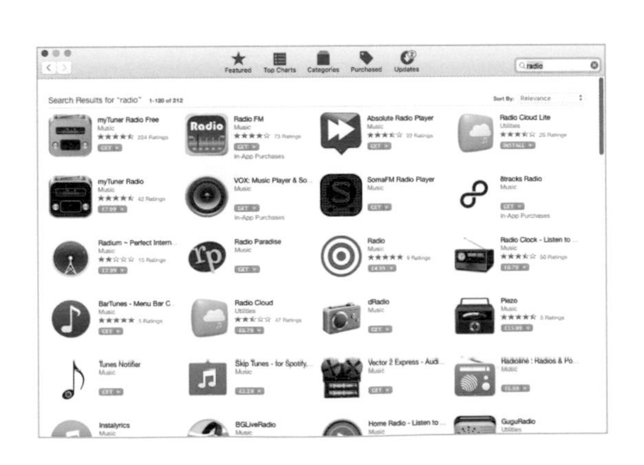

2. Preview the radio apps and select one as required

Don't forget

Several radio stations can also be accessed from the subscription service Apple Music.

Some radio apps are just for specific stations, while others provide a wide range of available stations.

Reading Books

iBooks is an eBook reading app that has been available with Apple's mobile devices, including the iPhone and the iPad, for a number of years. OS X El Capitan also brings this technology to desktop and laptop Macs. To use iBooks:

1. Click on this icon on the Dock or within the Launcher

2. Enter your Apple ID to access the iBooks Store or click on the Create Apple ID button to create a new Apple ID

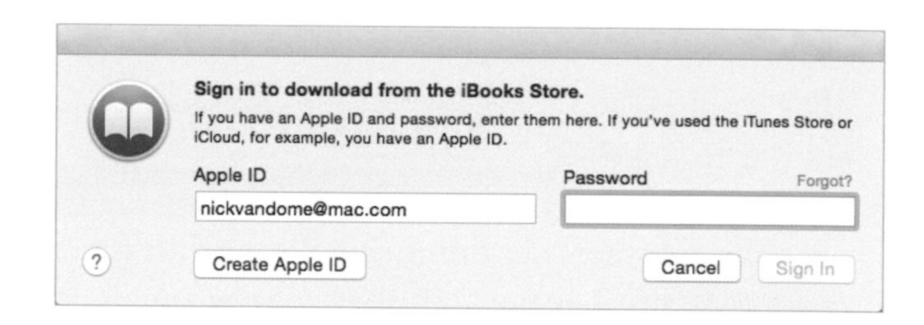

Sign in to download from the iBooks Store.
If you have an Apple ID and password, enter them here. If you've used the iTunes Store or iCloud, for example, you have an Apple ID.
Apple ID
Password
Forgot?
nickvandome@mac.com
?
Create Apple ID
Cancel
Sign In

3. Click on the **Sign In** button

4. Click on the **iBooks Store** button. The Store contains a wide range of books that can be previewed and downloaded

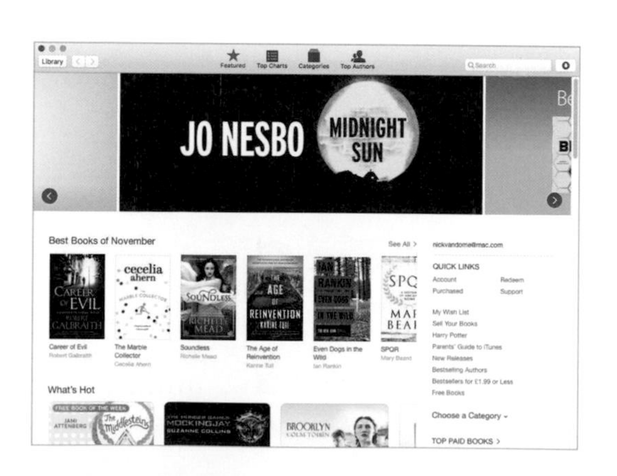

Don't forget

iBooks consists of your own library for storing and reading eBooks and also access to the online **iBooks Store** for buying and downloading new ones. Items that you have downloaded with iBooks on other devices will also be available in your iBooks Library.

Use these buttons on the top toolbar of the iBooks Store to view books by **Featured**, **Top Charts**, **Categories** and **Top Authors**.

5. Click on a title to preview details about it

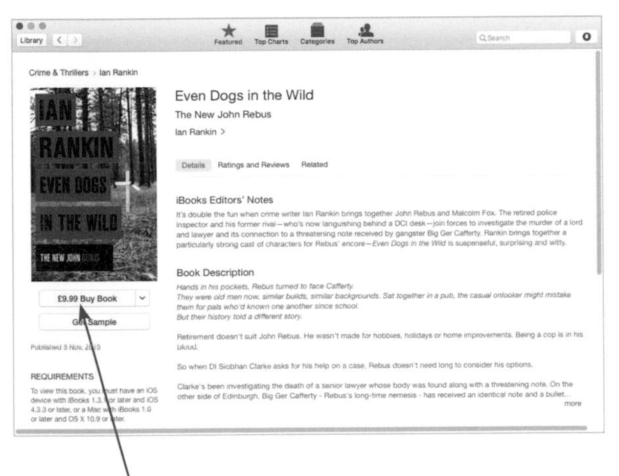

6. Click here to download the book (if it is a paid-for title this button will display a price)

7. The title will be downloaded into your iBooks Library. Double-click on the cover to open the book and start reading

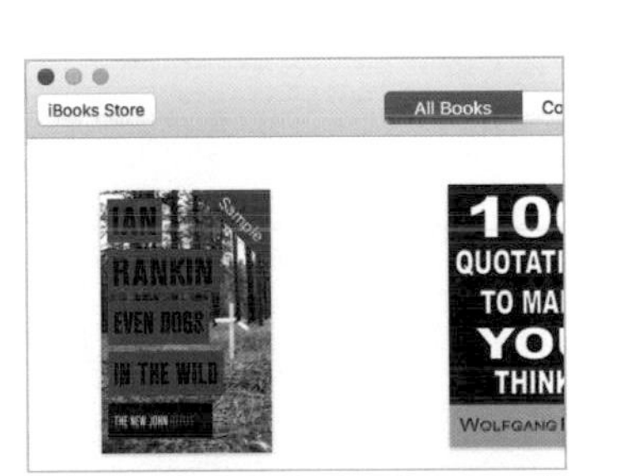

8. Click or tap on the right-hand and left-hand edges to turn a page. Move the cursor over the top of the page to access the top toolbar. The bottom toolbar displays the page numbers and location

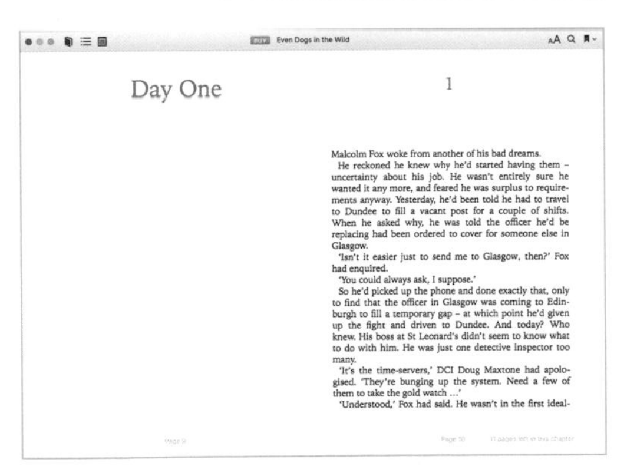

From the iBooks Store, click on the **Library** button in the top left-hand corner to go back to your own iBooks Library on your Mac.

Library

Use these buttons on the top toolbar to, from left to right, go back to your Library, view the Table of Contents or view any notes you have added to the text.

Creating a Home Movie

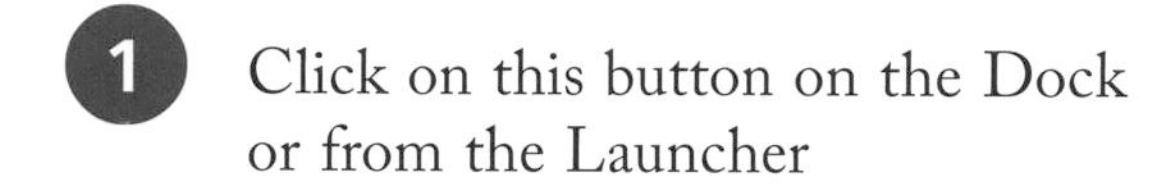

For home movie buffs, iMovie offers options for downloading, editing and publishing your efforts.

Video cameras can be connected with a USB or Thunderbolt cable. If you have a video camera with a FireWire cable you will need a FireWire adapter.

1. Click on this button on the Dock or from the Launcher

2. Click on the **Import Media** button to download video clips into iMovie

3. Select a location from which to download clips. This can be from a video camera, a removable device such as a pen drive, or on your Mac

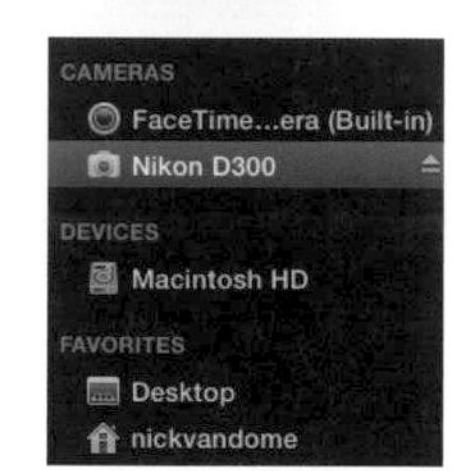

4. Once you have downloaded video clips, click on the **New** button to start your video project

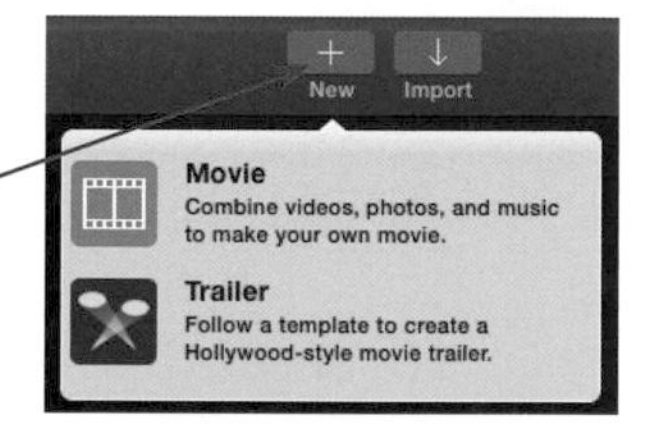

In the past, Apple produced an app called iDVD for creating artistic presentations from your own home movies. However, this has now been discontinued, but other DVD-creation apps can be obtained in the App Store.

5. Click on the **Theme** for your project and click on the **Create** button

6. Give your project a name and click on the **OK** button

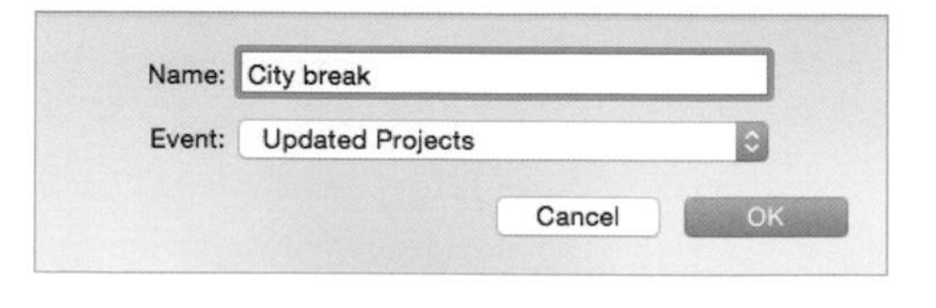

7. The video clip selected in Step 3 is added to the iMovie editing window

Video clips for using in projects

Preview window

Timeline, where the video project is created and edited. Drag the clip left or right to move it over the Playhead (the orange line). Projects are created in the **Library** area

8. Click on the **Enhance** button to apply editing enhancements to your video project

9. Click on these buttons for options that can be applied to video clips

10. Click on the **Share** button to share a complete movie in a variety of ways

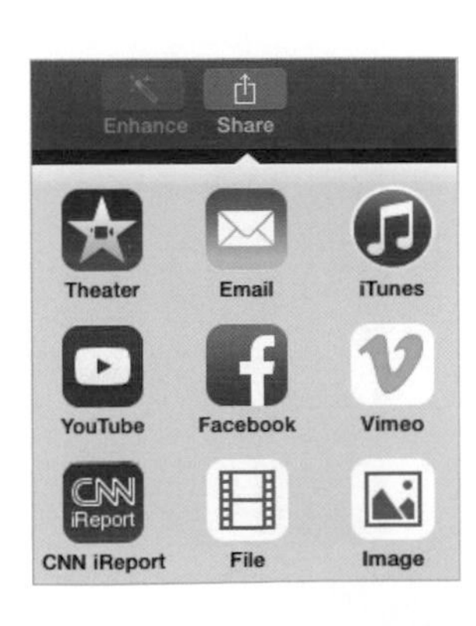

The name of a project is used for the opening title, but this can be changed by double-clicking on it.

Click on a clip on the timeline to trim it, by dragging at either end of the yellow box that appears around it.

The **Theater** area displays items that have been shared via iCloud. This can be used to view all of your iCloud video content. Click on this button to access it.

Theater

Playing Chess

Game playing relaxation is not ignored on the Mac, and many hours can be spent playing chess against the computer. To do this:

1. In Finder, click on the **Applications** button or access the Launchpad

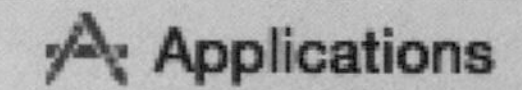

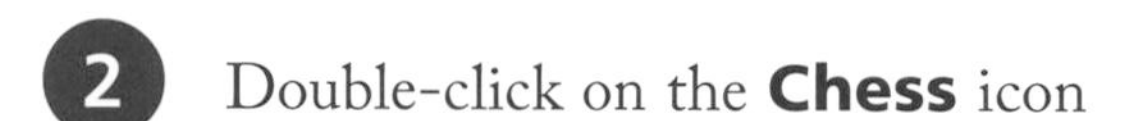

2. Double-click on the **Chess** icon

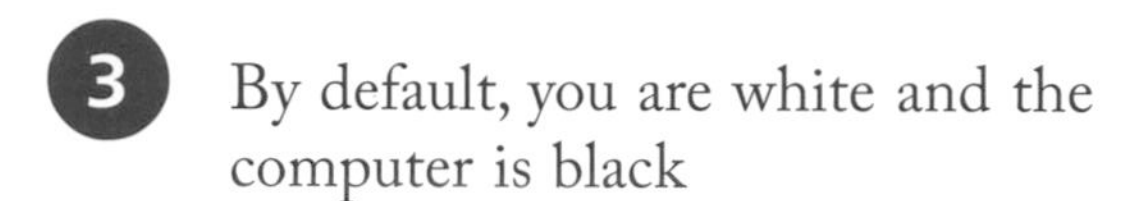

3. By default, you are white and the computer is black

4. Move your pieces by clicking on them and dragging them to the required square

5. Once you have moved, Black will move automatically

In the Chess application it is possible to play against the computer or another person. This can be specified when you select **Game > New** to start a new game.

Other similar games can be downloaded from the App Store. Type the name of a specific game into the Search box at the top right-hand side of the App Store window to view the available options.

5 At Home

This chapter reveals options for getting productive and creative by creating letters, household budgets and presentations.

Productivity Options

As well as using Macs for leisure and entertainment activities, they are also ideally suited for more functional purposes such as creating letters and documents, doing household expenses and creating posters or presentations. As always in the world of technology, there is more than one option for which app to use when performing these tasks. Some of these include:

Files in both iWork and Microsoft Office for the Mac can easily be saved for use elsewhere on a Windows PC. To do this, select the required file format in the **Save** window.

iWork

This is a suite of Apple apps that are designed specifically for the Mac. It contains productivity apps including those for word processing, spreadsheets and presentations. Although not as well known as the more ubiquitous Microsoft Office suite of apps, iWork is an easy-to-use and powerful option that will fulfill the productivity needs of most users. The iWork apps are Pages, Numbers and Keynote and they come pre-installed with new Macs. They can all also be downloaded from the App Store.

Where applicable, the productivity examples in this chapter use iWork.

If you already have versions of Pages, Numbers and Keynote, you can update them to the latest versions, for free, from the App Store. To do this, access the App Store and look in the Update or Purchased sections.

Microsoft Office

Even in the world of Apple it is impossible to avoid the software giant that is Microsoft. For users of Microsoft Office (the suite of apps containing the likes of Word, Excel, PowerPoint), the good news is that there is a version written specifically for the Mac. This works in the same way as the IBM-compatible PC version, and for anyone who has used it before, the Mac version will look reassuringly familiar. However, on the downside, Office is relatively expensive and the apps contain a lot of functionality that most users will never need.

TextEdit

For anyone who just wants to do some fairly basic word processing, the built-in Mac app TextEdit is an option. This can be used to create letters and other similar documents. However, it does not have the versatility of either iWork or Microsoft Office.

Accessing a Dictionary

A dictionary is a good starting point for any productivity function. On the Mac you do not have to worry about having a large book to hand, as there are two options that cover this task.

Applications dictionary

Within the Applications folder there is a fully-functioning dictionary. To use this:

1. In Finder, click on the **Applications** button or access the Launchpad

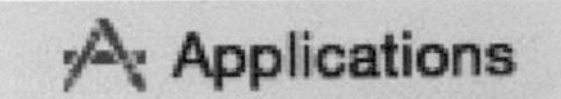

2. Double-click on the **Dictionary** app

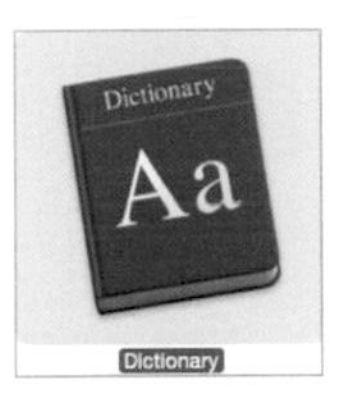

3. Select the option you want to use for looking up a word

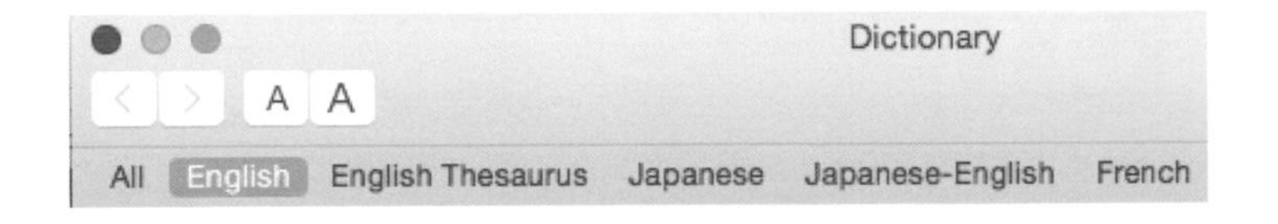

4. In the search box, type in the word you want to look up

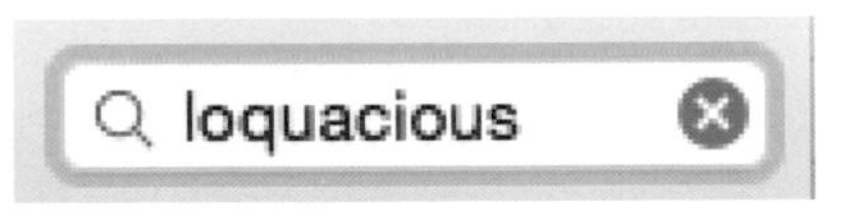

5. The results are displayed in the dictionary window

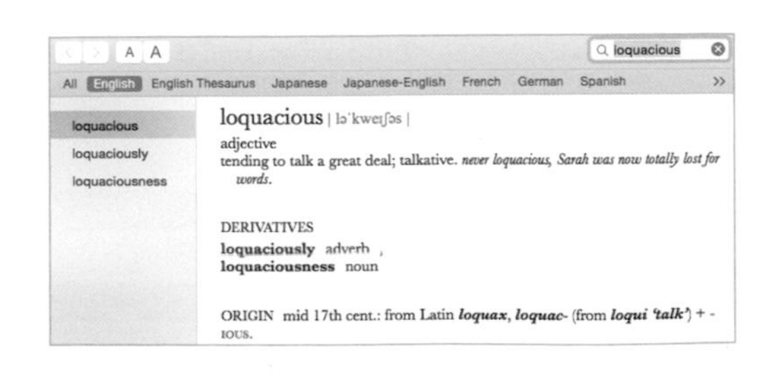

Always use a dictionary if you are unsure about the spelling of a word, even if you are using a spellchecker, as this may be set up for a different default language, e.g. US English or UK English.

Dashboard dictionary

The Dashboard is an app within Mac OS X that offers a number of widgets, or small apps, for a variety of useful tasks such as weather reports, maps, a clock and a calculator. It also has a dictionary. To use this:

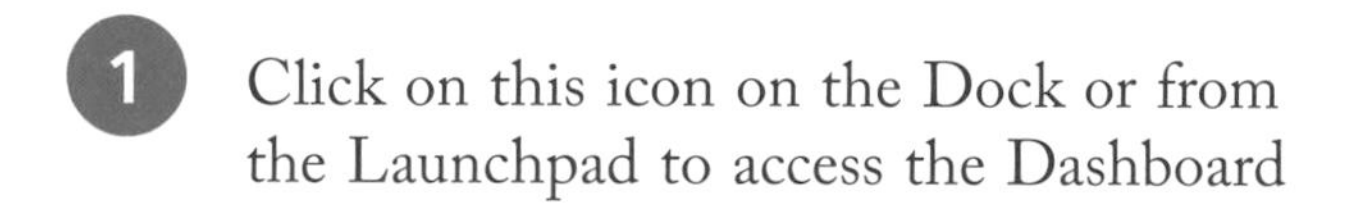

1. Click on this icon on the Dock or from the Launchpad to access the Dashboard

2. If the Dictionary widget is not showing, click on this button to view the available widgets

3. Click on the Dictionary widget to add it to the main Dashboard (which appears above the Desktop)

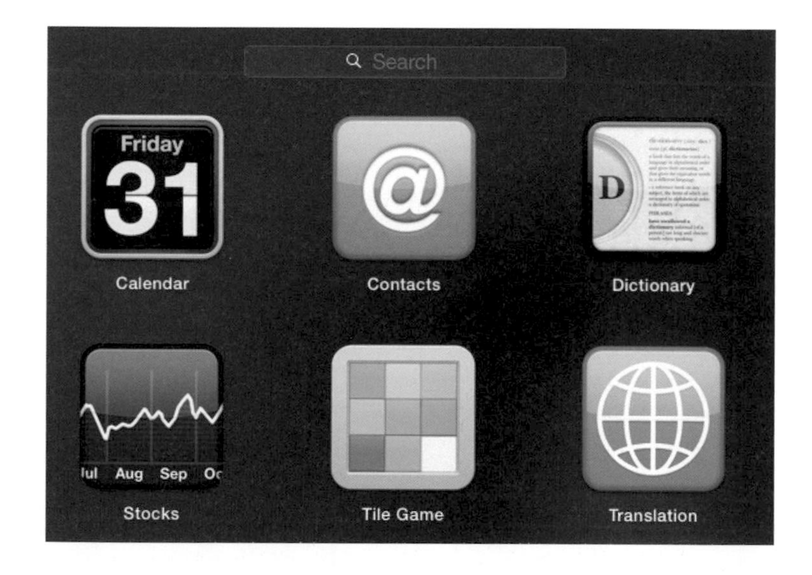

4. The Dictionary widget can be used in a similar way to the one on page 91

When you click on the Dashboard icon on the Dock, the available Dashboard widgets appear on the screen.

The Dashboard app is not as widely used now that there are a range of apps in the App Store that perform similar tasks and it may be the case that it begins to be phased out in subsequent versions of OS X.

Creating a Letter

One of the most common word processing tasks is writing a letter, and it is something that most of us have to do for either business or pleasure. This could be a letter to a family member or a letter of complaint. Whatever the subject matter it is worth making your letters look as professional, or as stylish, as possible. To create a letter in Pages:

1. In Finder, click on the **Applications** button or access the Launchpad

2. Click on the **Pages** app and select **File > New** from the menu bar

3. The template options are shown. Click on the **Stationery** option to view the letter-style templates

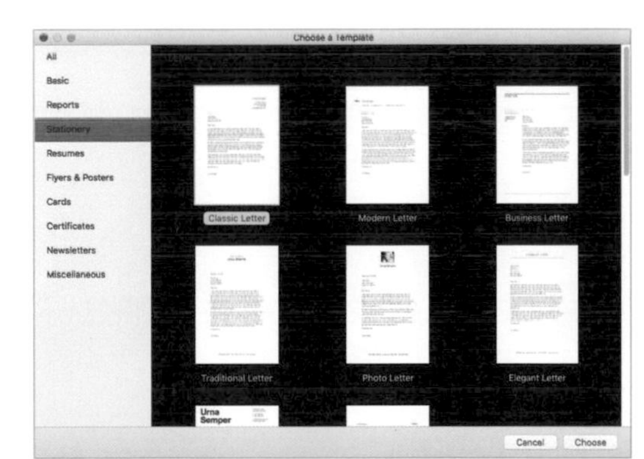

4. Click on one of the letter **Stationery** options and click on the **Choose** button

There are enough different letter templates in Pages for you not to need to create your own. If required, existing ones can be amended.

Use the **Basic** category in the left-hand panel and the **Blank** template to create a new file with no content in it.

...cont'd

5 An untitled letter is displayed based on the template you have selected

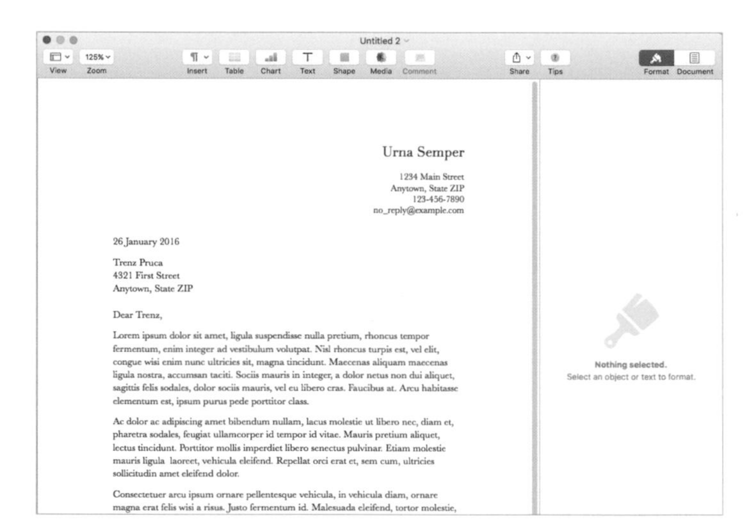

Don't forget

Use these buttons on the top toolbar to add a variety of types of content, including tables, charts, text boxes and images:

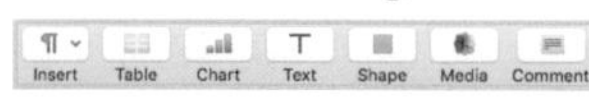

6 Click on an element of the letter and overtype to edit it

1234 Main Street¶
Anytown, State ZIP
123-456-7890
no_reply@example.com

Don't forget

Once you have added your own text, you can select items by double-clicking or triple-clicking on them.

7 Click once in the draft text of the letter. This will highlight all of the text. Enter your own text

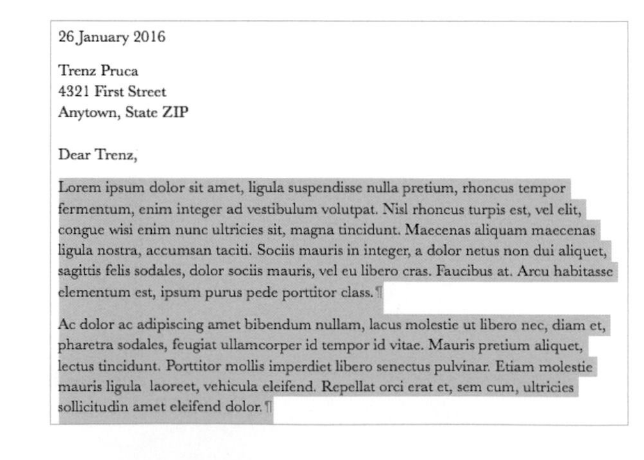

26 January 2016

Trenz Pruca
4321 First Street
Anytown, State ZIP

Dear Trenz,

Lorem ipsum dolor sit amet, ligula suspendisse nulla pretium, rhoncus tempor fermentum, enim integer ad vestibulum volutpat. Nisl rhoncus turpis est, vel elit, congue wisi enim nunc ultricies sit, magna tincidunt. Maecenas aliquam maecenas ligula nostra, accumsan taciti. Sociis mauris in integer, a dolor netus non dui aliquet, sagittis felis sodales, dolor sociis mauris, vel eu libero cras. Faucibus at. Arcu habitasse elementum est, ipsum purus pede porttitor class.¶

Ac dolor ac adipiscing amet bibendum nullam, lacus molestie ut libero nec, diam et, pharetra sodales, feugiat ullamcorper id tempor id vitae. Mauris pretium aliquet, lectus tincidunt. Porttitor mollis imperdiet libero senectus pulvinar. Etiam molestie mauris ligula laoreet, vehicula eleifend. Repellat orci erat et, sem cum, ultricies sollicitudin amet eleifend dolor.¶

8. Click on the **Format** button and select options for formatting your text, including font, size, bold, color and alignment

Use these buttons on the top toolbar to share a document and also access tip boxes.

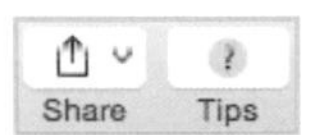

9. Once the letter has been completed, select **File > Save** from the menu bar

10. Give the letter a name in the **Save As** box

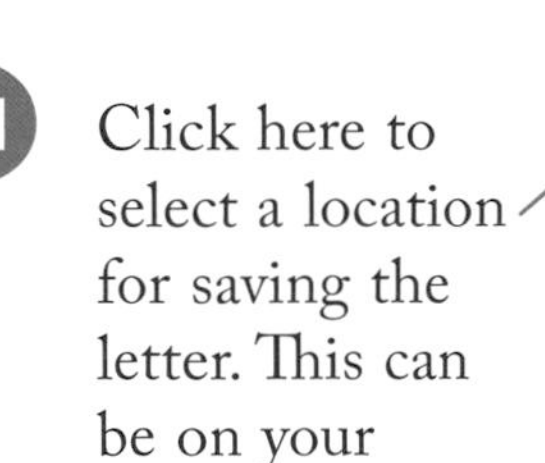

11. Click here to select a location for saving the letter. This can be on your Mac and also in the iCloud for online sharing and storage. Click on the **Save** button

For more information about using iCloud, see Chapter Nine.

Formatting a Newsletter

Newsletters are not just the preserve of the business world; they are a great source of information for local clubs, communities and also for family updates. To create and format a newsletter in Pages:

Keep newsletters relatively short (2-4 pages) so that they have the maximum impact without overwhelming the reader.

1. In Finder, click on the **Applications** button or access the Launchpad

2. Click on the **Pages** app

3. In the **Choose a Template** window, click on one of the **Newsletter** options

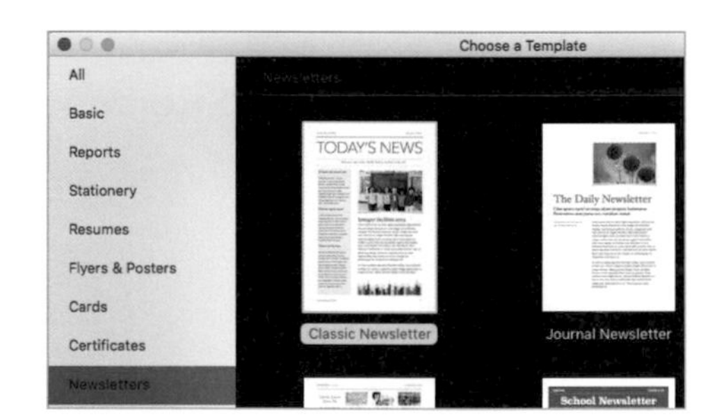

4. Click on the **Choose** button

Choose

5. A new document, based on the selected template, is displayed

A newsletter template consists of several text boxes with sample text. The text boxes can be selected by clicking on them once, and the text inside them can be selected by double-clicking on it and you can then enter your own text (see next page).

6. Click once to select a text box, or double-click to select text within a text box

7. Overtype the selection with your own text

8. Click on an image placeholder to replace a template image with your own photos, or

9. Click on the **Media** button on the toolbar to insert new content, including images

Use the Text tool on the top toolbar to create new text boxes.

When an element is selected it is highlighted by a box with small markers around its perimeter. By dragging these markers you can resize the item.

...cont'd

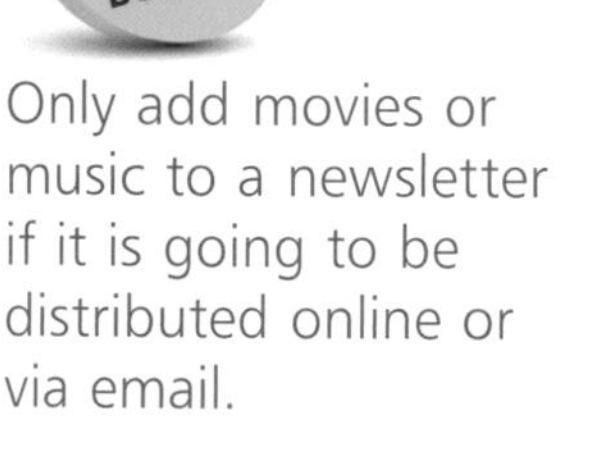
Only add movies or music to a newsletter if it is going to be distributed online or via email.

10. In the **Media** window, browse to the photo you want to use. (Click on the Music and Movies tabs to add this type of content)

The Media browser is a quick way to access your Photos app. However, photos must have been imported into the Photos app for them to be visible in the Media browser.

11. Click on a photo to add it to your newsletter, either by replacing the one in the placeholder, or inserting it as a new image

Include plenty of photos, at varying sizes, in your newsletter to make it visually appealing.

12. Click on an image to select it. Click on the **Format** button and click on the **Image** tab to replace the selected image or apply editing options to it

Style | Image | Arrange
File Info
DSC_0584-small.jpg
Replace
Edit Mask
Instant Alpha
Adjustments
Exposure 0%
Saturation 0%
Enhance Reset

...cont'd

13. Click on the **Style** tab for more options for editing the selected image

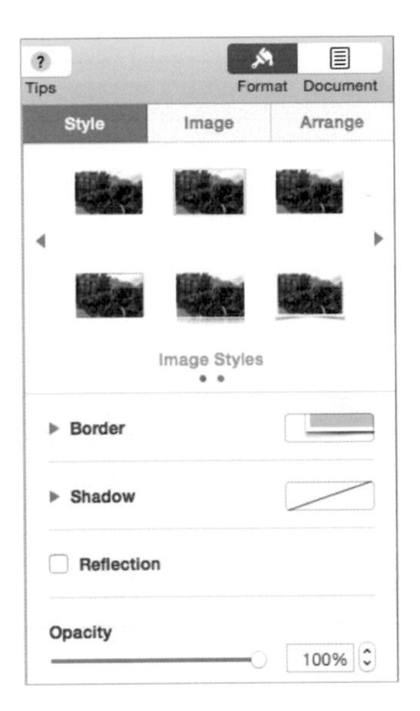

Photos can have a **Border** and a **Shadow** effect applied to them.

14. Click within a text box and click on the **Format** button to select formatting options for any selected text

Ensure that there is a good contrast between the color of text and its background.

15. Save the newsletter in the same way as a letter, i.e. either on your Mac or in the iCloud

Using a Calculator

Financial matters can sometimes be a chore but they are a necessary part of life, whether it is working out household expenses or calculating available spending money. Even for the best mathematicians, a calculator is a trusty friend when it comes to arithmetic. Luckily, the Mac has one ready-made:

Hot tip

Add the Calculator to the Dock so that it is readily available whenever you need to perform calculations.

1. In Finder, click on the **Applications** button or access the Launchpad

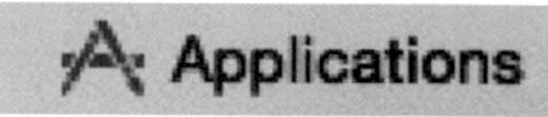

2. Double-click on the **Calculator** app

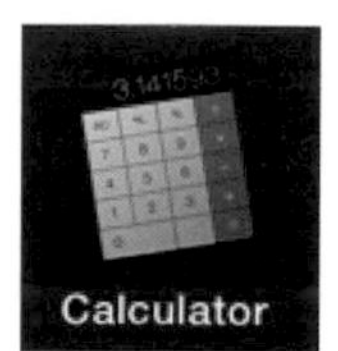

3. Click on the calculator's buttons to perform calculations

Don't forget

If you are going to be doing anything more than basic calculations, the scientific option may be more useful than the basic one.

4. Select **View** from the Menu bar and select an option for the type of calculator being displayed

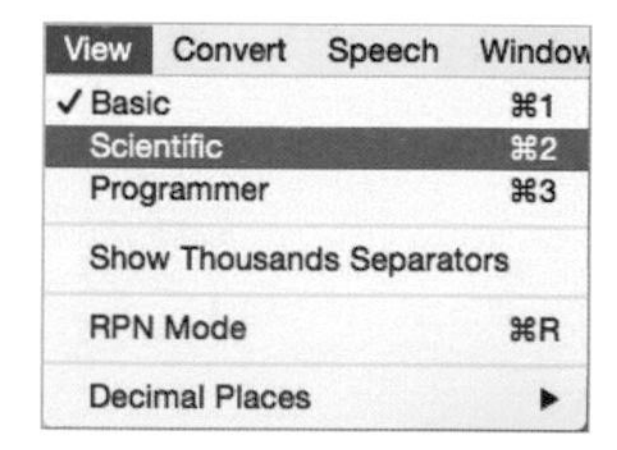

5. The option selected in Step 4 is now available

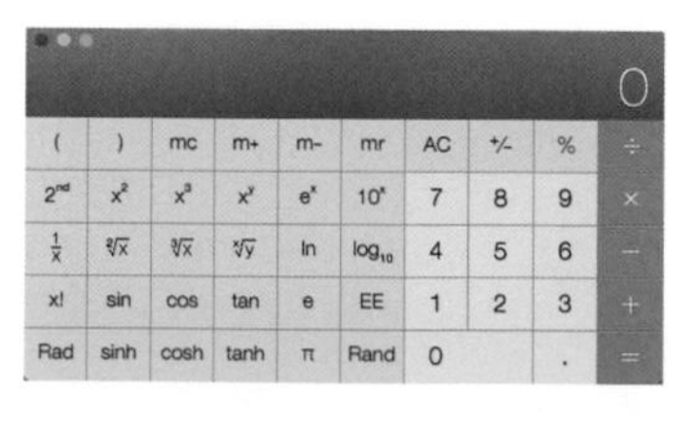

Doing Household Accounts

As well as being useful for word processing, iWork can also be used for financial accounting, such as keeping track of the household accounts. To do this:

1. In Finder, click on the **Applications** button or access the Launchpad

2. Double-click on the **Numbers** icon

3. Select **File > New** from the menu bar

4. In the template window, select one of the templates in the **Personal Finance** section

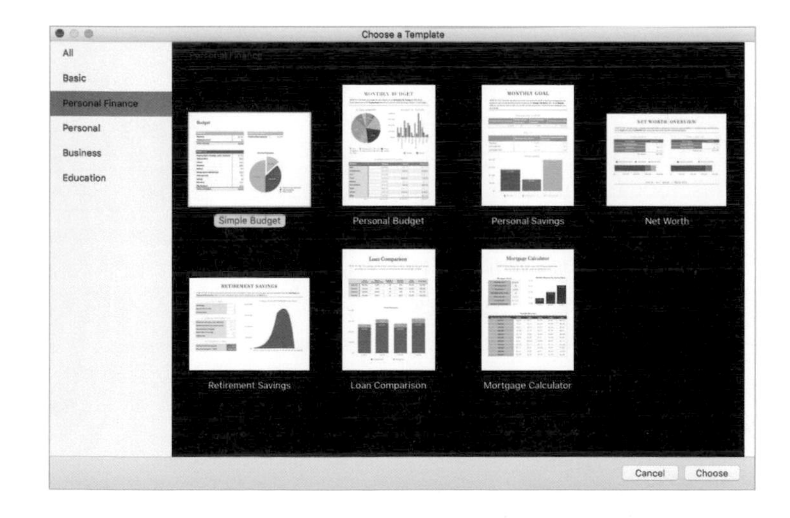

5. Click on the **Choose** button

Although any type of accounts are a chore, the more they are kept up-to-date the easier it is to control them.

Create an **Accounts** folder into which you can save all of your financial files.

...cont'd

6 The budget template is displayed. All of the items can be edited with your own information

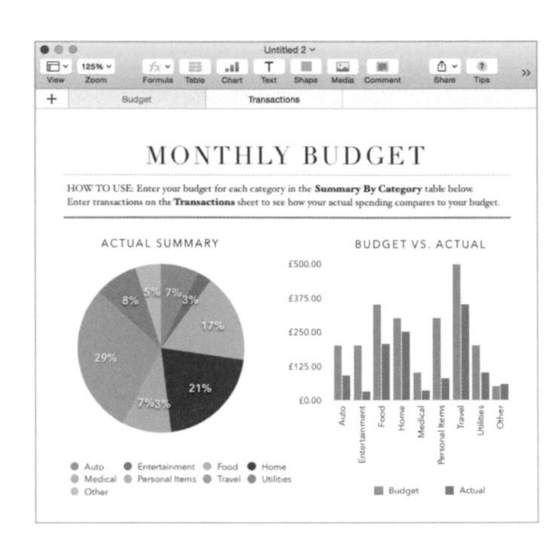

The text in a budget template can be edited as well as the numerical information. Double-click on an item of text and overtype as required.

7 Click on a cell to select it

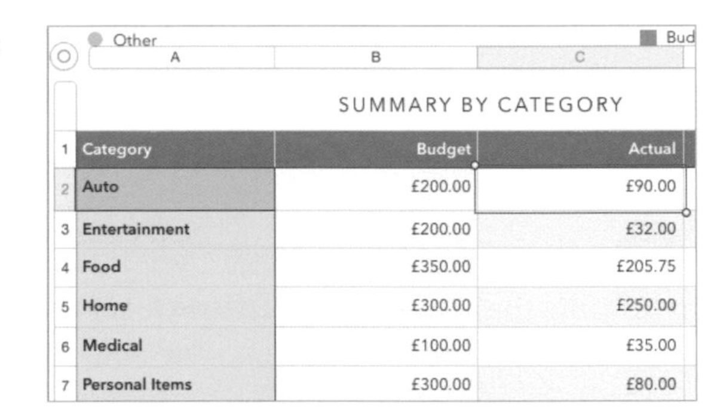

SUMMARY BY CATEGORY

	Category	Budget	Actual
2	Auto	£200.00	£90.00
3	Entertainment	£200.00	£32.00
4	Food	£350.00	£205.75
5	Home	£300.00	£250.00
6	Medical	£100.00	£35.00
7	Personal Items	£300.00	£80.00

Hot tip

Using a blank template and entering your own content from scratch can be a good way to become familiar with Numbers spreadsheets, before using a template with a lot of pre-inserted content.

8 Click on the **Format** button to select formatting options for the table, and also the selected cell. Use the **Table**, **Cell**, **Text** and **Arrange** tabs to format these items

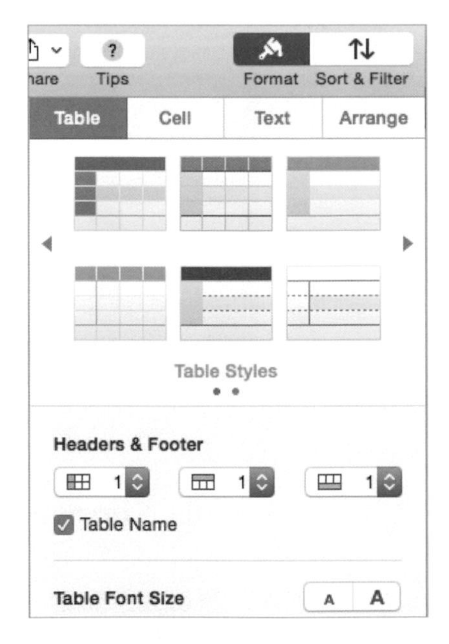

9. Double-click on an item within a cell to select it

10. Overwrite it with your own content as required. This can be text or numbers

11. Select a cell containing financial information. Edit the information, as required

2	£200.00	£90.00	£110.00
3	£200.00	£0.00	£200.00
4	£350.00	£205.75	£144.25
5	£300.00	£250.00	£50.00
Formula	SUMIF (Category , A3 , $Amount)		

12. Click on a cell and click on the **Formula** button to add a formula to a cell. Click on the **Format** button to view a wide range of functions

13. Save the spreadsheet in the same way as for a letter or a newsletter

Don't forget

Linked cells are controlled by a mathematical equation that ensures that if one is updated then the data in the linked cell changes too.

Functions can be relatively simple, such as adding up the sum of cells, but there are also numerous complicated functions that can be included.

Creating a Presentation

Presentations are a great way to produce customized slideshows of family photographs or promote activities in local clubs or charities. To do this in iWork:

Keynote is the iWork equivalent of Microsoft PowerPoint.

1. In Finder, click on the **Applications** button or access the Launchpad

2. Click on the **Keynote** icon

Generally, shorter presentations are more effective than longer ones, as the audience's attention span can be limited.

3. Select **File > New** from the menu bar
4. Select a template for your presentation, in the same way as for a letter or a spreadsheet

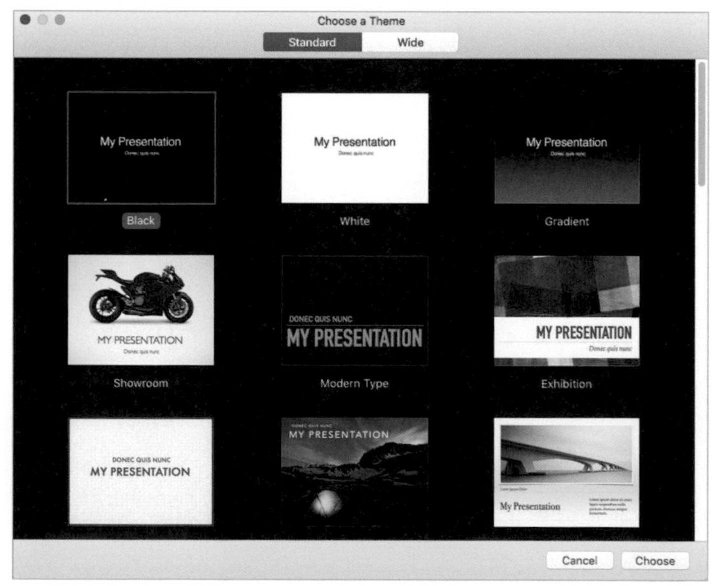

The template theme for a presentation is applied to all of the subsequent slides that are added to it.

5. Click on the **Choose** button

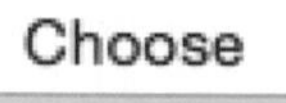

6. Double-click on the text to select it and overwrite it with your own text

My Slideshow

Double-click to edit

7. Click on the **Format** button to select options for formatting the selected text in your presentation

When adding text to a presentation, make sure that it is not too small and that there is not too much of it.

8. Click on the **Media** button on the menu bar to add more content

9. Browse to your content, including photos, music and movies. Click on an item or drag it onto a slide in your presentation. If you drag a photo onto a placeholder photo, this replaces the placeholder one

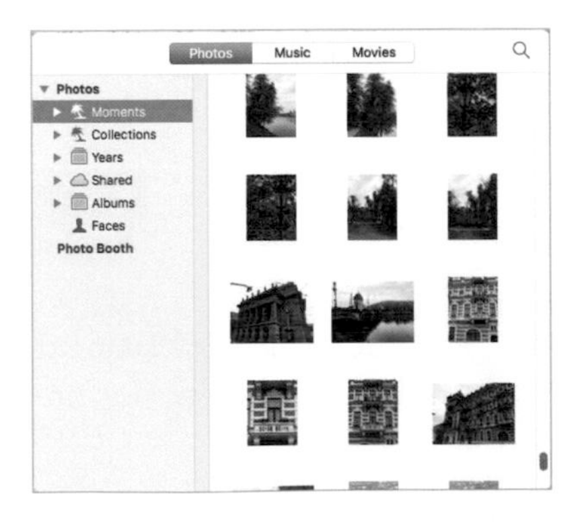

A placeholder photo is one that is inserted as part of a template to show how the photo will look in a slide.

...cont'd

10. To add more text to a slide, click on the **Text Box** button on the Menu bar

11. Drag the text tool on the slide to create a text box, and type the required text

Text boxes can be repositioned by dragging them around once they have been placed on a slide.

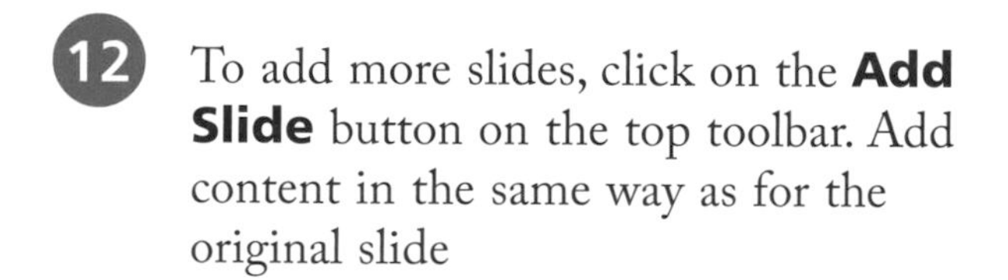

12. To add more slides, click on the **Add Slide** button on the top toolbar. Add content in the same way as for the original slide

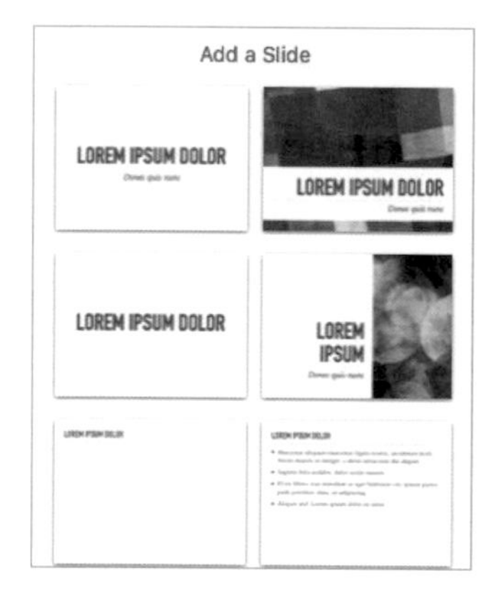

Build in and out effects can be added to images and text boxes from within the **Animate** section. Select an item in a slide and then select a Build effect. This determines how the item moves in, and out, of the slide when it is accessed.

13. Click on the **Animate** button on the top menu bar to add transition effects between slides. (Select the slides in the left-hand panel to add the effects to them)

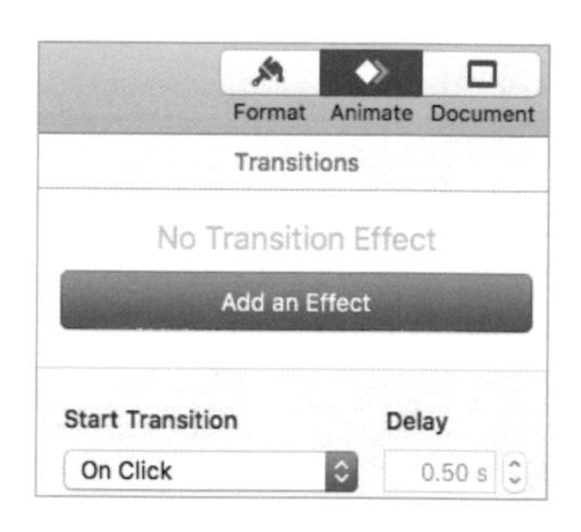

Animate

14. Click on the **Play** button on the Menu bar to preview the presentation

15. Save the presentation in the same way as a letter, a newsletter or a spreadsheet

6 Getting Online

This chapter shows how to get online with the internet and use your Mac to start browsing the web with the web browser Safari.

Accessing the Internet

Access to the internet is an accepted part of the computing world and it is unusual for users not to want to do this. Not only does this provide a gateway to the World Wide Web but also email, text and video communication. Access to the web is generally done through Wi-Fi, which requires a Wi-Fi router (for details about setting up your router, see pages 170-172). Connecting to the internet with a Mac is done through the System Preferences. To do this:

Don't forget

Before you connect to the internet you must have an Internet Service Provider (ISP) who will provide you with the relevant method of connection; usually cable or broadband. They will provide you with any login details if needed.

1. Open **System Preferences** and click on the **Network** icon

2. If your Wi-Fi is off, click on the **Turn Wi-Fi On** button

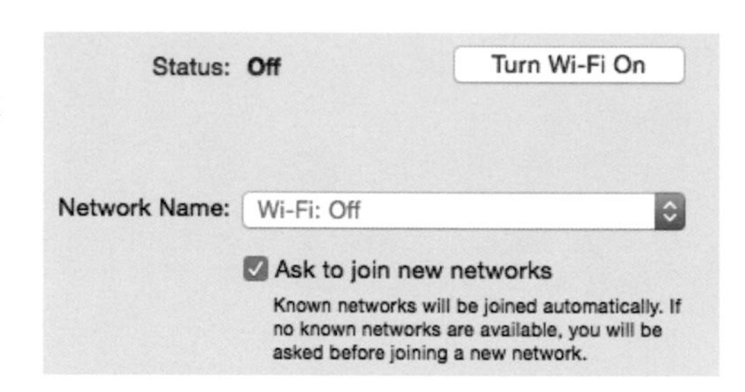

3. Your Mac connects to your router and this is displayed in the **Network Name** box

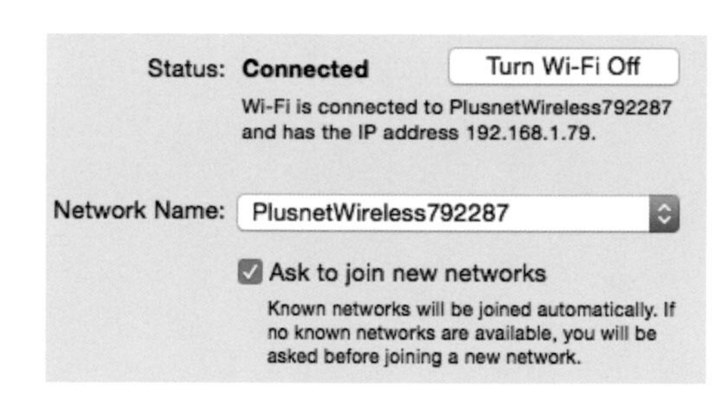

4. Your connection is denoted in the left-hand panel of the Network window, with a green dot next to an active connection. Ethernet connections (connecting to your router and Mac with an Ethernet cable) can also be made in the Network window by clicking on the Ethernet option in the left-hand panel

Hot tip

Check on the **Show Wi-Fi status in menu bar** to place a Wi-Fi icon on the Apple Menu bar. Click on this to view the status of your network.

Around the Web

When you are surfing the web it is important to feel comfortable with both your browser and also the websites at which you are looking. Most websites are a collection of linked pages that you can move between by clicking on links (also known as hyperlinks) which connect the different pages.

Macs have a built-in web browser known as Safari. This can be accessed from the Dock by clicking on this icon:

Address bar

The Address bar is the box at the top of the browser, and displays the address of the web page that is currently being displayed. Each web page has a unique address, so the address changes whenever you move to a different page. In Safari, the Address bar also serves as a search box so that you can either select a web page, or search for the item on the web. When you click in the Smart Search Address bar, the Safari Favorites page is also displayed, so that you can open one of your favorite pages in one click.

Main content

The full content of a web page is displayed in the main browser window:

Safari is a full-screen app and can be expanded by clicking on this button in the top left-hand corner. For more information on full-screen apps, see pages 40-41.

...cont'd

Toolbar

This is a collection of icons at the top of the browser. It has various options for navigating around web pages and accessing options such as sharing and printing pages:

Hot tip

The Toolbar can contain a Homepage button which takes you to your own Homepage, i.e. the page that is accessed when you first open up your browser.

Menu bar

This contains various menus with options for navigating around, and customizing web pages. In Safari it is located at the top of the Safari window:

Navigation bars

These are groups of buttons that appear on websites to help users navigate within the site. Generally, the main navigation bars appear in the same place on every page of the site:

The items that make up the navigation bar are buttons, or textual links, which take you to another location within the site.

Search box

Most websites have a search box, into which keywords or phrases can be entered to search over the whole site:

Links

This is the device that is used to move between pages within a website, or from one website to another. Links can be in a variety of styles, but most frequently they are in the form of buttons, underlined text or a roll-over (i.e. a button or piece of text that changes appearance when the cursor is passed over it):

The cursor usually turns into a pointing hand when it is passed over a link on a website.

Tabs

Safari has an option for using different tabs. This enables you to open different web pages within the same browser window. You can then move between the pages by clicking on each tab, at the top of the window. They can also be minimized so that you can swipe through available tabs:

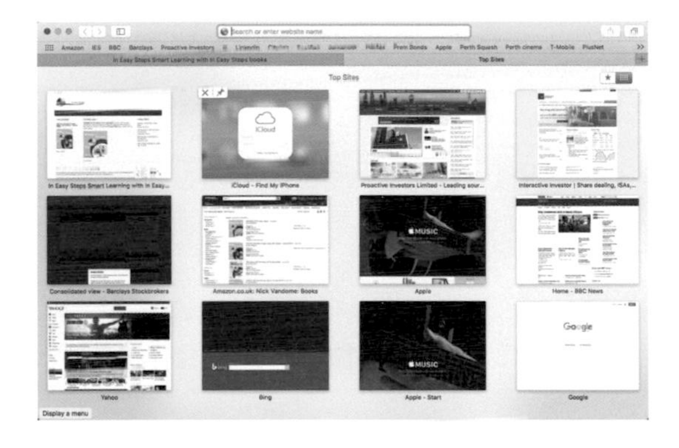

Tabs can be closed by clicking on the small cross that appears when you move the cursor over the left-hand corner of the tab's title bar.

Bookmarks

Everyone has their favorite web pages that they return to again and again. These can be added to a list in a browser so that they can be accessed quickly when required. There is usually a button at the top of the browser which can add the current page to the list of bookmarked items:

Setting a Homepage

A Homepage is what a browser opens by default whenever it is first launched. This is usually a page associated with the company that created the browser, i.e. the Apple Homepage for Safari. However, it is possible to customize the browser so that it opens with your own choice of Homepage. To do this in Safari:

Don't forget

A unique web page address is known as a URL. This stands for Uniform Resource Locator and means that every page on the web is unique.

1. Open Safari and click on **Safari > Preferences...** from the Menu bar

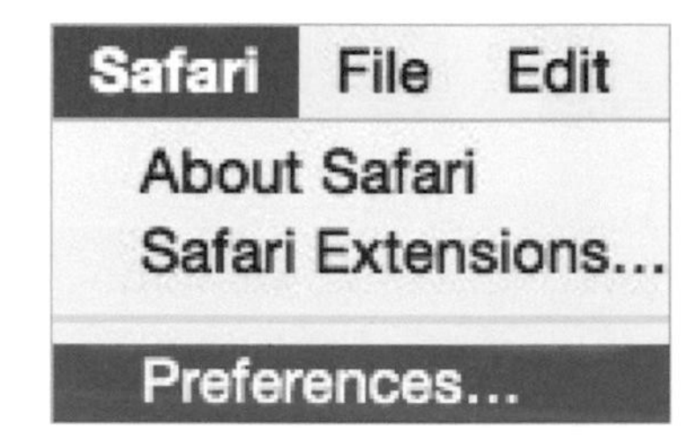

2. Click on the **General** tab

Once a Homepage has been set, this will be the one that first appears whenever Safari is opened.

3. Click on **Set to Current Page** if you want the current page you are viewing to be your Homepage, or

4. Enter a web address in the **Homepage** box to set this as your Homepage

5. Click on this button to close the Preferences window

About Safari

Safari is a web browser that is designed specifically to be used with OS X. It is similar in most respects to other browsers, but it usually functions more quickly and works seamlessly with OS X.

Safari overview

1. Click here on the Dock to launch Safari

2. All of the controls are at the top of the browser

Beware

If Safari is being viewed in full-screen mode, the top Menu bar is only visible if you move the cursor over the top of the screen.

Smart Search box

One of the innovations in Safari is that the Address bar and the Search box have been incorporated into one. You can use the same box for searching, or enter a web address to go to that page.

1. Click in the box to enter an item

2. Results are presented as web pages or search results. Click on the appropriate item to go to it, i.e. directly to a website or to the search results page

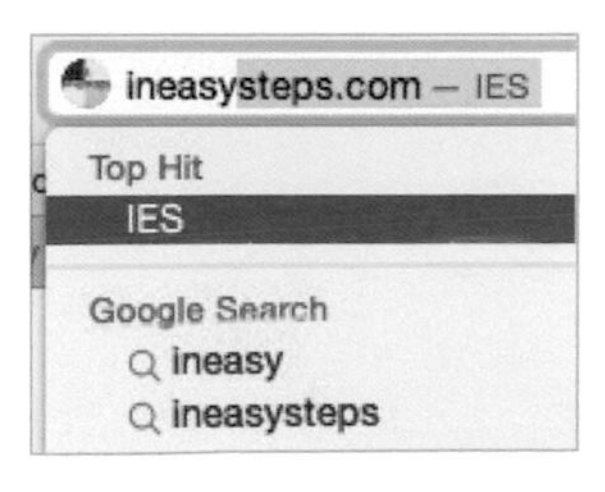

Hot tip

To avoid your browsing history being recorded, select **File > New Private Window** from the Safari Menu bar. This will mean that nothing is recorded from your browsing session.

...cont'd

Safari Tabbed Browsing

Tabs are now a familiar feature on web browsers, so you can have multiple sites open within the same browser window.

New tabs can also be opened by selecting **File > New Tab** from the Safari Menu bar.

1. When more than one tab is open, the tabs appear at the top of the web pages

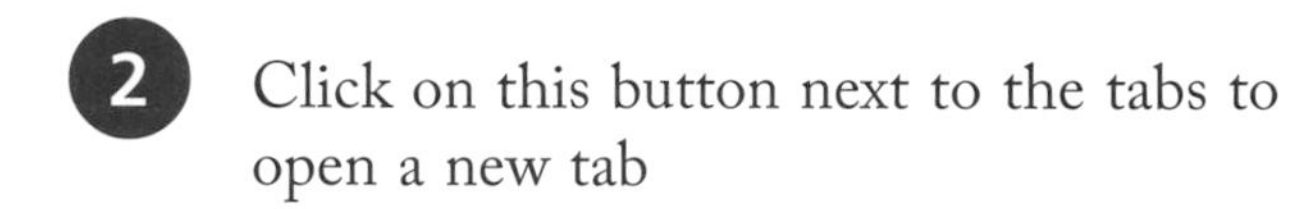

2. Click on this button next to the tabs to open a new tab

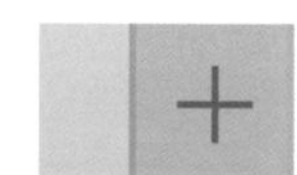

3. Click on one of the **Top Sites** (see next page) or enter a website address in the Smart Search Address bar to open a page

4. Click on this button next to the new tab button to minimize all of the current tabs

5. Move left and right to view all of the open tabs in thumbnail view. Click on one to view it at full size

Web pages that are open on any of your other Apple devices are also shown in the thumbnail view.

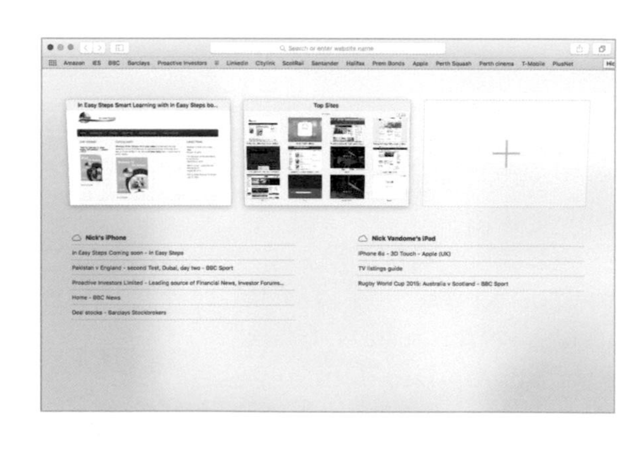

Safari Top Sites

Within Safari there is a facility to view a graphical representation of the websites that you visit most frequently. This can be done from a button on the Safari Menu bar. To do this:

The **Top Sites** window is also accessed if you open a new tab within Safari.

1. Click on this button to view the **Top Sites** window

2. The Top Sites window contains thumbnails of the websites that you have visited most frequently with Safari (this builds up as you visit more sites)

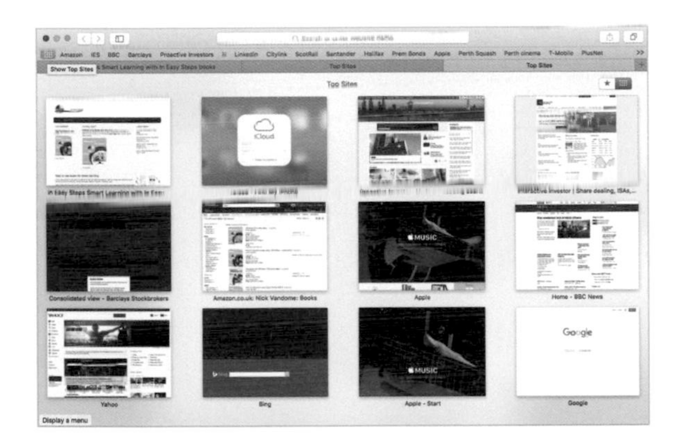

The thumbnails in the Top Sites window can be reordered by clicking and holding on them and dragging them into new positions as required.

3. Move the cursor over a thumbnail and click on the cross to delete a thumbnail from the **Top Sites** window. Click on the pin to keep it there permanently

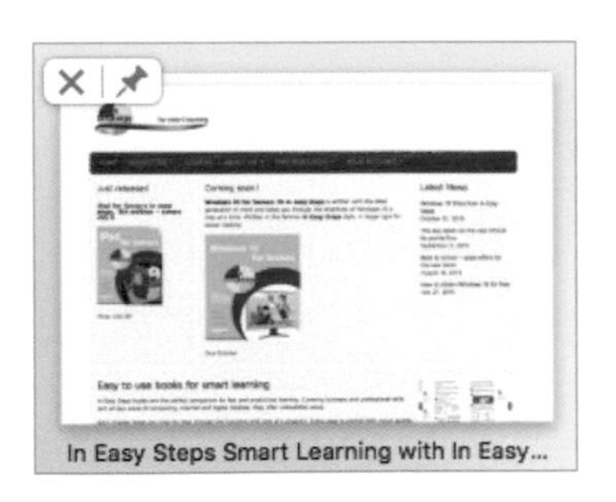

4. Click on a thumbnail to go to the full site

Adding Bookmarks

Bookmarks is a feature by which you can create quick links to your favorite web pages or the ones you visit most frequently. Bookmarks can be added to a menu or the Bookmarks bar in Safari, which makes them even quicker to access. Folders can also be created to store the less frequently used bookmarks. To view and create bookmarks:

Hot tip

If the Sidebar is not visible, select **View > Show Sidebar** from the Safari Menu bar.

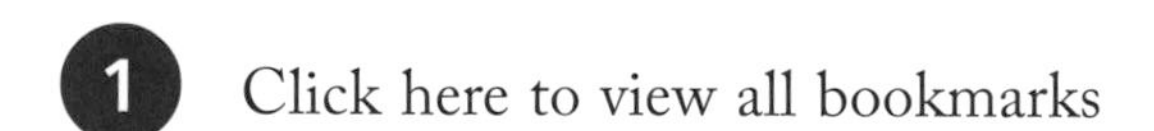

1. Click here to view all bookmarks

2. All of the saved bookmarks can be accessed from the Sidebar. Click on this button to view them

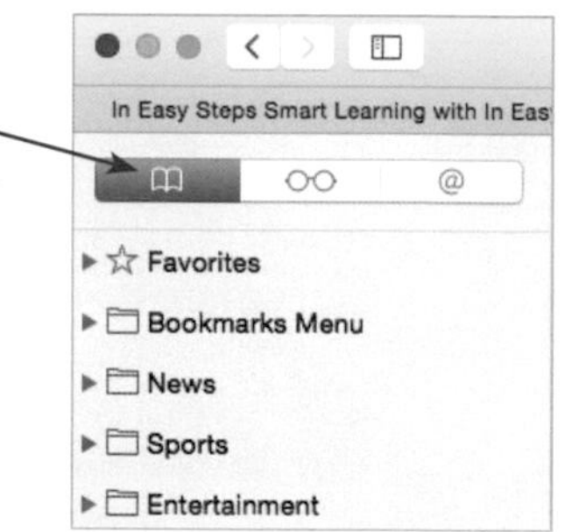

3. Click on the **Share** button and click on the **Add Bookmark** button to create a bookmark for the page currently being viewed

Hot tip

Bookmarks can be selected to appear on the **Favorites** bar, which is underneath the Smart Search Box. Select the **Favorites** option in Step 4 in the **Add this page to** box to add a page.

4. Enter a name for the bookmark and select a location for it

5. Click on the **Add** button

Viewing Your Online History

In any web session it is possible to look at dozens, or hundreds, of websites and pages. To make it easier to retrace your steps and return to previously-viewed pages, the History option in Safari can be used. To do this:

1. Select **History** from the Safari Menu bar

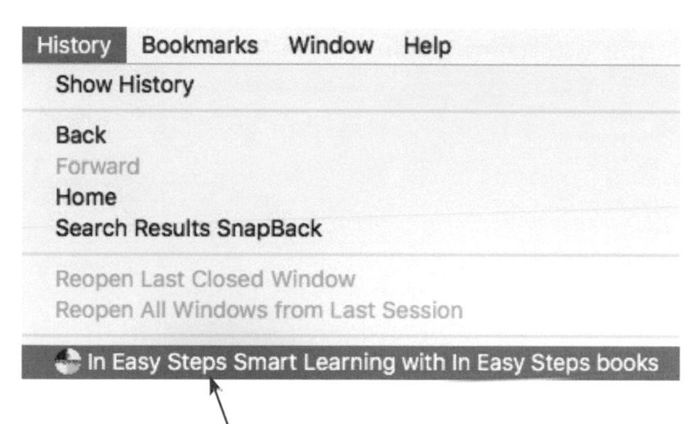

2. Click on an item here to return to a page that has been viewed in your current browsing session

3. Click on a date to view items that have been accessed previously

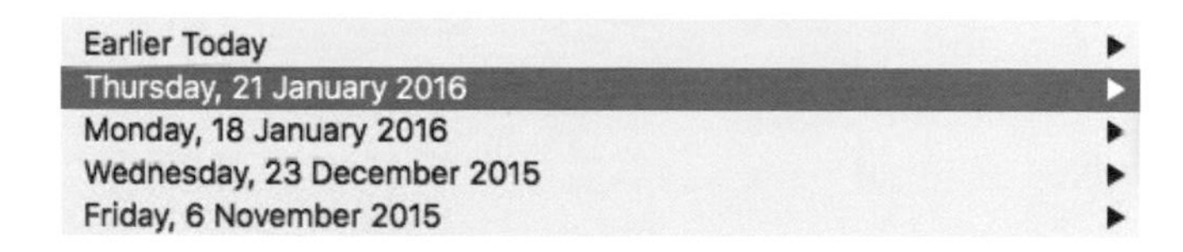

4. Click on **Clear History** to remove all of the items in your browsing history

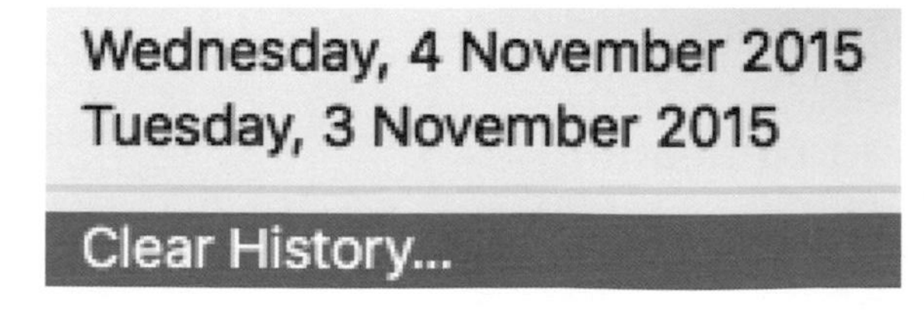

If you clear your browsing history your browser will not remember any address that you have previously entered. If the history is not cleared, the browser will remember them as soon as you start typing the address.

If you have been using Private Browsing (**File > New Private Window** from the Safari Menu bar) then there will be no record in your History and no browsing data will be recorded.

Safari Reader

Web pages can be complex and cluttered things at times. On some occasions, you may want to just read the content of one story on a web page without all of the extra material in view. In Safari this can be done with the Reader function. To do this:

Not all web pages support the Reader functionality in Safari.

The menu in Step 5 can be used to save pages so that they can be read even when you are offline.

1. Select **View > Show Reader** from the Safari menu bar

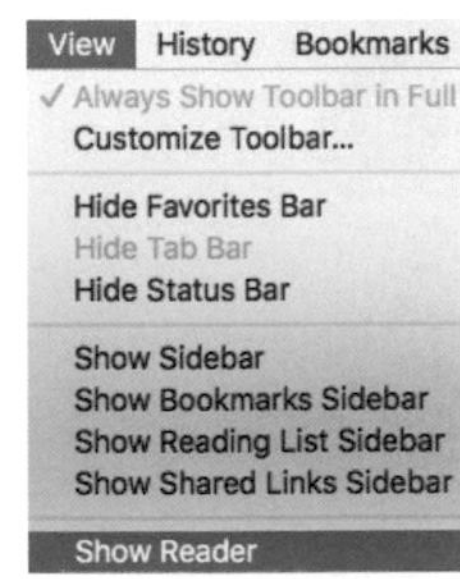

2. Click on the **Reader** button in the address bar of a web page that supports this functionality

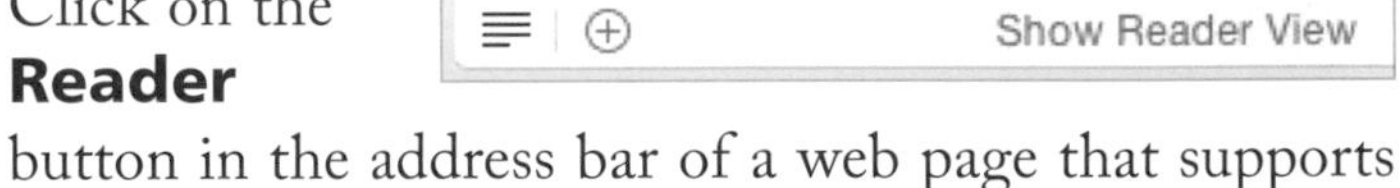

3. The button turns darker once the Reader is activated

4. The content is displayed in a text format, with a minimum of formatting from the original page

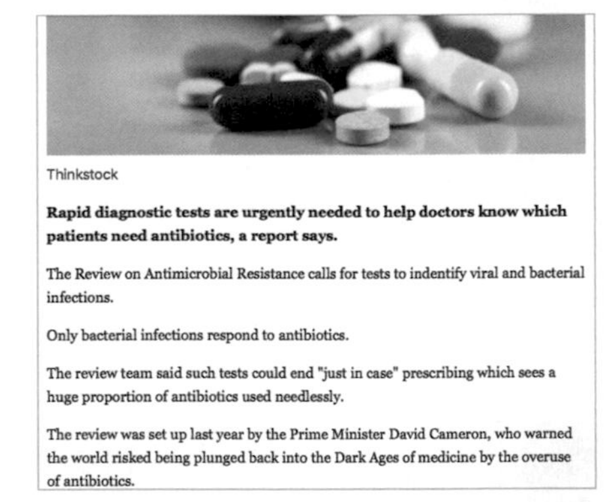
Thinkstock

Rapid diagnostic tests are urgently needed to help doctors know which patients need antibiotics, a report says.

The Review on Antimicrobial Resistance calls for tests to indentify viral and bacterial infections.

Only bacterial infections respond to antibiotics.

The review team said such tests could end "just in case" prescribing which sees a huge proportion of antibiotics used needlessly.

The review was set up last year by the Prime Minister David Cameron, who warned the world risked being plunged back into the Dark Ages of medicine by the overuse of antibiotics.

5. Click on this button on the Safari toolbar and select **Add to Reading List** if you want to save a page to read at a later date

7 Being Interactive Online

This chapter shows some of the activities that can be done on the web. It includes planning and booking a vacation, social networking, delving into your family history and playing games.

Shopping Online

The web is a lot more than just a means of discovering facts and figures. It is also a means of doing business in terms of buying and selling. This can be for small or large purchases, but either way, online shopping has revolutionized our retail lives.

Be careful when shopping online as you can quickly get carried away, since making purchases can be so easy.

When you are shopping online there are some guidelines that should be followed to try to ensure you are in a safe online environment and do not spend too much money:

- Make a note of what you want to buy and stick to this once you have found it. Online shopping sites are adept at displaying a lot of enticing offers and it is a lot easier to buy something by clicking a button than it is to physically take it to a checkout.
- Never buy anything that is promoted to you via an email, unless it is from a company that you have asked to send you promotional information.
- When paying for items, make sure that the online site has a secure area for accepting payment and credit card details. A lot of sites display information about this within their payment area, and another way to ascertain this is to check in the Address bar of the payment page. If it is within a secure area, the address of the page will start with "https" rather than the standard "http". Alternatively, it may show a locked padlock.

If the full website address is not showing in the Safari Address bar, select **Safari > Preferences** from the Menu bar. Click on the **Advanced** tab and check **On** the **Show full website address** checkbox, for **Smart Search Field**.

Using online shopping

The majority of online shopping sites are similar in their operation:

- Goods are identified
- Goods are placed in a shopping basket

- Once the shopping is completed you proceed to the checkout
- For some sites, you have to register before you can complete your purchase, while with others you do not
- You enter your shipping details and pay for the goods, usually with a credit or debit card

In some cases, if you are registered on a site, you can complete your shopping by using a 1-click system. This means that all of your billing and payment details are already stored on the site and you can buy goods simply by clicking one button without having to re-enter your details. One of the most prominent sites to use this method is Amazon.

Using cookies

A lot of online shopping sites use cookies, which are small programs that store information about your browsing habits on the site. Sites have to tell you if they are using cookies and they can be a good way to receive targeted information about products in which you are interested. This can be done on the sites when you are logged in, or via email.

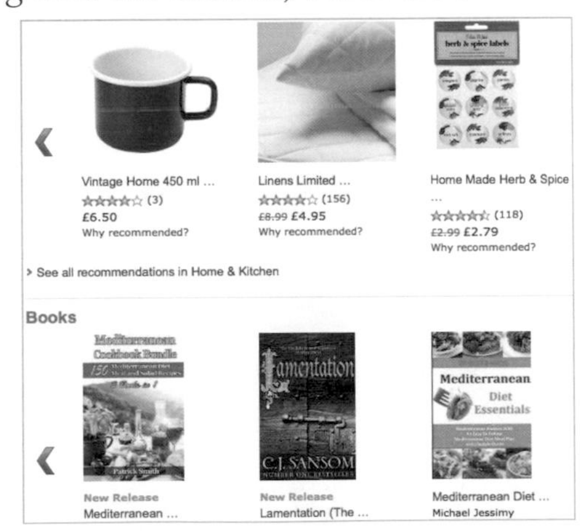

If you receive emails as a result of buying items from a site, you can choose to opt out or unsubscribe so that you do not receive them anymore. This is usually done from a link at the bottom of the email.

Booking a Vacation

Just as many retailers have been creating an online presence, the same is also true for vacation companies and travel agents. It is now possible to book almost any type of vacation on the web, from cruises to city breaks.

Several sites offer full travel services where they can deal with flights, hotels, insurance, car hire and excursions. These sites include:

- **www.expedia.com**
- **www.kayak.com**
- **www.orbitz.com**
- **www.travelocity.com**

These sites usually list special offers and last-minute deals on their Homepages and there is also a facility for specifying your precise requirements. To do this:

Hot tip

It is always worth searching different sites to get the best possible price. In some cases, it is cheapest to buy different elements of a vacation from different sites, e.g. flights from one site and accommodation from another.

1. Select your vacation requirements. This can include flight or hotel only, or both, and car hire

Most travel websites have specific versions based on your geographic location. You will be directed to these by default.

2. Enter flight details
3. Enter dates for your vacation
4. Click on the **Search** button

TripAdvisor

One of the best resources for travelers is TripAdvisor. Not only does the site provide a full range of opportunities for booking flights and hotels, it also has an extensive network of reviews from people who have visited the countries, hotels and restaurants on the site. These are independent, and are usually very fair and honest. In a lot of cases, if there are issues with a hotel or restaurant, the proprietor posts a reply to explain what is being done to address any problems.

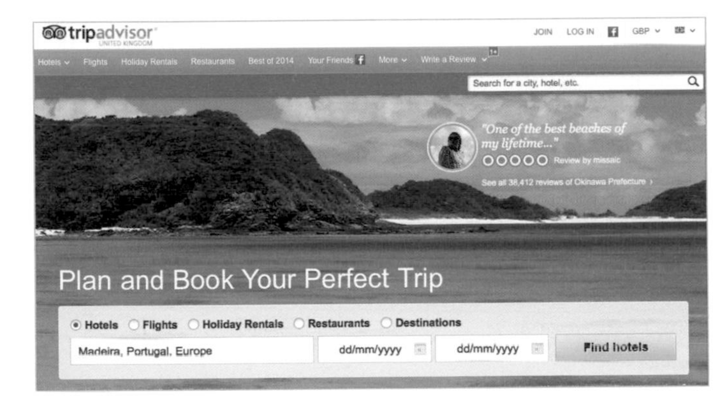

TripAdvisor has a certain sense of community, so post your own reviews once you have been places, to let others know about your experience.

Cruises

There are also websites dedicated specifically to cruises:

- **www.carnival.com**
- **www.cruises.com**
- **www.princess.com**

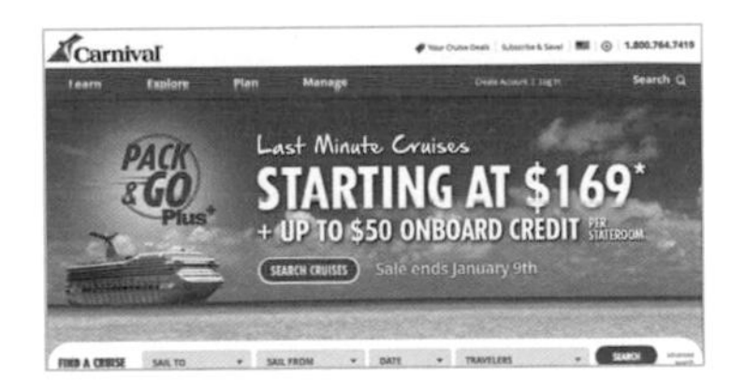

When booking holidays online, use the Private Browsing feature in Safari (**File > New Private Window**) so that the retailer does not know you are browsing from an Apple device, as there have been some instances where this has resulted in higher prices being returned.

Hotels

There is a range of websites that specialize in hotel bookings, a lot of them at short notice to get the best price:

- **www.choicehotels.com**
- **www.hotels.com**
- **www.laterooms.com**
- **www.trivago.com**

Travel Apps

While the practicalities of booking a vacation are important, the really fun part is researching destinations and planning the details of your trip. In the App Store there is a Travel category with a range of apps to help you on your way, and you can also make use of the ones already on your Mac:

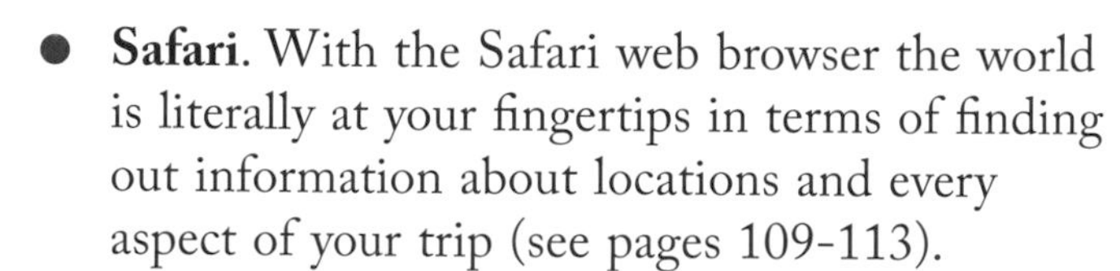

- **Safari**. With the Safari web browser the world is literally at your fingertips in terms of finding out information about locations and every aspect of your trip (see pages 109-113).

- **Notes**. Use this to create notes relating to your trip, ranging from Things to Pack lists to health information and travel details such as your itinerary. It is also a good option for keeping track of important items such as passport numbers (see pages 56-57).

- **iBooks**. Books are an ideal vacation companion and with this app you do not have to worry about being weighed down by a lot of heavy volumes (see pages 84-85).

- **Maps**. This is the perfect app for researching cities abroad so that you can start to feel at home as soon as you arrive (see pages 126-127).

- **FaceTime**. You can use your Mac to send emails and text messages when you are away from home, but FaceTime allows you to see people too with video calls (see page 143).

- **iTunes**. Use this to take all of your favorite music on vacation with you, and download more with an internet connection (see pages 74-78).

- **Photos**. This is an excellent app for downloading your vacation photos when you are away, and playing them back to family and friends when you get home (see pages 66-72).

To use Safari, Mail, Messages or FaceTime you will need an internet connection while you are away from home. This will probably be in the form of a Wi-Fi hotspot, which are widely available in hotels and other vacation locations.

If you have any music stored in the iTunes Store that has not yet been downloaded to your Mac, i.e. it is stored in the cloud, you will only be able to play it if you have a Wi-Fi connection. This can be used to play it by streaming, or you could also download it onto your Mac so that you can play it when you are offline.

App Store travel apps

To further expand your travel horizons, the App Store offers opportunities for every armchair traveler:

1. Click on the **App Store** app

2. Click on the **Categories** button

3. Click on the **Travel** category

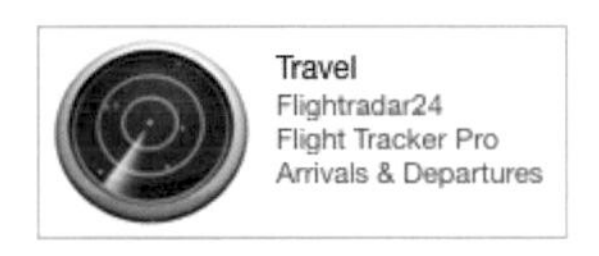

There is a good range of apps in the Travel category and some to look at include:

- **Stuck on Earth**. An excellent app for getting the travel juices flowing, this details interesting places around the world to visit, explore and photograph.
- **World Explorer**. Another app for looking at locations around the world including virtual walking tours.
- **Universal Translator**. This can be used to translate words and phrases in over 50 languages.
- **Flightradar24**. Use this to track flights in different regions of the world.
- **Language apps**. There are apps covering numerous different languages. Some of these are extensive language courses, while others are in the form of flashcards.
- **Transit apps**. There are apps that cover the transport systems in major cities around the world, such as the London Tube, New York Subway, Paris Metro and Madrid Metro.
- **Currency convertors**. For the financially-minded there are several apps for converting international currencies.

If you have an iPhone or an iPad, the range of travel apps will be different in the mobile version of the App Store. Some apps are available in both, but not all of them.

The Maps app also provides transit directions for certain locations.

Getting Around with Maps

With the Maps app you need never again wonder about where a location is, or worry about finding locations or getting directions to somewhere.

Viewing maps

Enable **Location Services** and then you can start looking around maps, from the viewpoint of your current location:

1. Click on this button on the Dock or in the Launcher

2. Click on this button to view your current location

3. Double-click to zoom in on a map. Alt + double-click to zoom out. Or, swipe outwards with thumb and forefinger to zoom in, and pinch inwards to zoom out

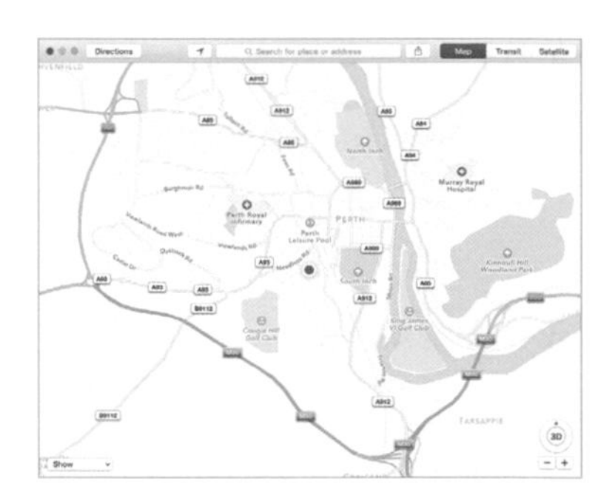

4. Or, click on these buttons to zoom in and out on a map

Don't forget

Location Services can be enabled in **System Preferences > Security & Privacy** and check on the **Enable Location Services** checkbox. Maps can be used without Location Services but this would mean that Maps cannot use your current location or determine anything in relation to this.

Finding locations

Locations in Maps can be found for addresses, cities or landmarks. To find items in Maps:

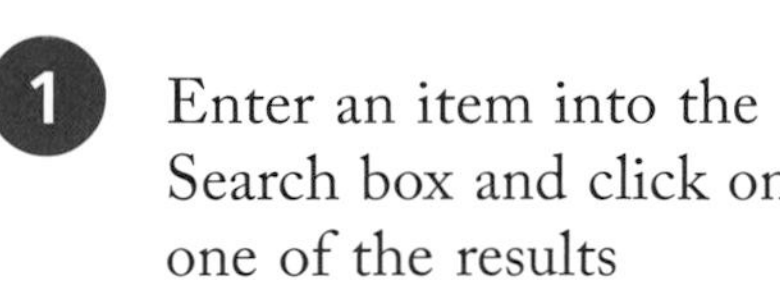

1. Enter an item into the Search box and click on one of the results

2. The selected item is displayed and shown on a map. Pins are also dropped at this point

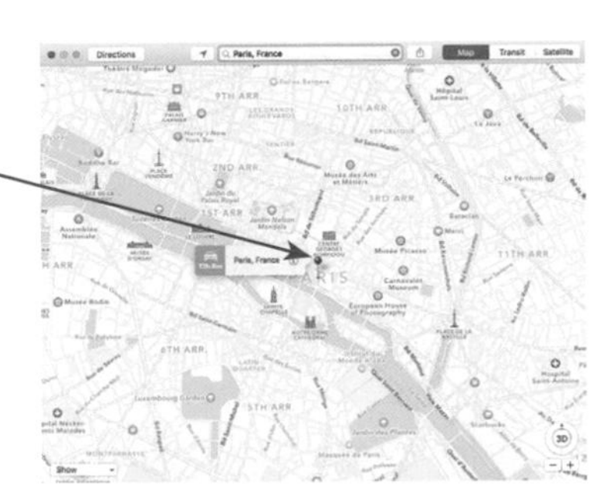

Click on a pin and the **i** symbol to view more information about a location.

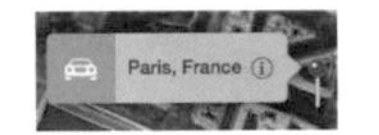

3. Click on one of the buttons on the top Maps toolbar to view a **Map** (Standard view), **Transit** (where available) or **Satellite** view of the map

Getting directions

Within Maps you can also get directions to almost any location around the world.

The **Transit** button on the top toolbar displays transit information for locations (where available) such as subway routes, trains, trams and buses. The **Transit** button underneath the directions boxes displays transit details for the selected journey (where available).

1. Click on the **Directions** button

2. By default, your current direction is used for the **Start** field. If you want to change this, click once and enter a new location

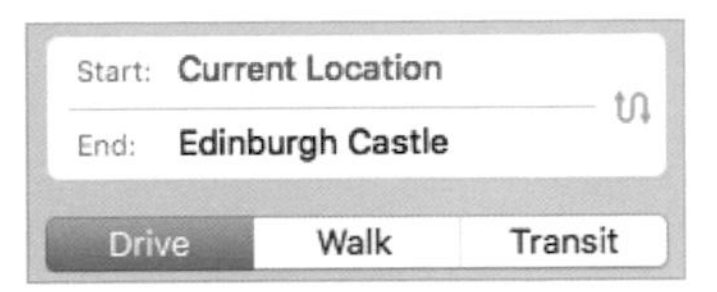

3. Enter an **End** location or address

4. The route is shown on the map, with the directions down the right-hand side of the window. The default mode of transport is by car

Researching Family History

A recent growth industry on the web has been family history, or genealogy. Hundreds of organizations around the world have now digitized their records concerning individuals and family histories, and there are numerous websites that provide online access to these records. Some of these sites are:

- **www.ancestry.com**
- **www.genealogy.com**
- **www.familysearch.org**
- **www.rootsweb.com**

When you are researching a family history, some of the areas you can look at include: births, deaths and marriages, military records, census records, professional association records and court records.

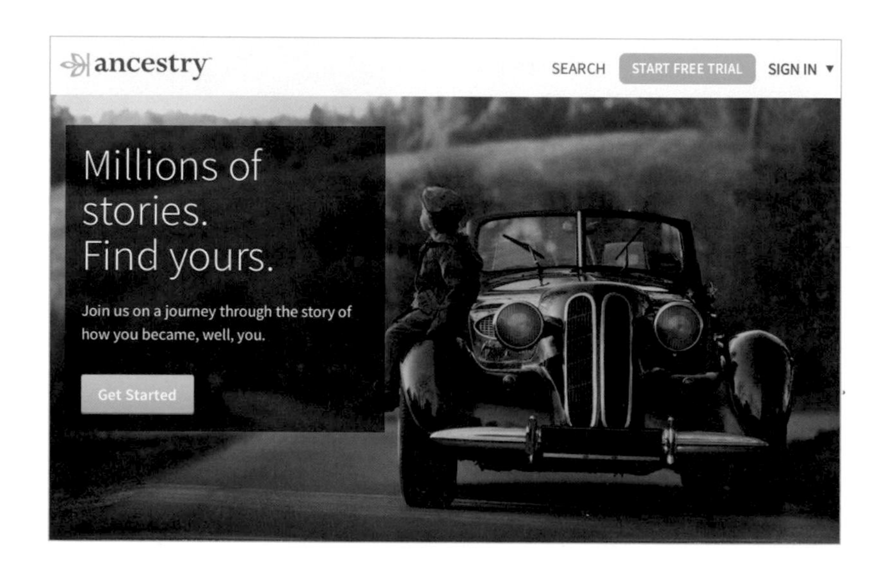

Most genealogy sites require you to register, for a fee, before you can conduct extensive family research on their sites, but once you do the process is similar on them all:

1. Enter the details of the family members in the search boxes

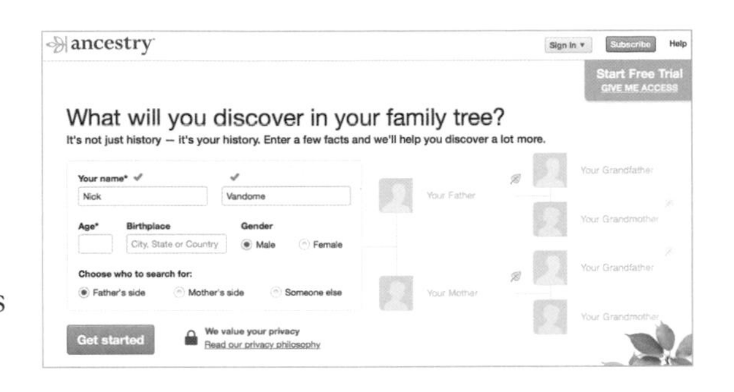

2. Click on the **Get started** button

3. The results are displayed for the names searched

4. Click on the **Search for Records** button to get a detailed report for your information. This may require registering on the site

5. On some sites there is a facility for creating your family tree. Enter the relevant details

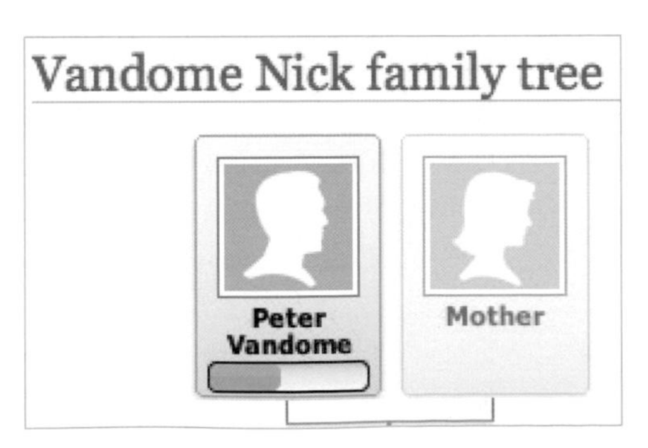

Some sites offer a free initial search, but after that you will have to pay for each search.

Saving Money

Everyone likes to get value for money when shopping or, better still, a bargain. On the web it is possible to try to find the best possible prices for items before you buy them. This is done through price comparison sites that show the prices for items from a range of online retailers. Some of the price comparison sites include:

- **www.pricegrabber.com**
- **www.pricerunner.com**
- **www.pricewatch.com**
- **www.shopping.com**

To use a price comparison site:

1. Select one of the online price comparison sites

2. Select a category for the type of product you want to buy or enter an item into the Search box

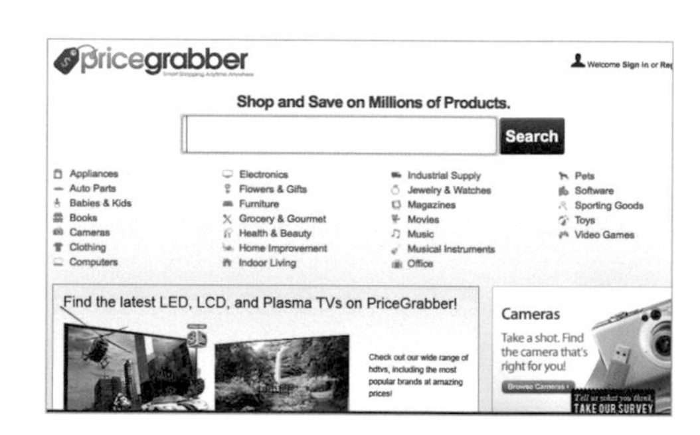

3. Locate the product you want to buy, then click on the **Compare** button to view the websites on which the product is available, and the different prices at which it is being offered. You can then buy the product from one of the sites

Price comparison sites do not actually sell anything: they just direct you to different retailers.

Just because certain items are displayed on a price comparison site does not mean that you cannot get them cheaper elsewhere.

Some geographic regions have websites dedicated to saving money on items such as mortgages, utility bills and insurance. Enter **money saving** into a search engine to see the options for your country or region.

Social Networking

Social networking is one of the communications revolutions of the 21st century, and sites like Facebook and Twitter provide excellent platforms to stay in touch with family and friends around the world. You have to register for these sites, which is free, and you can then use them to post comments, messages and photos and view what other people are saying and reply to them.

Facebook

This is now the most widely-used social networking tool and it offers a range of functionality (once you have registered): you can link up with your friends by searching for them and inviting them with a Friend Request; you can also be invited by other people and you have to accept their request before you can be friends; and you can post photos and messages and create and join groups.

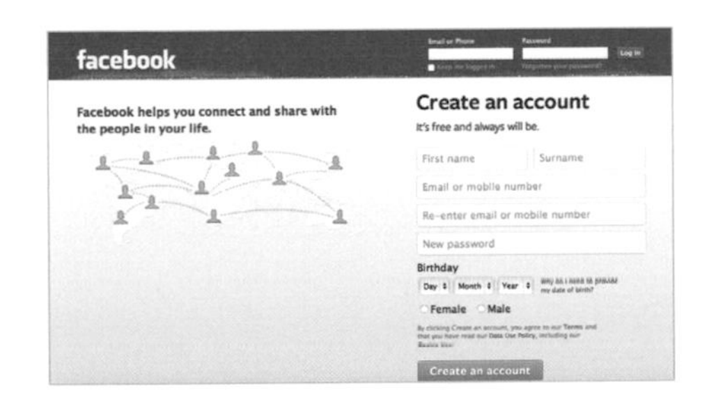

There is no dedicated Facebook app in the App Store for Mac computers but there is a **MenuTab for Facebook** app that acts like a mini version of the site. You can also log in online at www.facebook.com

Twitter

Twitter was launched in 2006 and has grown at a remarkable rate. It is a microblogging site where users post short messages, called tweets, of up to 140 characters, and is now one of the most visited websites in the world. Once you have joined Twitter, you can follow other users to see what they are saying and have people follow you too. You can log in to Twitter at the website at **www.twitter.com** or download the Twitter app from the App Store and use this to view your Twitter content.

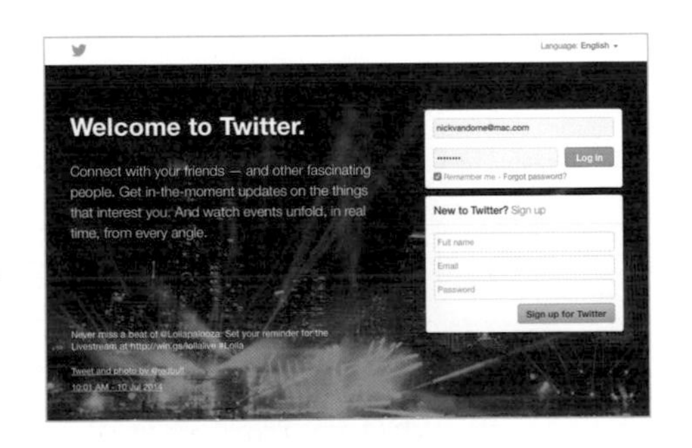

Other social networking sites to look at are Flickr for photo sharing and YouTube for sharing and viewing videos.

Shopping on eBay

eBay is one of the phenomena of the online world. Started as a small site in California, it has grown into a multi-billion dollar business, with online auctions and also standard online retailer transactions. To buy and sell items on eBay you have to be registered. This can be done from the eBay Homepage by clicking on the Register button or link. This takes you through the registration process, which is free.

Most people are honest on eBay but you do sometimes get unscrupulous buyers and sellers, so be sure to view a seller's feedback before you commit to buying anything.

Buying items

Once you have registered, you can start buying and selling items. In some ways, it is better to start by buying some cheaper items just to get used to the system. The two main options are **Auctions** and **Buy It Now** (single price purchase). For **Buy It Now** items, click on the relevant button to purchase the item without an auction. For auction items, enter a bid in the Place Bid box and click on the **Place Bid** button. If you win the auction, you will be notified on eBay and also via email. At this point you pay the vendor for the item and they should mail it to you.

Once you have completed the transaction you can leave feedback about the seller.

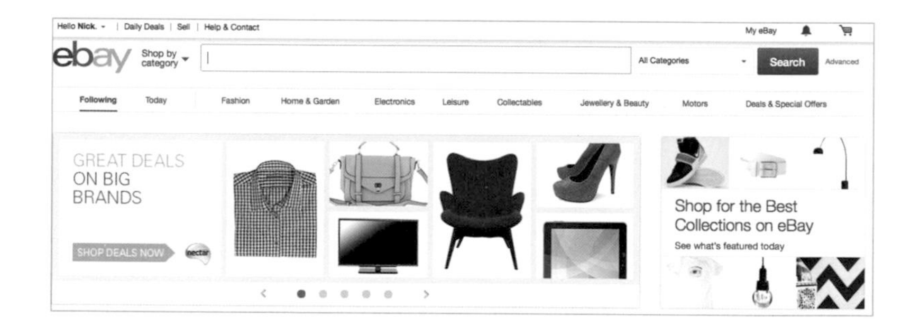

Selling items

To list items on eBay for sale, first click on the **Sell** button at the top of the eBay window. Complete the wizard for selling items. This includes a detailed description of the item and photographs. Choose a price for your item, the cost of postage and also the duration of the auction. Complete the sale wizard to list your item on eBay. Keep an eye on the auction to see the amounts that are being bid. If you have a **Buy It Now** price this means that someone can buy it for this price and thus end the auction.

eBay charges a fee when items are sold, which is a percentage of the sale price. This is not charged if the item is not sold.

Online Finances

Online banking

Online banking has helped to transform our financial activities in the same way as online shopping has transformed our retail ones. Most major banks have online banking facilities and they can be used for a number of services, including:

- Managing your accounts
- Transferring money
- Paying bills
- Applying for credit cards
- Paying credit cards
- Applying for loans

Before you can use any of these online services you have to first register and apply for an online account:

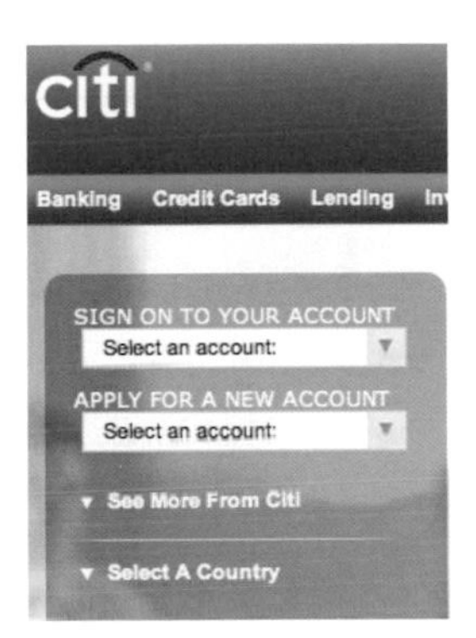

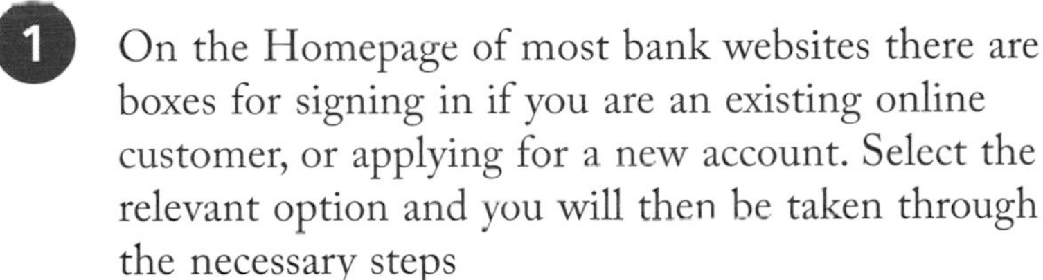

1. On the Homepage of most bank websites there are boxes for signing in if you are an existing online customer, or applying for a new account. Select the relevant option and you will then be taken through the necessary steps

Stocks and shares online

An extension of online banking is being able to deal in stocks and shares on the web. You can buy and sell on the stock market without having to leave the comfort of your own home. A number of financial services websites offer this facility, and they also provide a lot of background information as well as the buying and selling function. If you are going to be trading stocks and shares on the web it is a good idea to find out as much about them before you start trading. In this respect, the websites of relevant stock markets provide a very useful source of information.

Online banking is generally as secure as any other form of banking transaction and it has the advantage that you can check your accounts as frequently as you like.

Never buy stocks and shares from any offers you receive by email.

Online Games

Online gambling has developed in some countries in recent years but it is also possible to play online games, such as Bridge and Backgammon, without the need to gamble away your life savings. Although some of these sites do allow you to play for money, others offer a less financially pressurized environment. For both Bridge and Backgammon sites, you can either play against the computer or other people who are on the site. Either way, you are usually presented with a graphic interface of the action:

Websites for online Bridge or Backgammon can be found by entering these keywords into the Google Search box.

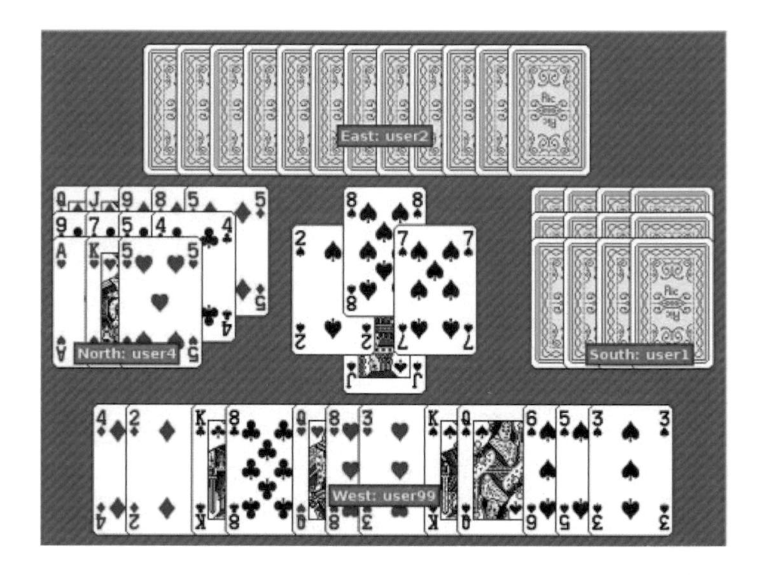

The Game Center app can also be used for downloading games from the App Store.

8 Keeping in Touch

Communication, as much as money, makes the world go round. This chapter shows how to use the Mac tools to communicate, using email and text, and FaceTime video calls.

Setting up Email

Email is an essential element for most computer users, and Macs come with their own email app called Mail. This covers all of the email functionality that anyone could need.

When first using Mail you have to set up your email account. This can be done with most email accounts and also a wide range of web mail accounts, including iCloud. To add email accounts:

Mail is a full-screen app and can be expanded by clicking the double arrow in the top right-hand corner. For more information on full-screen apps, see pages 40-41.

1. Click on this icon on the Dock

2. Check on the button next to the type of account that you want to create. If you have an Apple ID you will already have an iCloud email address which can be entered

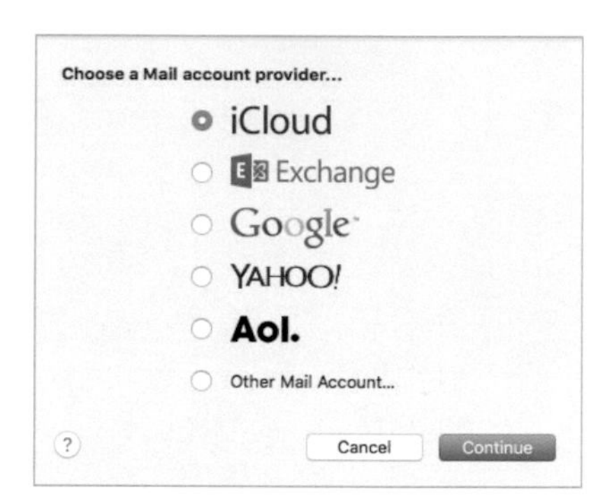

3. Enter details of the account and click on the **Sign In** button

You can set up more than one account in the Mail app and you can download messages from all of the accounts that you set up.

4. Check on the **Mail** option for iCloud to sync your iCloud email across any other Apple devices and also the online account at **www.icloud.com**

Adding Mailboxes

When you are dealing with email it is a good idea to create a folder structure (mailboxes) for your messages. This will allow you to sort your emails into relevant subjects when you receive them, rather than having all of them sitting in your Inbox. To add a structure of new mailboxes:

1. Click on this button to view your current mailboxes

Different mailboxes can be used to store emails according to their subject matter.

2. Move the cursor over the **Mailboxes** heading and click on the plus sign to the right of it

3. Enter a name for the Mailbox and a location for where you would like it to be stored, and then click on the **OK** button

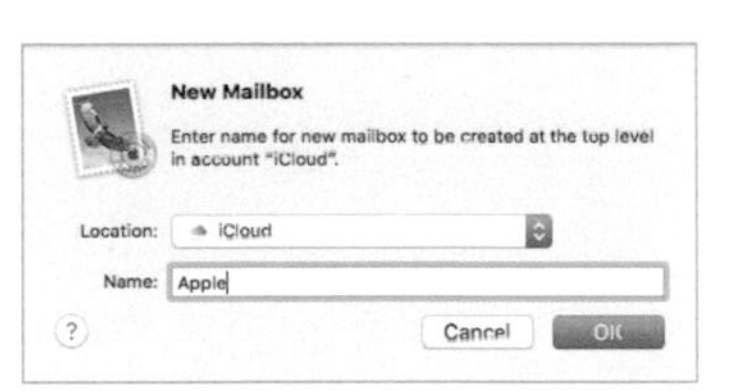

Mailboxes can be located on your Mac computer and also within iCloud, Apple's online sharing and backing up service.

4. The new mailbox is added to the current list

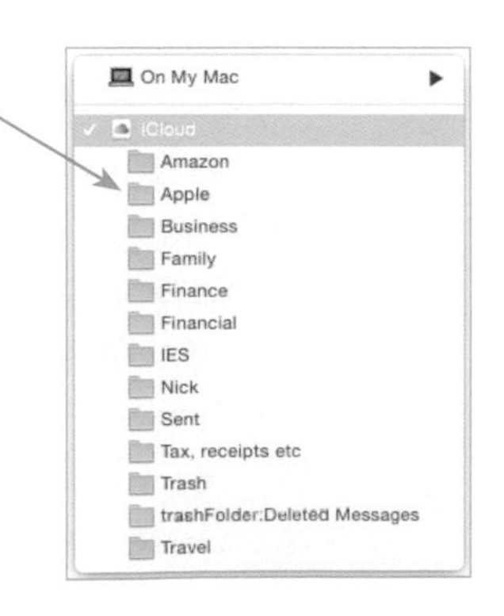

Creating Email

Mail enables you to send and receive emails and also format them to your own style. This can be simply formatting text or adding customized stationery. To use Mail:

1. Click on the **Get Mail** button to download available email messages

2. Click on the **New Message** button to create a new email

3. Enter a recipient in the **To** box, a title in the **Subject** box and then text for the email in the main window

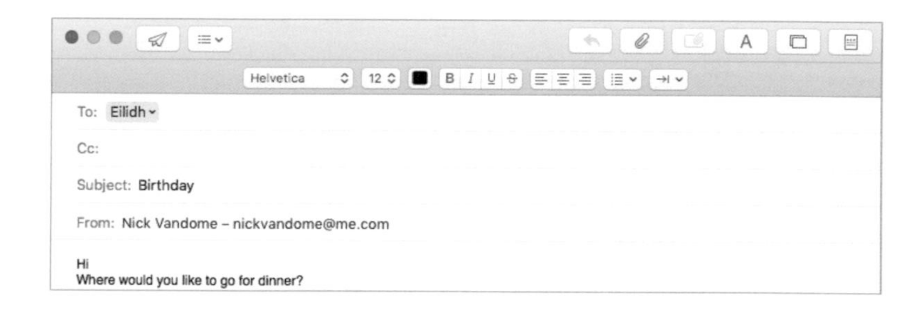

4. Click on the **Format** button to access options for formatting the text in the email

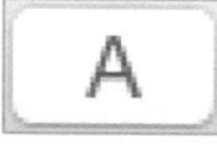

5. Click on these buttons to **Reply** to, **Reply to All** or **Forward** an email you have received

Reply Reply All Forward

6. Select or open an email and click on the **Delete** button to remove it

Select a reasonably large font size to ensure that your email can be read easily.

If you **Forward** an email with an attachment then the attachment is included. If you **Reply** to an email the attachment will not be included.

Email Conversations

Within Mail you can view conversations, i.e. groups of emails on the same subject. There is also a facility for showing your own replies within a conversation. To view a conversation:

1. Select **View > Organize by Conversation** from the Mail menu bar

2. Emails with the same subject are grouped together as a conversation in the left-hand pane. The number of grouped emails is shown at the right-hand side

Stuart Home, Allan, Geoff & James 14:29
Happy new year 7
yep, i'll be there from 6.20 on and can stay after 7 On 6 January 2015 at 12:49, Allan -- Stuart...

3. Click here to view the full list of emails

Stuart Home, Allan, Geoff & James 14:29
Happy new year 7
yep, i'll be there from 6.20 on and can stay after 7 On 6 January 2015 at 12:49, Allan -- Stuart...
Stuart Home 14:29
Allan 14:23
Allan 12:50
Geoff Bush 09:19
Stuart Home Yesterday

4. The full conversation is shown in the right-hand pane

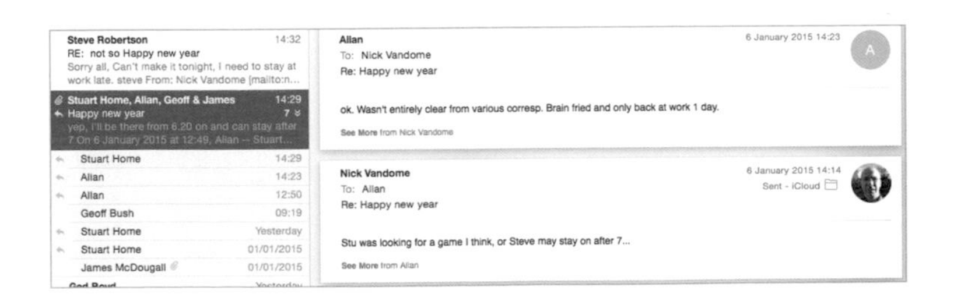

If messages are set up to be organized by conversation, you could miss some messages if they are grouped with the conversation rather than appearing individually. Check within the conversation to view all of the messages.

When replying to a message in a group conversation, use **Reply All** to copy your reply to everyone in the conversation, or **Reply** to answer one person directly.

Attaching Photos

Emails do not have to be restricted to plain text, and attachments are an excellent way to send photos to family and friends around the world. There are two ways to do this:

Attach button

To attach photos using the Attach button:

1. Click on this icon on the Mail toolbar

2. Select a photo from within the Finder

3. Click on the **Choose File** button

4. The photo is added to the body of the email

Do not send files that are too large in terms of file size, otherwise the recipient may find it takes too long to download.

Photo Browser

To attach photos using the Photo Browser:

1. Click on this icon on the Mail toolbar

2. Browse the **Photo Browser** for the photo(s) that you want to include

3. Drag the selected photo(s) into the open email to include them in the message

The Photo Browser is available from a variety of other applications.

Email Stationery

You do not have to settle for conservative formatting options in emails, and Mail offers a variety of templates that can give your messages a creative and eye-catching appearance. It can also be used to format any photos that you have attached to your message. This is done through the use of the Stationery function. To use this:

1. Click on this icon on the Mail toolbar

2. Select a category for the stationery

3. Double-click on a style to apply it to the email

4. The stationery incorporates any photos that have been attached from the Photo Browser

Once the Stationery effect has been applied the message will be sent in the same way as for a standard email.

If the recipient has an older email app on their computer (or one that is not compatible with Mail) they may not be able to see the full Stationery effect.

Dealing with Junk Email

Spam, or junk email, is the scourge of every email user. It consists of unwanted and unsolicited messages that are usually sent in bulk to lists of email addresses. In Mail there is a function which limits the amount of junk email that you receive in your Inbox. To do this:

It is worth occasionally checking in your Junk Mailbox, in case something you do want is there.

1. When you receive a junk email, click on the **Junk** button on the Mail toolbar (initially, this will help to train Mail to identify junk email)

2. Once Mail has recognized the types of junk that you receive, it will start to filter them directly into the Junk Mailbox

To empty your Junk Mailbox completely, select **Mailbox > Erase Junk Mail** from the Menu bar.

3. To set the preferences for junk email, select **Mail > Preferences** from the Menu bar and click on the **Junk** tab

4. Junk email is displayed in the **Junk Mailbox**

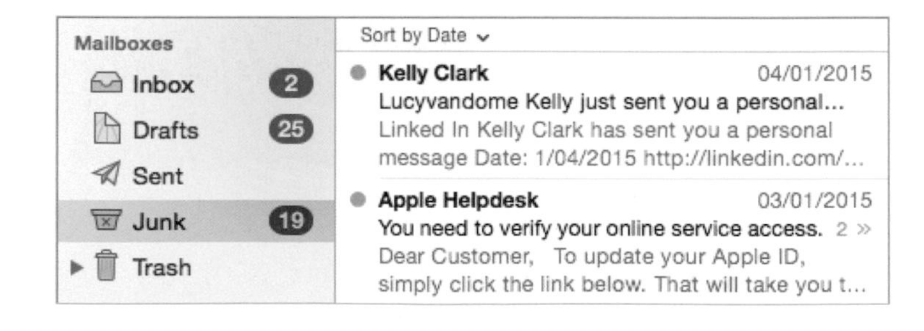

FaceTime

FaceTime is an app that was originally used on the iPhone and iPod Touch to make video calls to other compatible devices. However, it is now also available with OS X so that you can make and receive video calls from your Mac via other Macs, iPhones, iPads and iPod Touches. To do this:

To use FaceTime you need to have an in-built FaceTime camera on your Mac or use an external one that is compatible.

1. Click on this icon on the Dock

2. You require an Apple ID to use FaceTime. Enter your details or click on the **Create New Account** button

3. Once you have logged in you can make video calls by selecting people from your address book, or adding their phone number, providing they have a device that supports FaceTime. When you connect, you see them in the main video window, with your own image minimized as a thumbnail

Your contacts are displayed next to the main video window. Click on a contact to connect for a FaceTime call to them.

Messaging

Text messaging is now a common part of life and the Messages app enables you to send text messages (iMessages) to other OS X users or those with an iPhone, iPad or iPod Touch. It can also be used to send photos, videos and audio clips. To use Messages:

You require an Apple ID to use Messages and you will need to enter these details when you first access it. If you do not have an Apple ID you will be able to create one at this point.

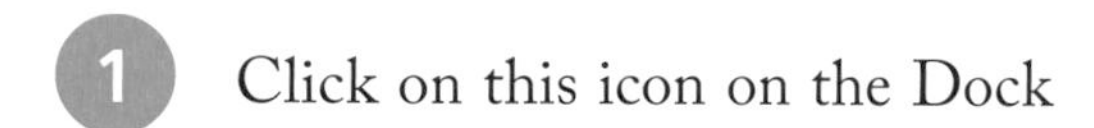

1. Click on this icon on the Dock

2. Click on this button to start a new conversation

3. Click on this button and select a contact (these will be from your Contacts app). To send an iMessage the recipient must have an Apple ID

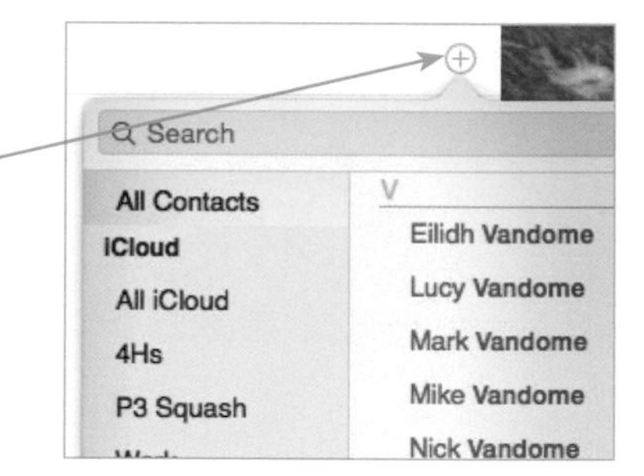

4. The person with whom you are having a conversation is displayed in the left-hand panel

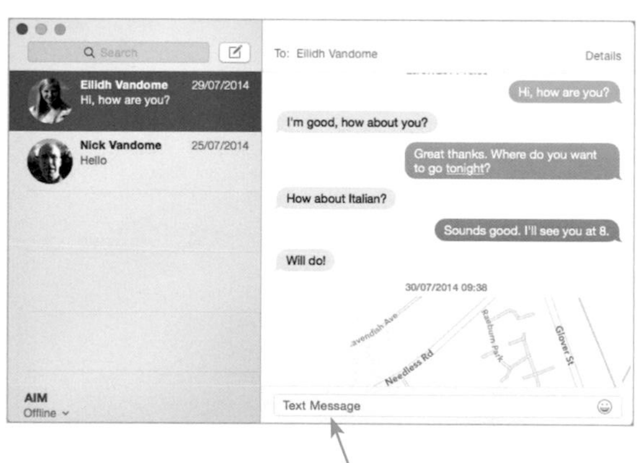

5. The conversation continues down the right-hand panel. Click here to write a message, and then press **Return** to send it

To delete a conversation, roll over it in the left-hand panel and click on this cross.

Adding photos and videos

Photos and videos can be added to messages:

1. Select the photo or video in the Finder, next to the Messages app

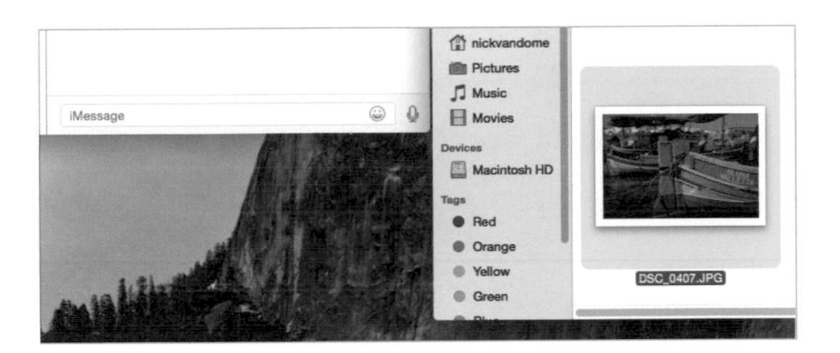

2. Drag the photo or video into the text box to include it in a message

3. Add text to the message as required and send it in the same way as a text-only message

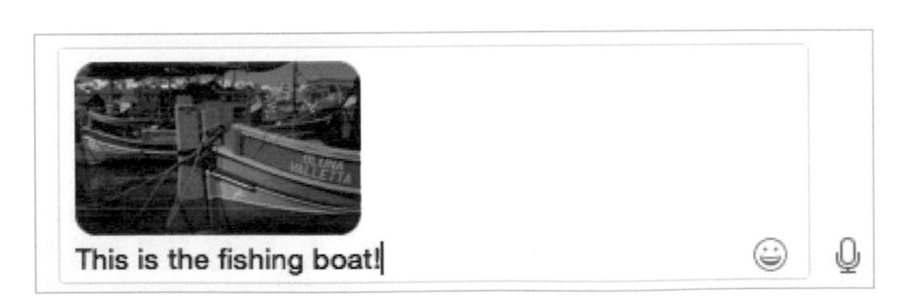

Don't forget

Keep photos and videos in the Pictures folder so that they can be quickly found in the Finder. (Create separate folders for specific topics or events.)

Hot tip

Add text to a message first and then add the image, so that you can be sure you are not sending an image on its own, with no explanation.

...cont'd

Adding emojis

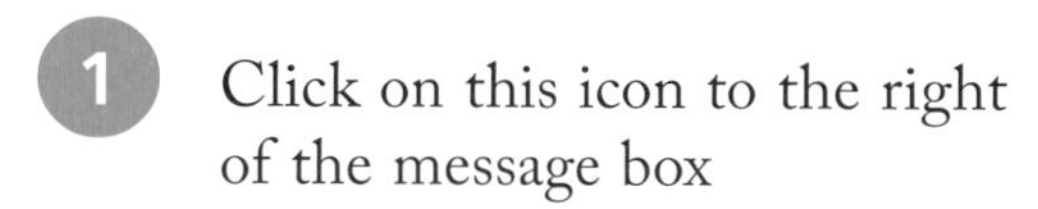

Emojis are the small graphical symbols that can be inserted into text messages. To include them in an iMessage:

Do not add too many emojis to a message, unless you know that the recipient is a fan of them.

1. Click on this icon to the right of the message box 

2. Click on an emoji to include it in a message, or click here to view more options

Adding an audio clip

The Messages app can also be used to send short audio clips:

You need to have an internal or external microphone attached to your Mac in order to add an audio clip to an iMessage.

1. Click on this icon to the right of the message box 

2. Record your audio message and click on the red button once you have finished

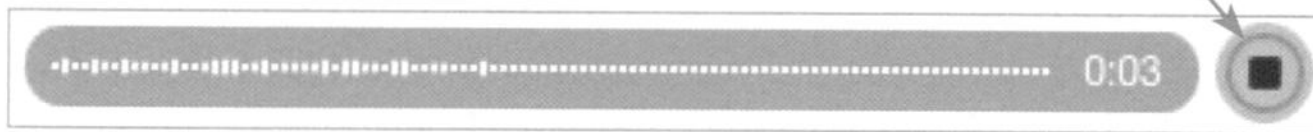

3. Click on the **Send** button to send the audio clip

4. When an audio clip has been included in a message, click on the Play button to listen to it

9 Apple Mobility

Apple is so much more than just computers. This chapter looks at using mobile devices and how to share content using iCloud and Family Sharing.

About El Capitan and iOS 9

OS X El Capitan and iOS 9 are two separate and distinctive operating systems, designed specifically for their own devices, i.e. OS X for Mac computers and laptops; and iOS 9 for iPhones, iPads and iPod Touches. However, they share certain similarities and have been designed to interact with each other so that content can be shared between the two different platforms. They should be thought of as two halves of the Apple operating system family.

iOS 9 includes Siri, the digital voice assistant that can be activated by speaking to your iPad, iPhone or iPod Touch. It can be used to operate apps on your devices, e.g. set up reminders, or search for items over the web or Wikipedia.

For the family

One of the aims of OS X El Capitan and iOS 9 is enabling you to store your content so that it is not only backed up, but also so that you can edit it on different devices and also share it with other people. The main way for doing this is with the Family Sharing feature that is used with OS X El Capitan and iOS 9.

Family Sharing works in conjunction with the online iCloud service and, once it has been set up, you can use it to share content that you have bought from the iTunes Store, and the App Store, with up to six family members. You can also share items such as photos and calendars. See pages 154-159 for more details about Family Sharing.

Linking it Together

Apple iOS 9 devices and those using OS X El Capitan are designed to work together so that you can share content between them. This is done through the use of the iCloud service which means that all of your Apple computing activities can be available across various devices. As shown in Chapter One, this is done from within System Preferences on computers using OS X El Capitan. On iOS 9 devices iCloud is set up through the Settings app. To do this:

1. Tap on the **Settings** app

2. Tap on the **iCloud** button in the left-hand panel of the Settings

3. Drag these buttons to On (showing green) to enable the relevant features for iCloud. This means that the content will be available across any iOS 9 devices that you have and also any OS X El Capitan devices (as long as they have been enabled for iCloud too)

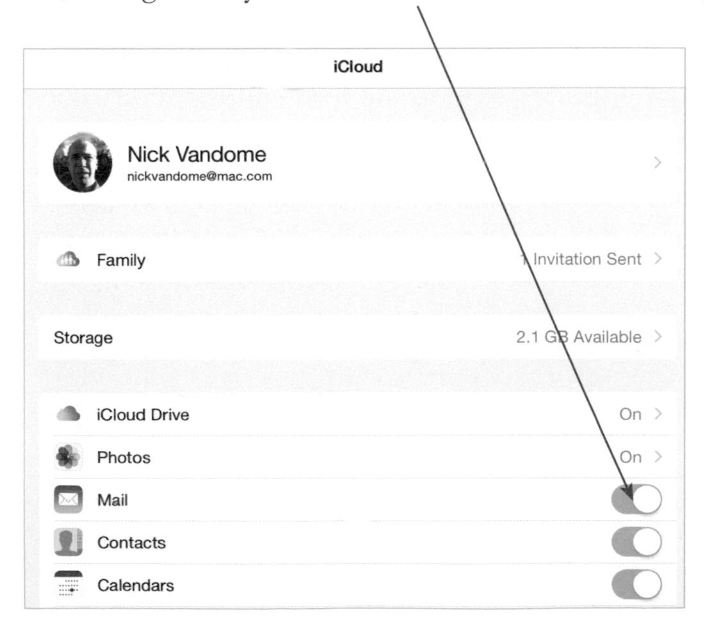

One of the options for iOS 9 devices under iCloud is Find My iPad. This provides a service for locating a lost or stolen iPad (also works for iPhone) via the online iCloud website: **www.icloud.com**

iPhone

The iPhone 6s, 6s Plus and iPhone SE can also be used with Apple Pay, Apple's method of contactless payment that operates with the iPhone's Touch ID feature, which involves setting a fingerprint ID for the Home button. You can add debit or credit cards to your iPhone and then use these at participating outlets.

The **Apple Watch** can be used in conjunction with the iPhone (iPhone 5 and later, running iOS 8 or later) for a variety of tasks such as receiving email and text message notifications, health and fitness monitoring and using the digital voice assistant, Siri. It can be used without an iPhone, but its functionality is much more limited.

Launched in 2007, the iPhone is one of the products that has helped propel Apple to be the world's most valuable technology company. It is a smartphone that is capable of accessing the web, using email, taking photos, recording videos and playing multimedia content such as music and movies. In essence, it is really a mini computer that can also be used to make phone calls and send and receive texts.

The user interface of the iPhone is a touchscreen with a virtual keypad, rather than the traditional screen and physical keypad. The screen is navigated around by using swiping gestures with your fingers and tapping to access items. The keypad appears whenever you need to input text, such as when using the Notes app or typing a web address into the Safari app.

iPhone 6s and iPhone 6s Plus

These were announced in September 2015 and this further enhanced Apple's reputation for innovation and style. Some of the features are:

- iOS 9 operating system so that the iPhone 6s and 6s Plus can be used independently and also linked to other iOS 9 devices, such as the iPad and the iPod Touch, and also computers using OS X El Capitan.
- Two models: the iPhone 6s, which has a screen size of 4.7 inches and the iPhone 6s Plus, which has a screen size of 5.5 inches (measured diagonally).
- Two cameras, one for high resolution photos and one for video calls (FaceTime).
- All of the latest apps from the online App Store.

In March 2016 Apple released the iPhone SE. With a smaller 4-inch screen, it still runs on iOS 9 and can perform all of the same functions as the iPhone 6s and 6s Plus. It will suit users who prefer a smaller phone.

iPad

Apple has a knack of changing the way people look at computers and computing and the iPad was another product that continued this trend. It is a tablet computer that is primarily designed for multimedia content, such as movies, video games, music and books, but it can also be used for productivity options such as word processing or creating presentations and spreadsheets.

The first iPad was released in 2010 and operates in a similar way to the iPhone, with iOS 9 and a large touchscreen and a virtual keyboard that appears when you need to type anything. All iPads come with Wi-Fi connectivity for access to the web and some models have 3G (or 4G in some locations) connectivity so that you can connect to the internet in the same way as you would with an iPhone.

The majority of apps for the iPad can be downloaded from the App Store, in the same way as for the iPhone.

iPad Air, iPad Mini and iPad Pro

The iPad comes in three sizes: the original version which has a screen measuring 9.7 inches (measured diagonally), now known as the iPad Air; the iPad Mini 3 which has a screen measuring 7.9 inches; and the iPad Pro, which is marketed as a replacement for a laptop and has a 9.7 inch or a 12.9 inch screen. All three have high resolution Retina Display screens for exceptional clarity and they all use iOS 9.

In terms of functionality, there is little difference between the iPad Air and the iPad Mini, and the choice may depend on the size of screen that you prefer. Both the iPad Air 2 (and later) and the iPad Mini 3 (and later) have Touch ID functionality, whereby the Home button can be used as a fingerprint sensor for unlocking the iPad.

A Smart Cover can be added to an iPad. This is a firm cover that protects the iPad and it can also be used to support it by folding it behind the iPad. The Smart Covers come in a range of colors.

The iPad Air 2 (and later) has a Split View option so two apps can be viewed on the screen simultaneously.

The iPad Pro comes with either 32GB or 128GB of memory and can also be used with the Apple Pencil and the detachable Apple Smart Keyboard.

Using iOS 9

iOS 9 works with touchscreen devices, which means its functionality is performed by tapping and swiping on the screen of an iPhone, iPad or iPod Touch. Some of this functionality includes:

To open an iOS 9 app, tap on it once on the Dock or the device's Home screen.

The Dock

This is the collection of icons at the bottom of the screen. It works in a similar way to the Dock in OS X El Capitan, in that items can be opened from here and also added to, and removed from, the Dock.

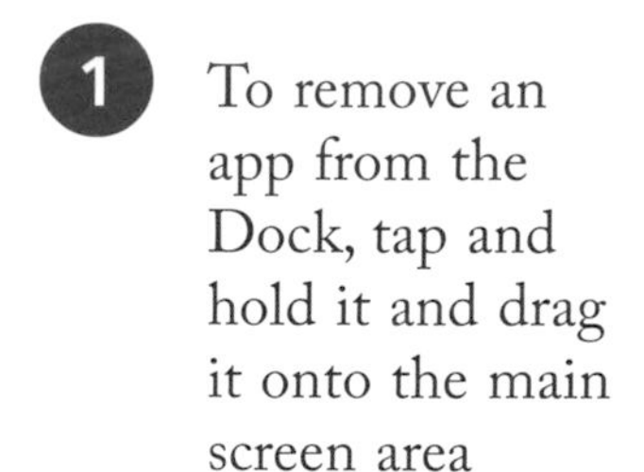

1. To remove an app from the Dock, tap and hold it and drag it onto the main screen area

Apps that have been downloaded to an iPhone, iPad or iPod Touch from the App Store, i.e. not the pre-installed apps, can be deleted by pressing and holding on the app until it starts to jiggle and a cross appears next to it. Tap on the cross to delete the app.

2. To add an app to the Dock, tap and hold it and drag it onto the Dock

Closing apps

iOS 9 devices deal with open apps very efficiently. They can be open in the background, without using up a significant amount of processing power, so it is not always necessary to close apps. However, you may want to close them if you feel you have too many open or if one stops working. To do this, double-click on the Home button to access the App Switcher window. Swipe left and right to view all open apps and drag one to the top of the screen to close it.

Settings

This is similar to the System Preferences in OS X El Capitan and is where you can customize your iOS 9 devices in dozens of ways, using different categories.

1. Tap on the **Settings** app

2. The categories are listed in the left-hand panel, with the items for each to the right

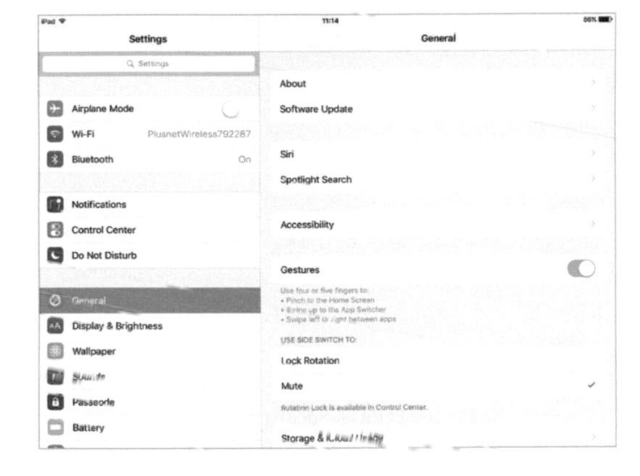

3. To turn an option On, drag this button to the right so that it shows green

Home button

The Home button on iOS 9 devices can be used for a variety of functions:

- Click once on the **Home** button to return to the Home screen at any point.
- Double-click on the **Home** button to access the **App Switcher** window. This can also be accessed by swiping up from the bottom of the screen with four or five fingers.
- Press and hold on the **Home** button to access the **Siri** voice assistant function. This can be used to search for information on your iOS 9 devices or from the web or Wikipedia by using voice commands.

The Settings for iOS 9 include options for setting up Wi-Fi, setting the background wallpaper, specifying system sounds, setting up iCloud and privacy settings. There are also settings for the specific apps on your device.

For more information on using iOS 9 on mobile devices, have a look at **iPad for Seniors in easy steps** and **iPhone for Seniors in easy steps** in this series.

About Family Sharing

As everyone gets more and more digital devices it is becoming increasingly important to be able to share content with other people, particularly family members. With OS X El Capitan, iOS 9 and iCloud, the Family Sharing function enables you to share items from the iTunes Store and the App Store, such as music, movies and apps, with up to six other family members, as long as they have an Apple Account. Once this has been set up, it is also possible to share items such as family calendars, photos and even see where family members' devices are located. To set up Family Sharing in OS X El Capitan:

Don't forget

On iOS 9 devices, Family Sharing is set up from the iCloud option from within the Settings app.

1. Click on the **iCloud** button in System Preferences

2. Click on the **Set Up Family Sharing** (or the **Manage Family** button if Family Sharing has already been set up)

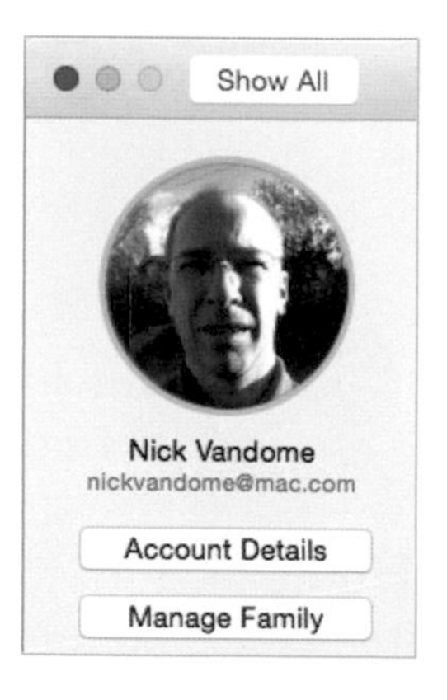

Don't forget

To use Family Sharing, other family members must have an Apple device using either iOS 8 (or later) for a mobile device (iPad, iPhone or iPod Touch) or OS X Yosemite (or later) for a desktop or laptop Mac computer.

3. One person will be the organizer of Family Sharing, i.e. in charge of it, and if you set it up then it will be you. Click on the **+** button to add other family members

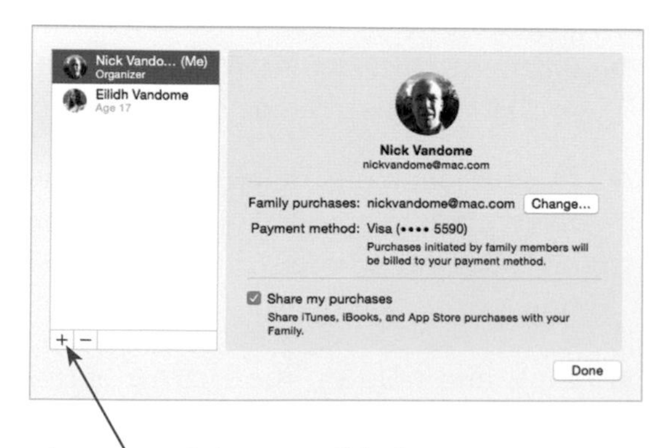

4. Enter the name or email address of a family member and click on the **Continue** button

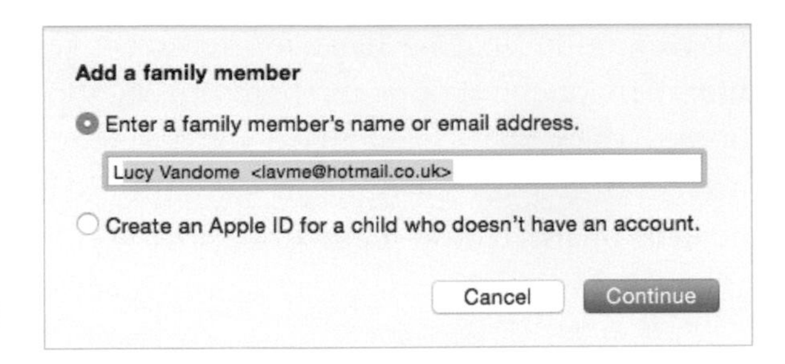

5. Verify your debit or credit card information for your iCloud account, as this will be used by the family member for making purchases. Click on the **Continue** button

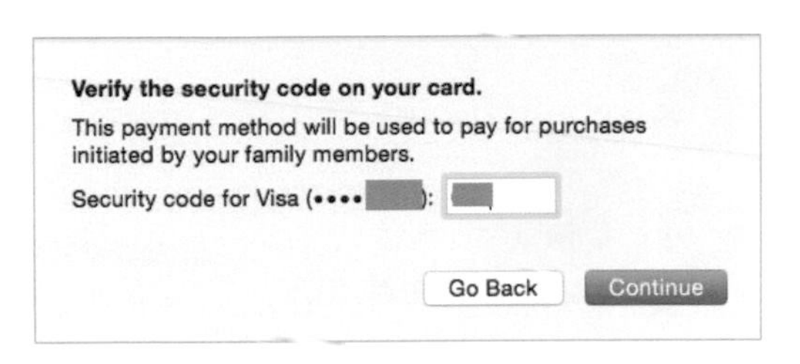

6. Enter your Apple ID password and click on the **Continue** button

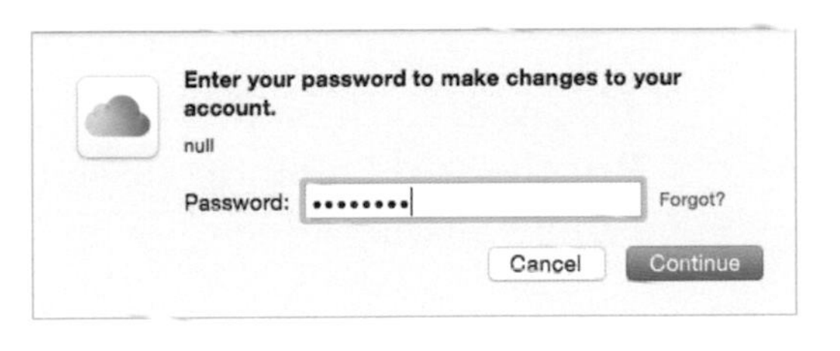

7. An invitation is sent to the selected person. They have to accept this before they can participate in Family Sharing

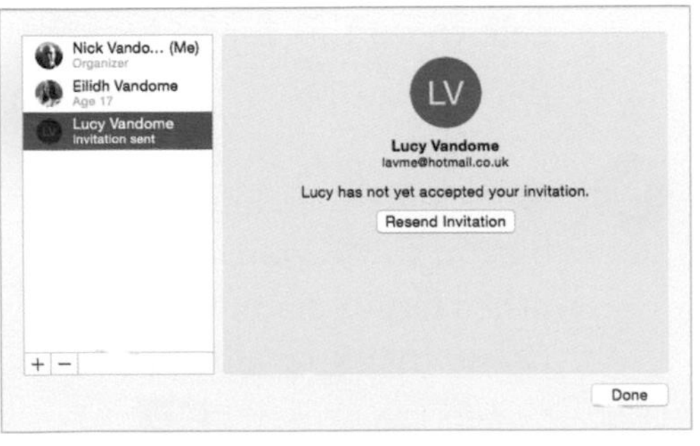

If children are part of the Family Sharing group you can specify that they need your permission before downloading any items from the iTunes Store, the App Store or the iBooks Store. To do this, click on **iCloud** in **System Preferences** and click on the **Manage Family** button. Select a family member and check **On** the **Ask to Buy** button. You will then receive a notification whenever they want to buy something and you can either allow or deny their request.

Using Family Sharing

Once Family Sharing has been set up, it can be used by members of the groups to share music, apps, movies and books. There is also a shared Family calendar that can be used and it is also possible to view the location of the devices of the family members.

Beware

If you are sharing any content with children within Family Sharing, make sure that it is appropriate for their age group.

Sharing music

To share music and other content from the iTunes Store, such as movies and TV shows:

1. Click on the **iTunes** app on the Dock

2. Click on the **Purchased** link

MUSIC QUICK LINKS
Redeem Account
Send iTunes Gifts Support
Purchased

3. By default, your own purchases are displayed. Click on the **Purchased** button to view other members of Family Sharing

Purchased Nick

4. Click on another family member to view their purchases (they will be able to do this for your purchases too)

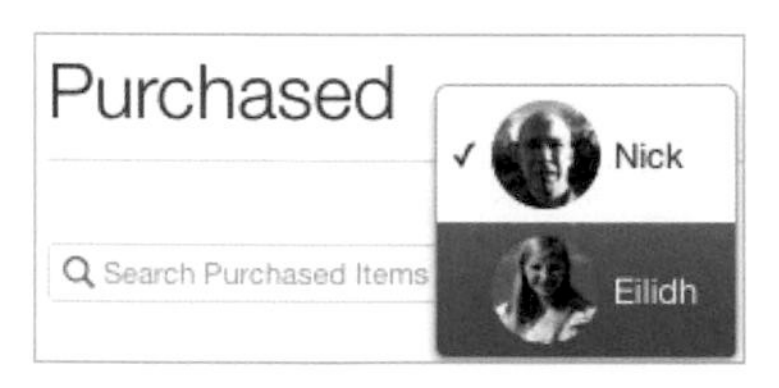

5. Click on the iCloud button to download the other family member's music tracks or albums

Hot tip

You have to be connected to the internet and online to access the iTunes Store and view purchases from other family members. When you do this, you can play their songs without having to download them. However, if you want to be able to use them when you are offline, then you will have to download them first, as in Step 5.

Sharing apps

Apps can also be shared from the App Store. To do this:

1. Click on the **App Store** app on the Dock

2. Click on the **Purchases** button

3. By default, your own purchases are displayed. Click on the **My Purchases** button to view other members of Family Sharing

4. Click on another family member to view and download their purchased apps (they will be able to do this for your apps too)

Sharing books

Books can also be shared in a similar way to items from the iTunes Store and the App Store. To do this:

1. Click on the **iBooks** app on the Dock

2. Click on the **iBooks Store** button

3. Click on the **Purchased** link

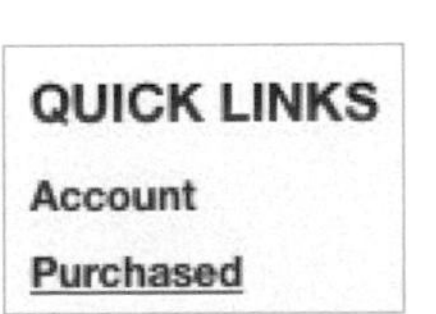

4. By default, your own purchases are displayed. Click on the **Purchased** button to view books downloaded by other Family Sharing members

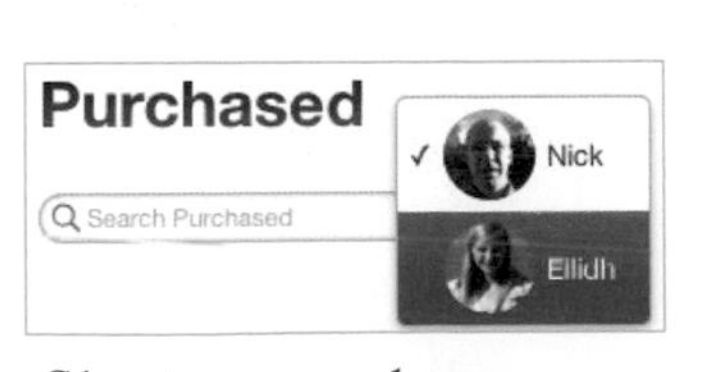

More than one family member can use content in the Family Sharing group at the same time.

...cont'd

Sharing calendars

Family Sharing also generates a Family calendar that can be used by all Family Sharing members:

If some family members are not part of the Family Sharing group, make sure that you invite them separately if you want them to come to the family event.

1. Open the **Calendar** app

2. Click and hold on a date to create a **New Event**. The current calendar (shown in the top right-hand corner) will probably not be the Family one. Click on this button to change the calendar

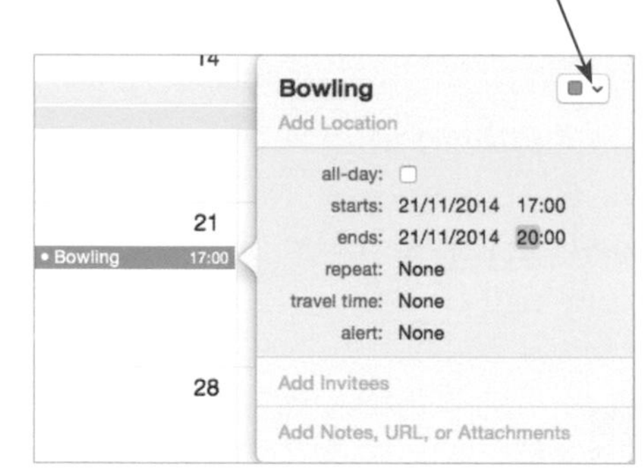

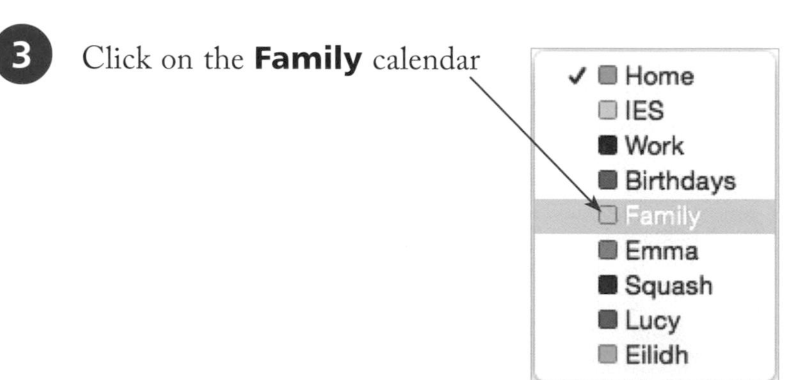

3. Click on the **Family** calendar

Other members of the Family Sharing group can add items to the Family calendar and, when they do, you will be sent a notification that appears on your Mac.

4. Complete the details for the event. It will be added to your calendar, with the Family tag. Other people in your Family Sharing circle will have this event added to their Family calendar too, and they will be sent a notification

Finding lost family devices

Family Sharing also makes it possible to see where everyone's devices are, which can be useful for locating people, but particularly if a device belonging to a Family Sharing member is lost or stolen. To do this:

The other person's device has to have **Share My Location** turned **On** (**Settings > Privacy > Location Services > Share My Location**) otherwise you will not be able to locate it.

1. Ensure that the **Find My Mac** function is checked **On** in the **iCloud** System Preferences, and log in to your online iCloud account at **www.icloud.com**

2. Click on the **Find My iPhone** button (this works for other Apple devices too)

3. Devices that are turned on, online and with iCloud activated are shown by green dots

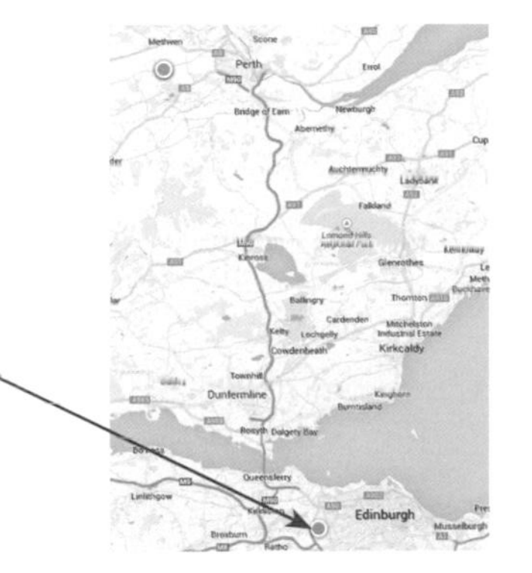

4. Click on a green dot to display information about the device. Click on the **i** symbol to access options for managing the device remotely

The location of devices is shown on a map and you can zoom in on the map to see their location more exactly.

5. There are options to send an alert sound to the device, lock it remotely or erase its contents (if you are concerned about it having fallen into the wrong hands)

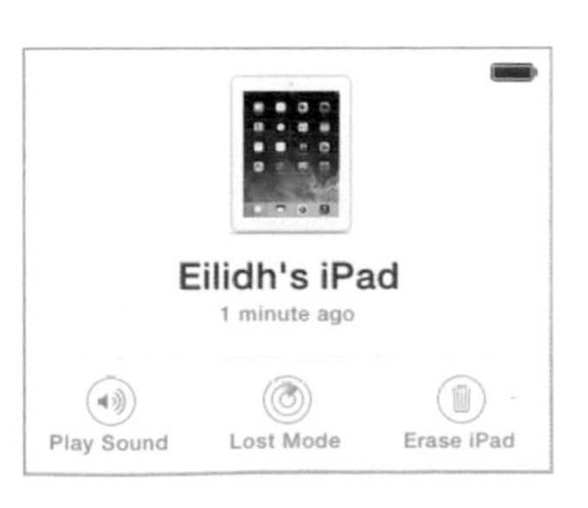

About the iCloud Drive

One of the options in the iCloud section is for the iCloud Drive. This can be used to store documents and other content so that you can use them on any other Apple devices that you have, such as an iPhone or an iPad. With iCloud Drive you can start work on a document on one device, and continue on another device from where you left off. To set up the iCloud Drive:

Don't forget

To save files into an iCloud Drive folder, select **File > Save As** from the Menu bar, click on the **iCloud Drive** button in the Finder Sidebar and navigate to the required folder for the file.

1. Click on the **iCloud** button in System Preferences

2. Check On the **iCloud Drive** option and click on the **Options** button

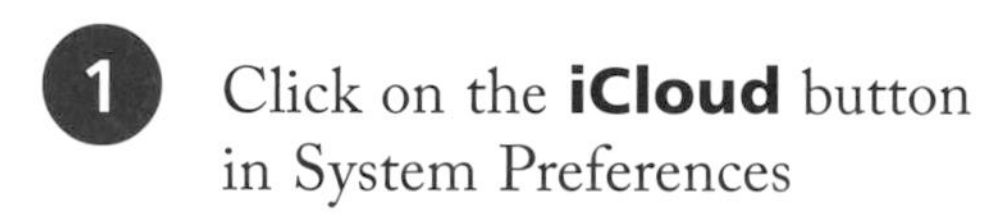

3. Select the apps that you want to use with the iCloud Drive

4. Click on the **Done** button

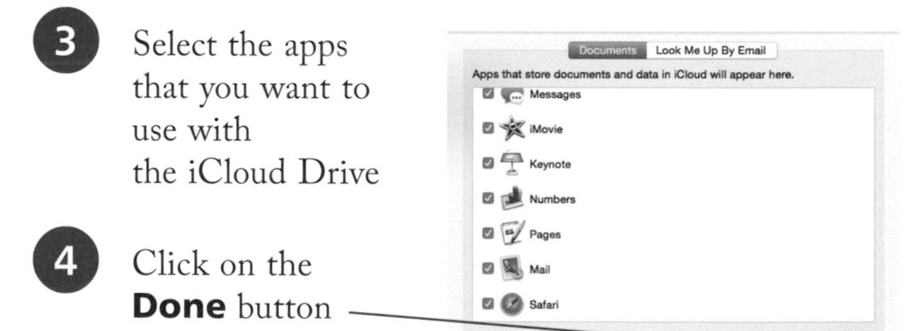

Don't forget

Files that have been saved into the iCloud Drive can also be accessed from the online iCloud website: **www.icloud.com** Enter your Apple ID and password to log in to your account.

5. In the Finder Sidebar click on the **iCloud Drive** button

6. Certain iCloud Drive folders are already created, based on the apps that you have selected in Step 3. These are the default folders into which content from their respective apps will be placed (although others can also be selected, if required). Double-click on a folder to view its contents

10 Expanding Your Horizons

This chapter shows how you can develop your skills on a Mac, from adding new users, to setting up a network.

Adding Users

Due to the power and versatility of Macs it would seem a shame to limit their use to a single person. Thankfully, it is possible to set up user accounts for several people on the same Mac. This means that each person can log in to their own settings and preferences. All user accounts can be password protected, to ensure that each user's environment is secure. To set up multiple user accounts:

Every computer with multiple users has at least one main user, also known as an administrator. This means that they have greater control over the number of items that they can edit and alter. If there is only one user on a computer, they automatically take on the role of the administrator. Administrators have a particularly important role to play when computers are networked together. Each computer can potentially have several administrators.

1. Click on the **System Preferences** icon on the Dock

2. Click on the **Users & Groups** button

3. The information about the current account is displayed. This is your own account and the information is based on details you provided when you first set up your Mac

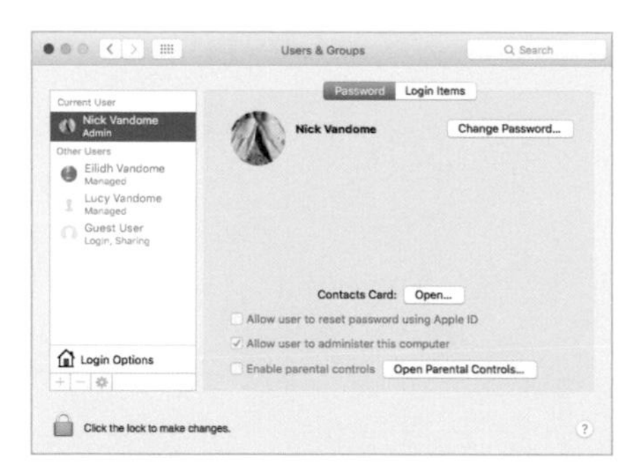

4. Click on this icon to enable new accounts to be added (the padlock needs to be open)

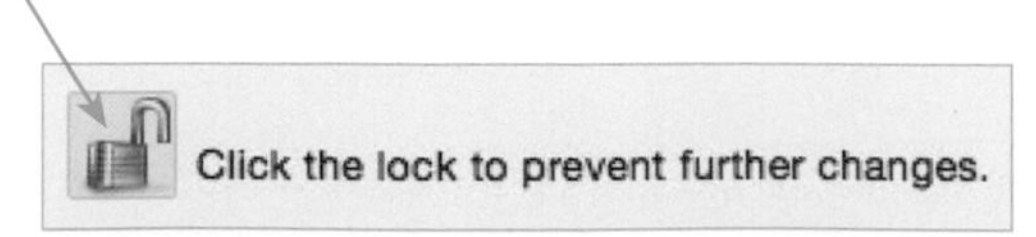

Each user can select their own icon or photo of themselves.

5. Click on the plus sign icon to add a new account

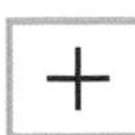

6. Enter the details for the new account holder

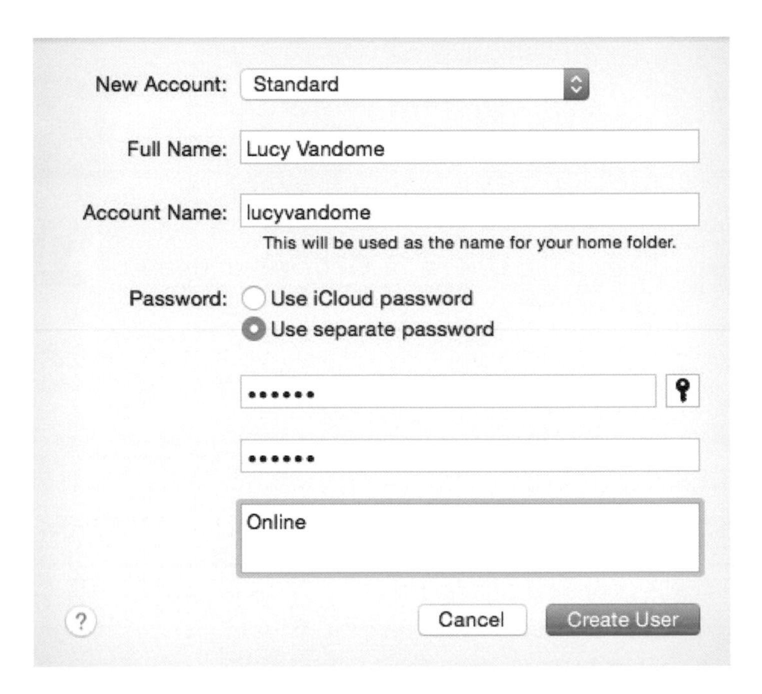

7. Click on the **Create User** button

8. The new account is added to the list in the Accounts window, under **Other Users**

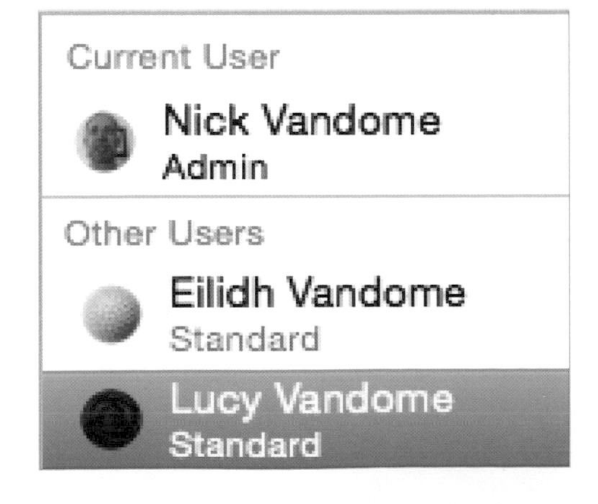

If the new user has an iCloud account (created with an Apple ID and a password) they can use this password when their Mac account is set up.

By default, you are the administrator of your own Mac. This means that you can create, edit and delete other user accounts.

Login Options

Once you have set up more than one user you can determine what happens at login, i.e. when the Mac is turned on. You may want to display a list of all of the users for that machine, or you may want to have yourself logged in automatically. To set login options:

1. Click on the **System Preferences** icon on the Dock

2. Click on the **Users & Groups** button and click on one of the current users

3. Click on the padlock to open it

4. Click on the **Password** tab to set a password for when you log in to your account

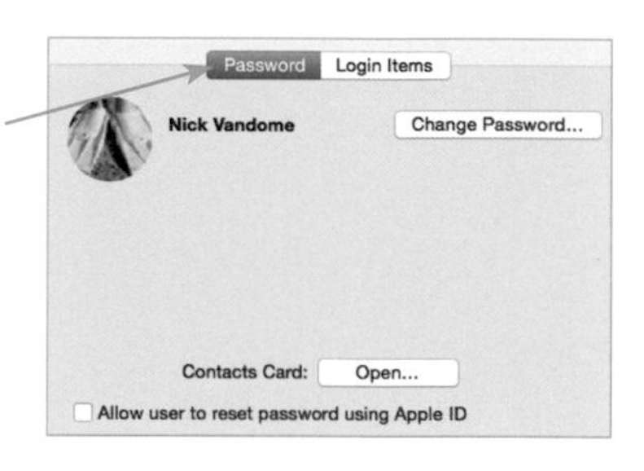

5. Click on the **Login Items** tab and click on this button to add items that open when you log in to your account

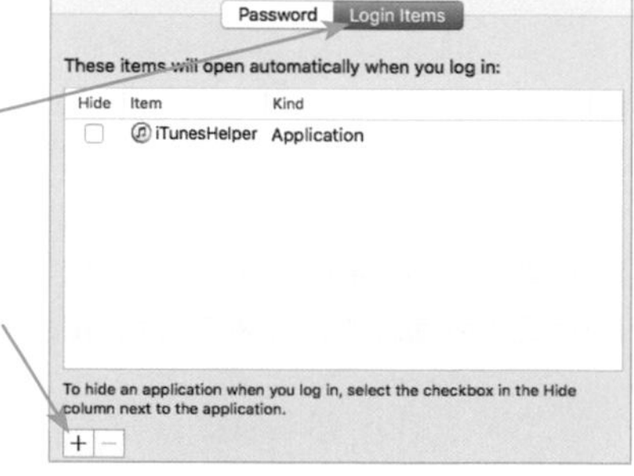

6. Click on the **Login Options** button

If the padlock is locked, no changes can be made within the **Accounts** window, not even by an administrator.

If a lot of Login Items are added at Step 3 it could cause your Mac to take longer to boot up and be ready for use when it is first turned on.

7. Click on the **Automatic login** box

Automatic login: Eilidh Vandome

8. Select a name from the list. (If **Off** is selected all of the users for that Mac will be displayed at login)

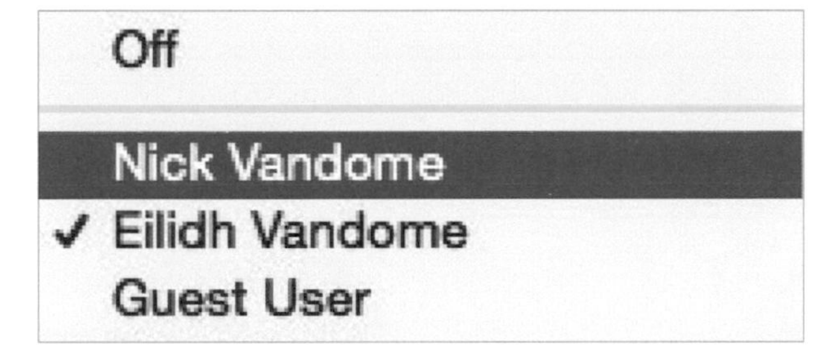

9. If **Off** is selected, select one of the options for how the login window is displayed

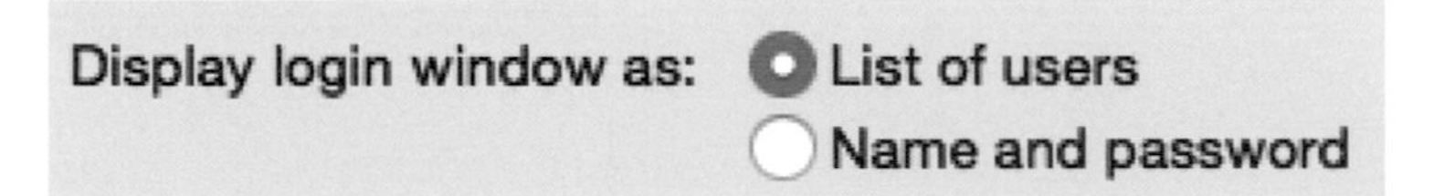

10. Check **On** this box to show the numbers and characters of passwords when they are entered (this only shows for about a second and then appears as a black dot)

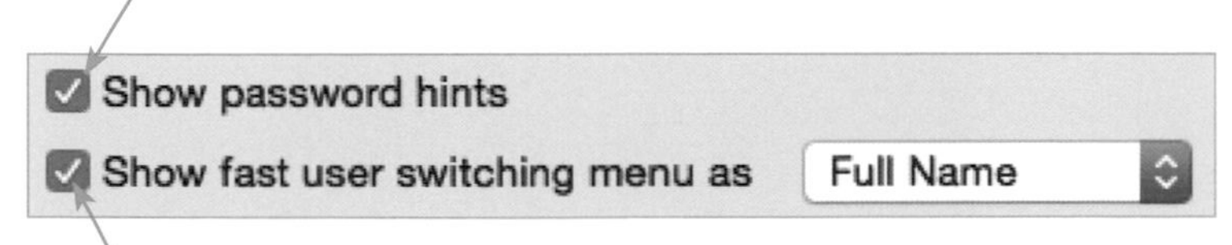

11. Check **On** this box if you want to make it as easy as possible to switch between users (see page 166)

If **Automatic login** is selected for a named user, no username or password needs to be selected when the Mac is turned on.

The **Show password hints** option is a good one for ensuring that you enter the correct password, but do not use it if you are worried that unwanted people may be able to see your password, such as if you are using a MacBook in an internet cafe.

Switching Between Users

If there are multiple users set up on a Mac it is useful to be able to switch between them as quickly as possible. When this is done, the first user's session is retained so that they can return to it if required. To switch between users:

When you switch between users, the first user remains logged in and their current session is retained intact.

1. Make sure **Fast User Switching** is enabled (see page 165)

2. At the top-right of the screen, click on the current user's name

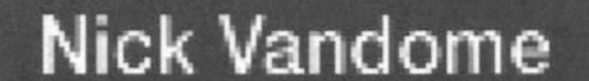

3. Click on the name of another user

If you want to log out of your current session and let someone else log on, select **Apple Menu > Log Out** from the main Menu bar. This will close your current session and a list of the other users will appear on the screen, ready for one of them to log on.

4. Enter the relevant password (if required)

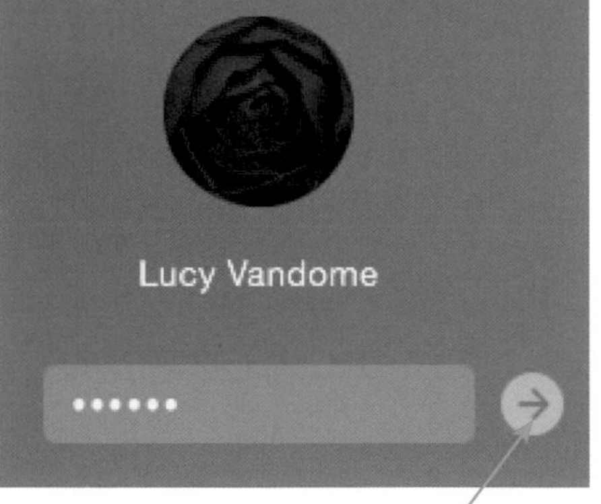

5. Click on this arrow to log in

Parental Controls

If children are using the computer, parents may want to restrict access to certain types of information that can be viewed, using Parental Controls. To do this:

1. Access **Users & Groups** and click on a username. Check **On** the **Enable parental controls** box and click on **Open Parental Controls...**

2. Click on the **Apps** tab 

Different types of parental controls can be set for each user account on a Mac.

3. Check **On** this box if you want to limit the types of app that a user can access

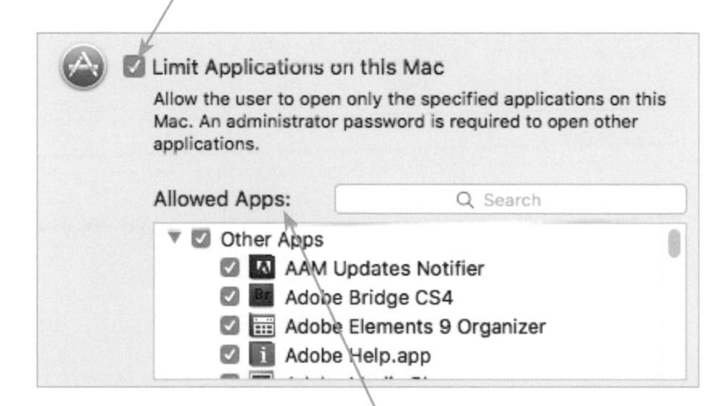

4. Under **Allowed Apps:** check **Off** the boxes next to the apps that you do not want used

If only certain apps are allowed, others will be visible but the user will not be able to open any of them.

5. Click here for options for using the Game Center and also limiting emails to allowed contacts (click on the **Manage...** button to specify allowed contacts)

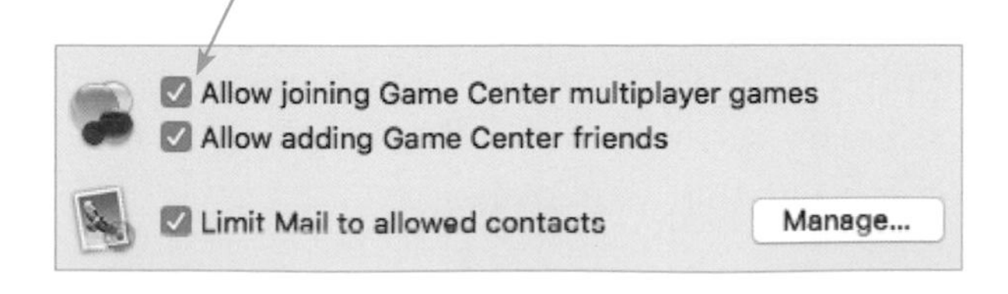

...cont'd

Web controls

1. Click on the **Web** tab 

2. Check **On** this button to try to prevent access to websites with adult content

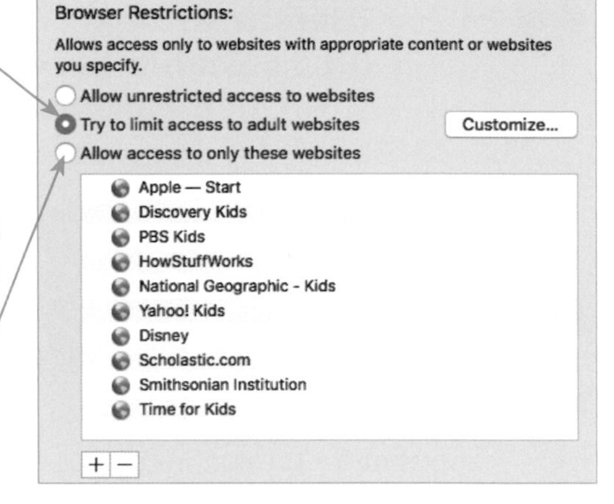

3. Check **On** this button to specify particular websites that are suitable to be viewed

The best way to ensure that children are not accessing inappropriate websites is to be in the same room as them when they are using the computer. Also, discuss these issues openly with them so that they do not feel that you are being secretive.

Stores controls

1. Click on the **Stores** tab 

2. Check **On** the items under **Disable** that you do not want available, and apply the necessary settings under **Restrict**, in terms of types of content that is permissible

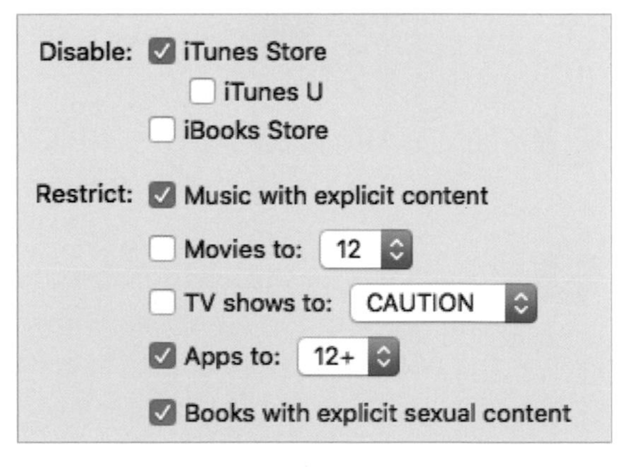

Time controls

1. Click on the **Time** tab
2. Check **On** this box to limit the amount of time the user can use the Mac during weekdays

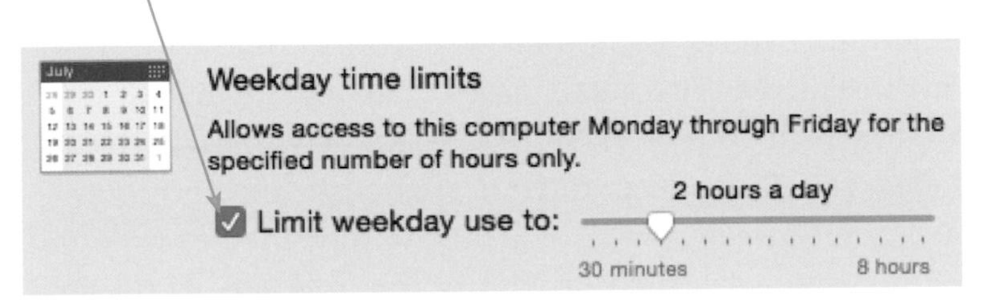

3. Check **On** this box to limit the amount of time the user can use the Mac during weekends

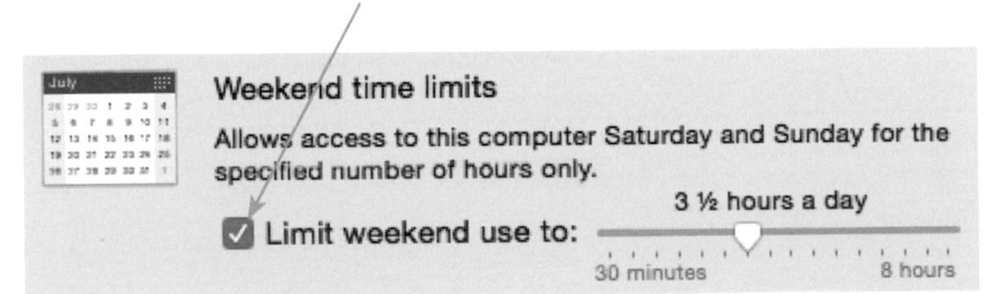

4. Check **On** these boxes to determine the times at which the user cannot access their account

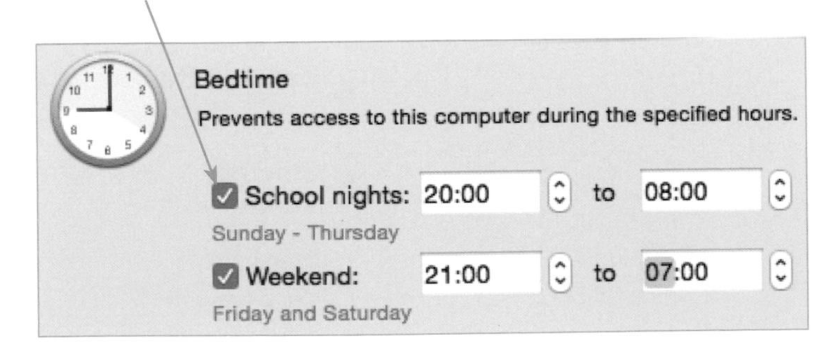

Time Limits, and other parental controls, have to be set for each individual user to whom you want them to apply.

Creating Your Own Network

Computer networks are two or more computers joined together to share information. A computer connected to the internet constitutes a network, as does one computer connected to another.

Networks can be set up by joining computers together, with cables or wirelessly. The latter is becoming more and more common and this can be done with a wireless router and a wireless card in the computer. New Macs come with wireless cards installed so it is just a case of buying a wireless router. (Apple sells its own version of this, known as AirPort.) A wireless router connects to your telephone line and then you can set up your Mac, or Macs, to join the network and communicate with each other and the internet. To do this:

Wireless routers should automatically detect a wireless card in a Mac.

1. Click on the **System Preferences** icon on the Dock

2. Click on the **Network** button

3. The **Network** window displays the current settings

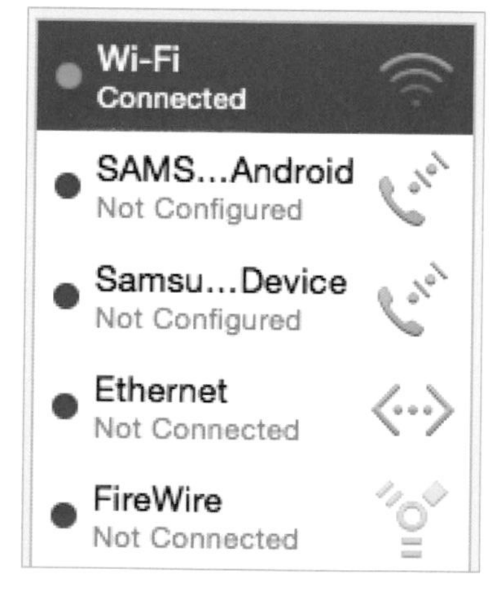

Click on the Ethernet option in Step 3 to access options for connecting to a network with an Ethernet cable connected to your Mac and your router.

4. Click on the **Assist Me...** button

5. The **Network Setup Assistant** is launched

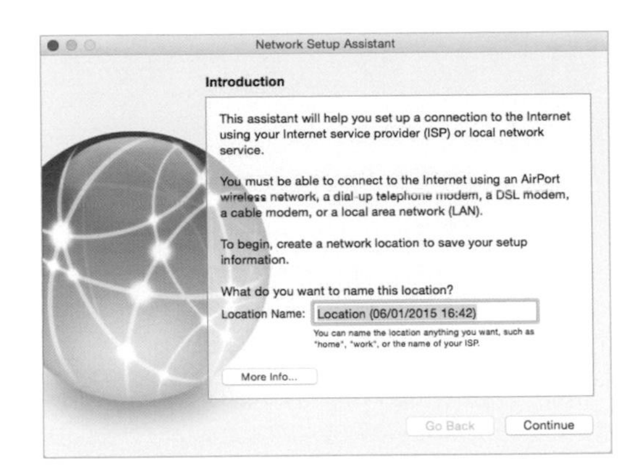

Network Setup Assistant
Introduction
This assistant will help you set up a connection to the Internet using your Internet service provider (ISP) or local network service.
You must be able to connect to the Internet using an AirPort wireless network, a dial-up telephone modem, a DSL modem, a cable modem, or a local area network (LAN).
To begin, create a network location to save your setup information.
What do you want to name this location?
Location Name:
Location (06/01/2015 16:42)
More Info...
Go Back
Continue

6. Enter a name for your network connection

Location Name: Home network
You can name the location anything you want, such as "home", "work", or the name of your ISP.

7. Click on the **Continue** button

Continue

8. Select how you connect to the internet

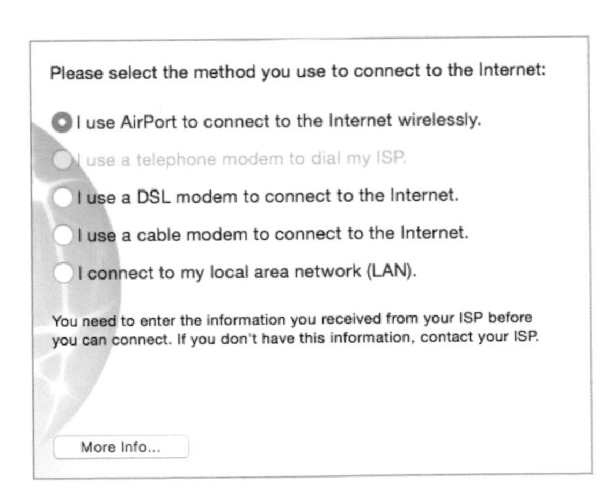

Please select the method you use to connect to the Internet:
I use AirPort to connect to the Internet wirelessly.
I use a telephone modem to dial my ISP.
I use a DSL modem to connect to the Internet.
I use a cable modem to connect to the Internet.
I connect to my local area network (LAN).
You need to enter the information you received from your ISP before you can connect. If you don't have this information, contact your ISP.
More Info...

9. Click on the **Continue** button

Continue

Give each network an easily recognizable name, in case you need to switch between different networks.

...cont'd

10 Select the name of your wireless router

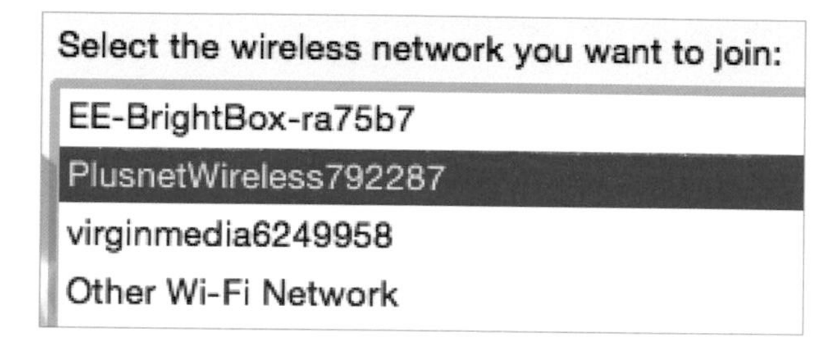

11 Enter the password for the router. This will have been set when you installed the router

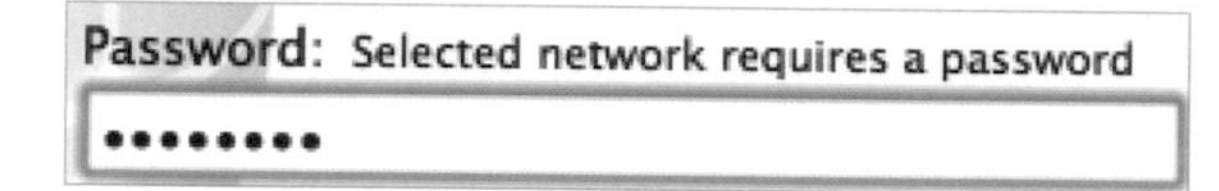

12 Click on the **Continue** button Continue

13 The **Ready to Connect** window confirms that you are ready to connect to your router

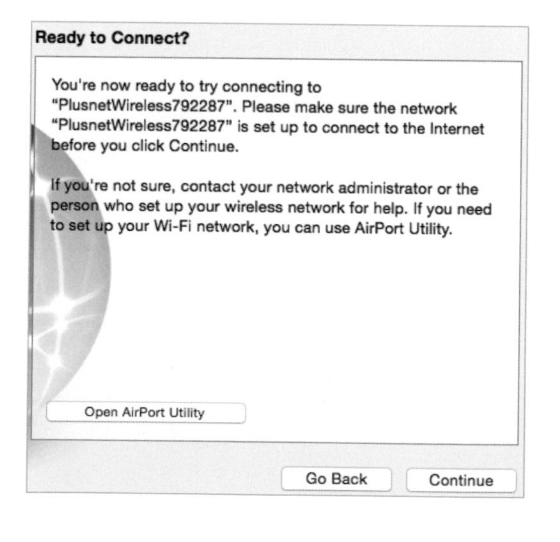

Ready to Connect?
You're now ready to try connecting to "PlusnetWireless792287". Please make sure the network "PlusnetWireless792287" is set up to connect to the Internet before you click Continue.
If you're not sure, contact your network administrator or the person who set up your wireless network for help. If you need to set up your Wi-Fi network, you can use AirPort Utility.
Open AirPort Utility
Go Back
Continue

14 Click on the **Continue** button Continue

In the wireless network window you may see other available networks. This could be because you are in receiving distance of your neighbor's wireless network. Do not try to connect to this as there can be legal implications.

If there is an error in any of the steps in setting up a network, this will be flagged up and you will be able to make a different selection.

Sharing on a Network

One of the main reasons for creating a network of two or more computers is to share files between them.
On networked Macs this involves setting them up so that they can share files, and then accessing these files.

Setting up file sharing

To set up file sharing on a networked Mac:

1. Click on the **System Preference** icon on the Dock

2. Click on the **Sharing** button

3. Check on the boxes next to the items you want to share (the most common items to share are files and printers)

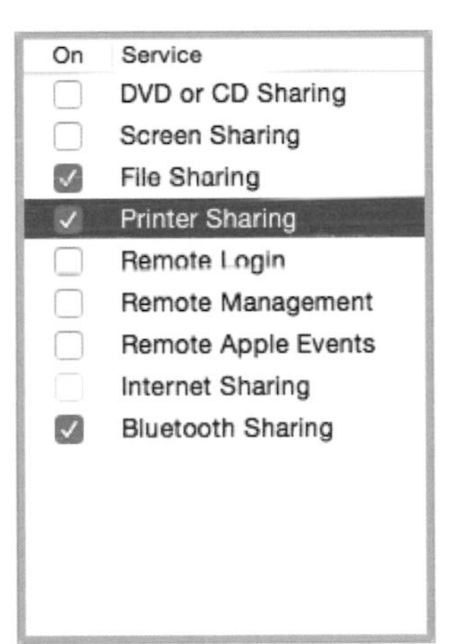

4. Click on a shared folder to specify the access permissions, i.e. whether you can just read the information there or edit it too

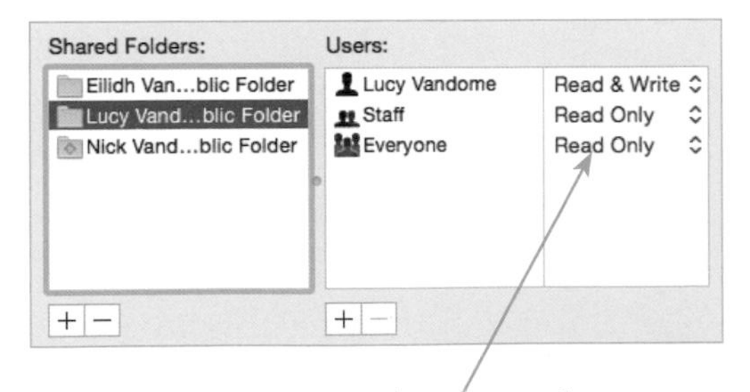

Only enable **Sharing** for people you trust. Do not do it for someone you do not know (such as when you are in a public place) regardless of their reason.

If you only use your network to connect to the internet then you do not need to worry about file sharing. This is mainly for sharing files between two different computers.

...cont'd

Accessing other computers

When you access other computers on a network you do so as either a registered user or a guest. If you are a registered user it usually means you are accessing another computer of which you are an administrator, i.e. the main user. This gives you greater access to the computer's contents than if you are a guest. To access another computer on your network:

You should be able to access other compatible Mac computers and also Windows ones.

1. Networked computers should show up automatically in the Finder. Double-click on one to access it

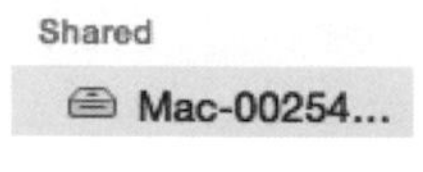

2. By default, you will be connected as a Guest, with limited access. Click on the **Connect As...** button in the Finder window

3. Check On the **Registered User** button

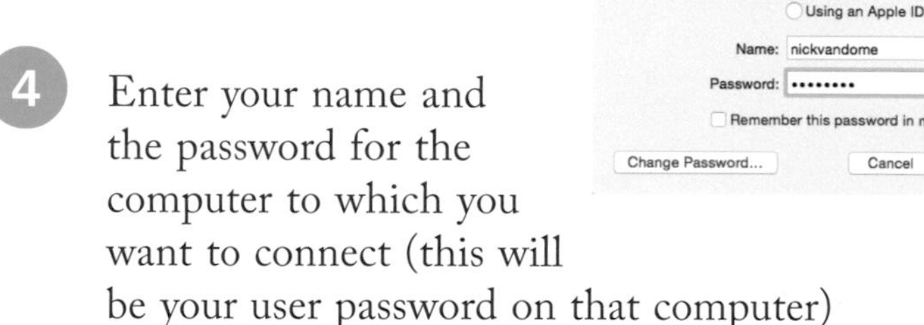

4. Enter your name and the password for the computer to which you want to connect (this will be your user password on that computer)

When connecting to another computer, it has to be turned on.

5. Click on the **Connect** button

6. In the Finder you will have access to the hard drive of the networked computer

7. You will then be able to access files and folders in the same way as if they were on the computer on which you are viewing them

Guest users

Guest users on a network are users other than yourself, or other registered users, to whom you want to limit access to your files and folders. Guests only have access to a folder called the Drop Box in your own Public folder. To share files with Guest users you have to first copy them into the Drop Box. To do this:

1. Create a file and select **File > Save** from the Menu bar
2. Navigate to your own home folder (this is created automatically by OS X and displayed in the Finder Sidebar)

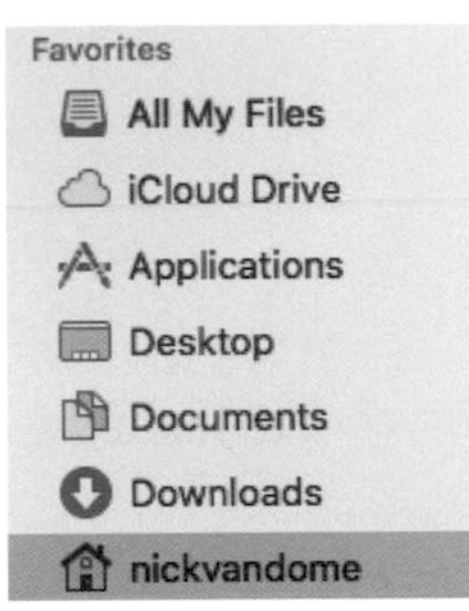

Your home folder is the one with your Mac username.

3. Double-click on the **Public** folder

4. Double-click on the **Drop Box** folder

The Drop Box folder should not be confused with DropBox, which is an online sharing and backing up service.

5. Save the file into the Drop Box

...cont'd

Accessing a Drop Box

To access files in a Drop Box:

The Drop Box can be thought of as a secure area for sharing files between users.

1. Double-click on a networked computer in the Finder
2. Click on the **Connect As...** button in the Finder window
3. Click on the **Guest** button
4. Click on the **Connect** button
5. Double-click on the administrator's folder

Set permissions for how the Drop Box operates by selecting it in the Finder and Ctrl + clicking on it. Select **Get Info** from the menu and apply the required settings under the **Sharing & Permissions** heading.

6. Double-click on the **Drop Box** folder to access the files within it

11 Safety Net

This chapter shows some of the ways to keep your Mac, and your files, as safe, as up-to-date and as secure as possible.

Mac Security

Modern computers are plagued by viruses, spyware and malware, all of which can corrupt data or impair the smooth running of the system. Thankfully, Macs are less prone to this than computers running Windows, partly due to the fact that there are a smaller number of Macs for the virus writers to worry about, and partly because the UNIX system, on which the Mac OS X is based, is a very robust platform.

However, this is not to say that Mac users should be complacent in the face of potential attacks and, as Macs become more and more popular, there are an increasing number of Mac viruses being developed by hackers. In order to minimize the threat of viruses and unwanted visitors, try some of the following steps:

OS X El Capitan has a security feature, known as **Gatekeeper**, that enables you to specify details about apps that are downloaded to your Mac. This can be from anywhere, the App Store and identified developers, or just from the App Store. This feature is found in the **Security & Privacy System Preference**, under the **General** tab.

- Install anti-virus software and a firewall. Although this is not as essential as for a computer running Windows, it is still important and will give you additional peace of mind. Norton and Sophos produce good anti-virus software for the Mac.
- Protect your Mac with a password. This means that no-one can log in without the required password.
- Download software updates from Apple, which, among other things, contain security updates (see next page).
- Do not open suspicious email attachments.
- In Safari, select **Safari > Preferences** and click on the **Security** tab. Deselect any items that you feel may put your computer at risk.

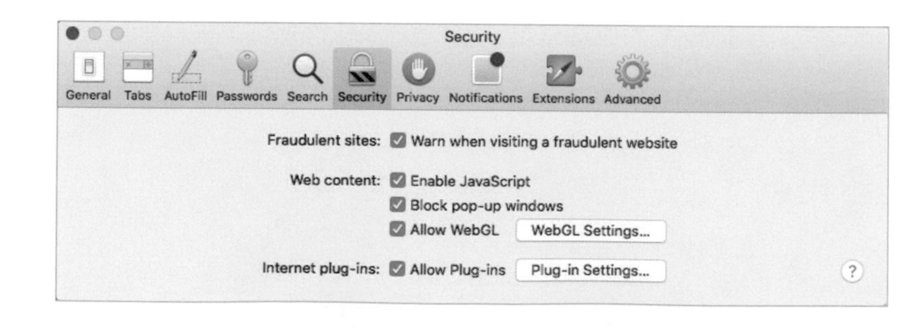

Updating Software

Apple periodically releases updates for its software; both its apps and the OS X operating system. All of these are now available through the App Store. To update software:

1. Open **System Preferences** and click on the **App Store** button

2. Click here to select options for how you are notified about updates and how they are downloaded

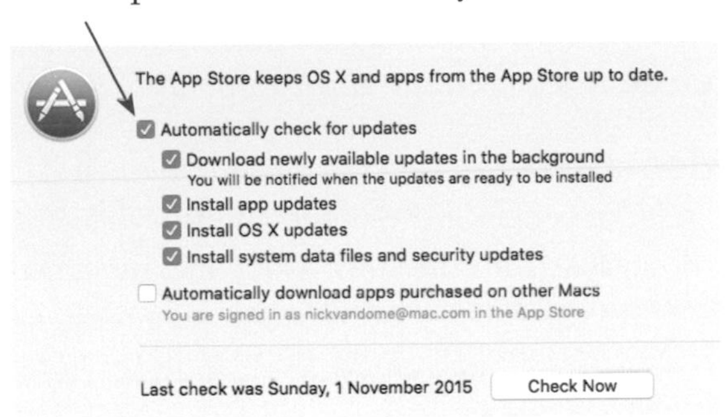

3. If you want to check for updates manually, click on the **Check Now** button

4. If you have selected **Download newly available updates in the background** in Step 2, updates will not be shown in the App Store window. However, if this option is checked Off, available updates will be displayed in this window

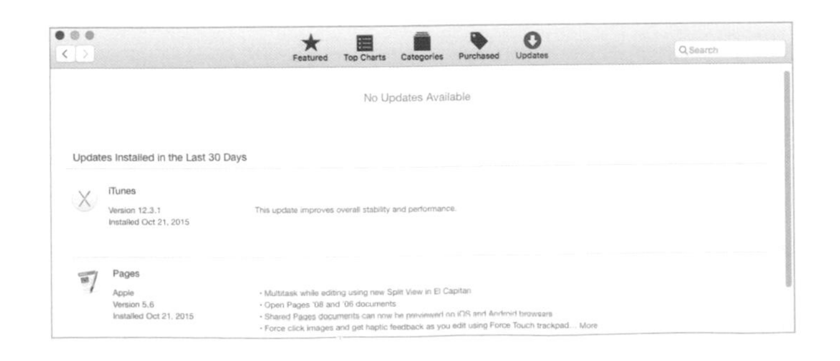

In OS X El Capitan, software updates can also be accessed from the Apple menu.

Check on the **Automatically download apps purchased on other Macs** box if you want to activate this function.

For some software updates, such as those to OS X itself, you may have to restart your computer for them to take effect.

Checking Your System

Macs have a couple of apps that can be used to check the overall health and condition of your system. These are utilities called Activity Monitor and System Information. To access these apps:

1. In the Finder, click on the **Applications** button or access it from the Launchpad
2. Double-click on the **Utilities** folder
3. Double-click on either app to open it

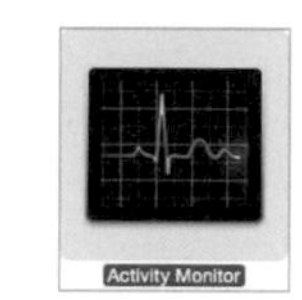

Activity Monitor

This can be used to check how much memory and data is being used up on your Mac, and by certain apps:

1. Click on the **CPU** tab to see how much processor capacity is being used up

System:	2.56%	CPU LOAD	Threads:	1037
User:	6.39%		Processes:	245
Idle:	91.04%			

2. Click on the **Memory** tab to see how much system memory (RAM) is being used up

MEMORY PRESSURE	Physical Memory:	8.00 GB	App Memory:	1.90 GB
	Memory Used:	2.94 GB	Wired Memory:	1.04 GB
	Cached Files:	1.30 GB	Compressed:	0 bytes
	Swap Used:	0 bytes		

3. Click on the **Disk** tab to see how much space has been taken up on the hard drive

RAM (Random-Access Memory) is the memory that is used to open and run apps. The more RAM you have, the more efficiently your Mac will run.

System Information

This can be used to view how the different hardware and software elements on your Mac are performing. To do this:

1. Open the **Utilities** folder and double-click on the **System Information** button

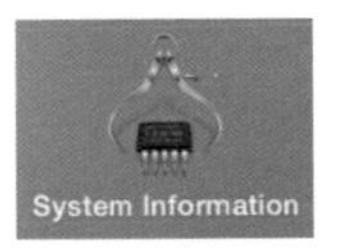

2. Click on the **Hardware** link and click on an item of hardware

3. Details about the item of hardware, and its performance, are displayed

MATSHITA DVD-R UJ-898:

Firmware Revision:	HE13
Interconnect:	ATAPI
Burn Support:	Yes (Apple Shipping Drive)
Cache:	1024 KB
Reads DVD:	Yes
CD-Write:	-R, -RW
DVD-Write:	-R, -R DL, -RW, +R, +R DL, +RW
Write Strategies:	CD-TAO, CD-SAO, DVD-DAO
Media:	To show the available burn speeds, insert a disc and choose File > Refresh Information

4. Click on software items to view their details

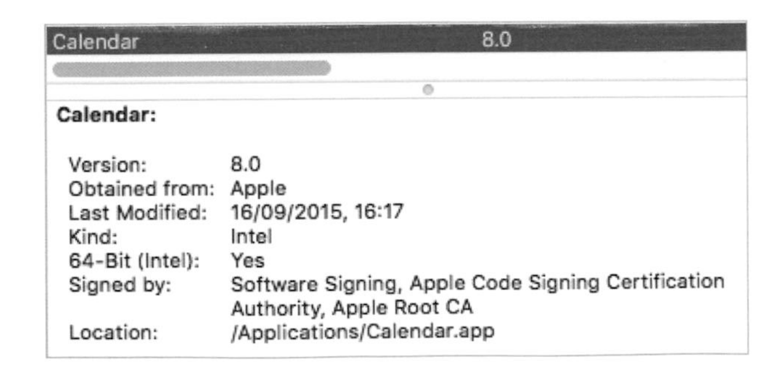

Another option for checking your system is Disk Utility, which is located in the **Applications > Utilities** folder. The Disk Utility can be used to check that disks are working properly and also erase disks, such as removable disks, if required.

Privacy

Within the Security & Privacy System Preferences are options for activating a firewall, and privacy settings.

OS X El Capitan apps are designed to do only what they are supposed to, so that they do not have to interact with other apps if they do not need to. This lessens the possibility of any viruses spreading across your Mac.

Click on the **Diagnostics & Usage** link and check **On** the **Send diagnostic & usage data to Apple** if you want to send information to Apple about the performance of your Mac and its apps. This will include any problems and helps Apple improve its software and apps. This information is collected anonymously and does not identify anyone personally.

1. Open **System Preferences** and click on the **Security & Privacy** button

2. Click on the **Firewall** tab Firewall
3. Click on the **Turn On Firewall** button to activate this

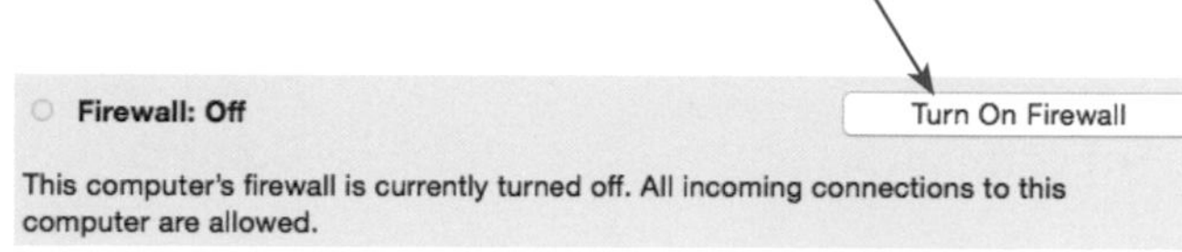

4. Click on the **Privacy** tab Privacy
5. Click on the **Location Services** link and check **On** the **Enable Location Services** option if you want relevant apps to be able to access your location

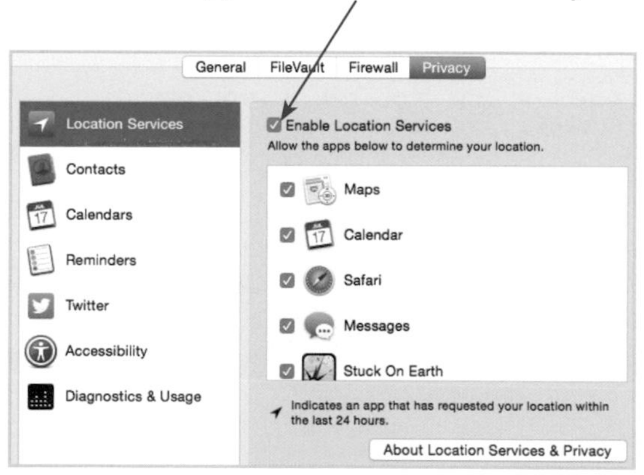

6. Click on the **Contacts** link and check **On** any relevant apps that want to access your Contacts

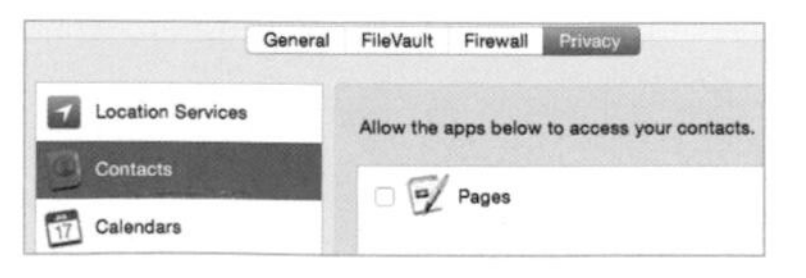

Dealing with Crashes

Although Macs are known for their stability, there are occasions when something goes wrong and an app crashes or freezes. This is usually denoted by a spinning, colored ball (known as the "Spinning Beach Ball of Death"). Only rarely will you have to turn off your Mac and turn it on again to resolve the problem. Usually, Force Quit can be used to close down the affected app. To do this:

1. Once the spinning ball appears, click on the **Apple Menu**

2. Select **Force Quit** from the Apple Menu

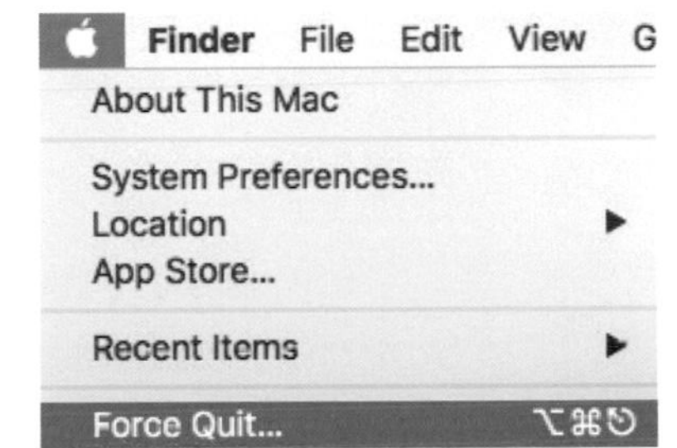

or

1. Hold down the Command (Apple), Alt and Esc keys at the same time

2. Select the non-responding app

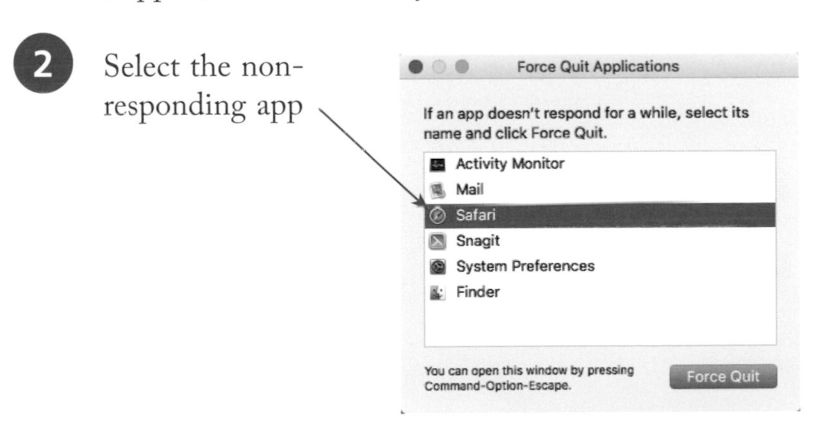

3. Click on the **Force Quit** button

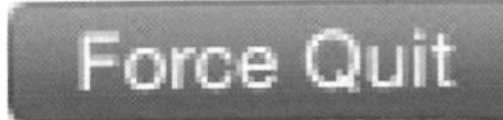

It is unusual for Macs to freeze completely. However, if this does happen, hold down the start button for a few seconds until your Mac turns off. You should then be able to start it normally.

Backing Up

Backing up data is a chore, but it is an essential one: if the worst comes to the worst and all of your data is corrupted or lost then you will be very grateful that you went to the trouble of backing it up. Macs have a number of options for backing up data.

Don't forget

iMacs, Mac Minis and the MacBook range no longer have an internal CD/DVD drive, but an external CD/DVD drive can be attached via a USB cable.

Burning discs

One of the most traditional methods of backing up data is to burn it onto a disc that can then be stored elsewhere. These days, this is most frequently done on CDs or DVDs. To do this, first attach an external CD/DVD drive:

1. Insert the CD/DVD into the CD/DVD slot
2. Select for the disc to be shown in the Finder

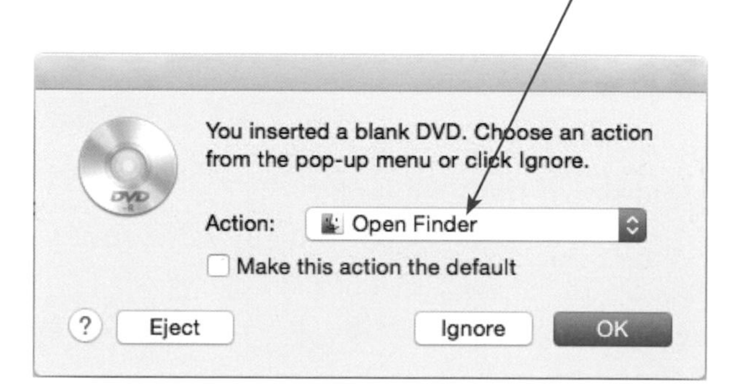

Hot tip

If a CD or DVD does not burn successfully, try a different brand of discs. Sometimes the coating on some discs can cause a problem with the disc burner.

3. Locate the item you want to copy
4. Drag it onto the disc name in the Finder

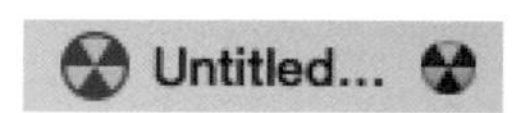

5. Click on this button to burn the disc

Time Machine

Time Machine is a feature of OS X that gives you great peace of mind. In conjunction with an external hard drive, it creates a backup of your whole system, including folders, files, apps and even the OS X operating system itself.

Once it has been set up, Time Machine takes a backup every hour and you can then go into Time Machine to restore any files that have been deleted or become corrupt.

Setting up Time Machine

To use Time Machine, it has to first be set up. This involves attaching a hard drive to your Mac. To set up Time Machine:

1. Click on the **Time Machine** app on the Dock, or access it in the **System Preferences**

2. You will be prompted to set up Time Machine

3. Click on the **Set Up Time Machine** button

4. Click on the **Select Disk...** button

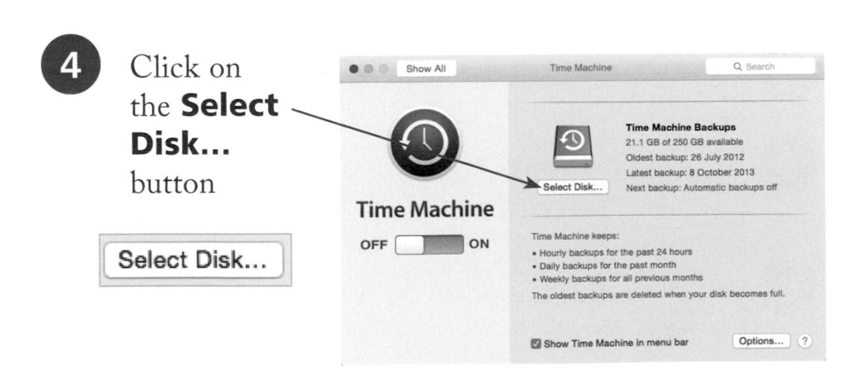

If an external hard drive is not attached to your Mac you will not be able to use Time Machine and a warning message will appear when you try to set it up.

...cont'd

5. Connect an external hard drive and select it via a USB cable

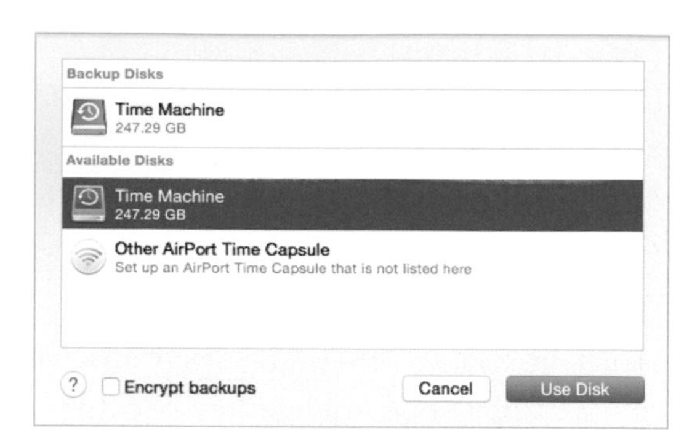

6. Click on the **Use Disk** button

7. In the Time Machine System Preferences window, drag the button to the **On** position

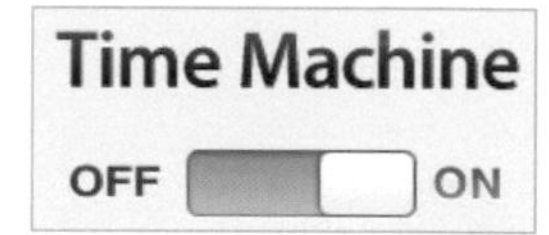

8. The backup will begin. The initial backup copies your whole system and can take several hours. Subsequent hourly backups only look at items that have been changed since the previous backup

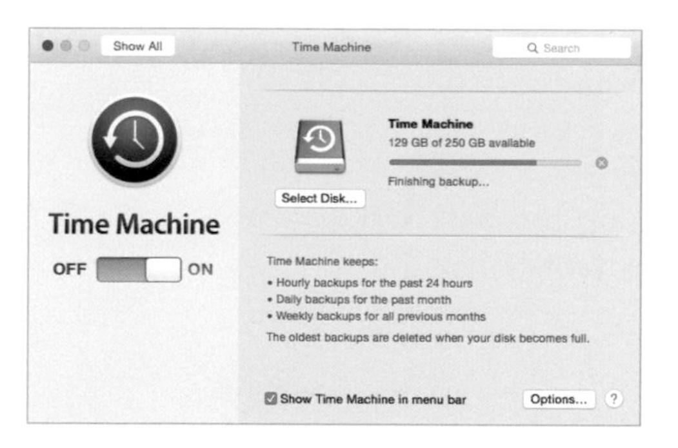

9. The progress of the backup is displayed in the System Preferences window and also here:

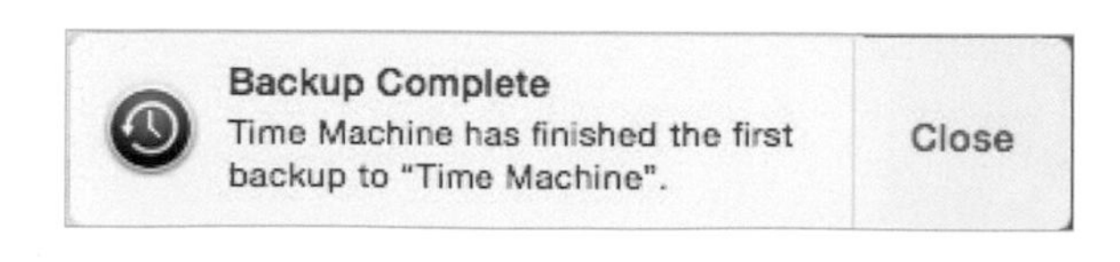

Once your Mac has been backed up, click on the Time Machine app on the Dock or from the Launchpad, to restore files from the backup. Your backup disc has to be connected for this, and you can scroll through Finder windows from different backup dates if you need to restore files from a specific time.

A

B

C

D

E

F

G

M

N

O

P

Q

R

S

T

U

V

W

Y